Criminal Case Dispositions through Pleas in Greater China

"This book stands as a joint enterprise by Chinese scholars in engaging with international dialogue on plea-based case disposition. It represents a unique and genuine contribution from a group of young and talented researchers, and a must-read for anyone interested in understanding criminal justice systems in Greater China. This compilation truly exemplifies the commitment and effort of Asian criminology in enriching the body of knowledge in criminology and criminal justice."

—Jianhong Liu, *Founder of the Asian Journal of Criminology and Asian Criminological Society Distinguished Professor, University of Macau*

"This fine collection deftly navigates the diversity of how plea bargaining reforms have been received across Greater China. It assembles distinguished authors. They reveal how path dependant legal institutions can be. The way plea negotiation reforms are actually received in Mainland China, Hong Kong, Macao and Taiwan are differently shaped by local legal cultures. The book tells a powerful story of the resilience and distinctiveness of local professional cultures. It is revealing on how they fail and succeed in allowing defendants to tell their side of the story. This is an important contribution that greatly advances our knowledge of new criminal justice trends in Greater China."

—John Braithwaite, *Emeritus Professor, Australian National University*

Enshen Li · Xiaoyu Yuan · Yan Zhang
Editors

Criminal Case Dispositions through Pleas in Greater China

Conception, Operation and Contradiction

palgrave
macmillan

Editors
Enshen Li
School of Law
City University of Hong Kong
Hong Kong, China

Xiaoyu Yuan
School of Criminal Justice
Shanghai University of Political Science and Law
Shanghai, China

Yan Zhang
Department of Sociology,
University of Macau
Zhuhai, China

ISBN 978-981-97-1855-9 ISBN 978-981-97-1856-6 (eBook)
https://doi.org/10.1007/978-981-97-1856-6

This Palgrave Macmillan imprint is published by the registered company Springer Nature Singapore Pte Ltd.
The registered company address is: 152 Beach Road, #21-01/04 Gateway East, Singapore 189721, Singapore

Preface

In many jurisdictions around the world, criminal convictions are becoming no longer a product of fair (contested) trials but an object in plea bargaining and related trial-avoiding mechanisms. Increasingly, a defendant's guilt is determined by non-judicial officials through streamlined, routinized and managerial proceedings. This approach to case dispositions is, more often than not, associated with the neglect of defendants' procedural rights and real checks and balances aimed at curtailing the miscarriage of justice. The plea bargaining system in the US is the most prominent illustration, but many similar initiatives—though termed differently (e.g., charge negotiation, resolution discussion or plea resolution)—have developed exponentially in the European, Latin American and Asian criminal law regimes. This edited volume is motivated by an emerging international research interest in plea-based case dispositions and their implications for the criminal justice system. A particular aim of this book is to speak to the cultural distinctiveness of plea bargaining and related mechanism given that the local context of law and culture plays a vital role in shaping the on-the-ground law enforcement and justice administration.

The idea of this edited collection can be traced back to 2016 when Mainland China piloted the 'Admission of Guilt and Acceptance of Punishment' system (known as 'plea leniency'). Following this, all four entities of the Greater China region (Mainland China, Taiwan, Hong

Kong and Macau) have adopted certain forms of trial-avoiding mechanisms in their criminal proceedings. Gathering scholars, practitioners and policy watchers with different perspectives, this book intends to provide fresh and pioneering perspectives on plea-based case dispositions in Greater China as a lens to examine their idiosyncratic roots, contours and patterns at the local level. The proposed volume is the product of a common aspiration of the editors and contributors to showcase research that explores the indigenous forms and characteristics of criminal case dispositions through guilty pleas in jurisdictions that are not so familiar to Western audiences engaged in the study of crime, criminal justice and criminology. The existence of culturally different Chinese-speaking societies presents a unique opportunity to create new knowledge in the field of comparative criminal justice and criminology. Chapters included in this book are therefore to examine important legal, social and cultural issues found throughout plea-based case dispositions in Greater China, but in a geographically specific manner—providing an in-depth view of issues that can help forge connections and inspire creative solutions for scholars gaining understanding of common problems across the societies in question. At the same time, this book seeks to unfold Western influences on developments of plea-based initiatives in Greater China while placing the lessons learned in this region into a larger global comparative context.

Hong Kong, China — Enshen Li
Shanghai, China — Xiaoyu Yuan
Macau, China — Yan Zhang

Contents

List of Contributors

Hui Chen SGLA (Sino-Global Legal Alliance) Law Firm, Shanghai, China

Kevin Kwok-yin Cheng Faculty of Law, The Chinese University of Hong Kong, Shatin, Hong Kong

Mong-Hwa Chin National Yang Ming Chiao Tung University School of Law, Hsinchu, Taiwan

Xueke Fan School of Law, City University of Macau, Macau, China

Chengchen He The Chinese University of Hong Kong, Shatin, Hong Kong, People's Republic of China

Xin He Faculty of Law, The University of Hong Kong, Hong Kong, China

Enshen Li School of Law, City University of Hong Kong, Hong Kong, China

Zhe Li School of Law, University of Macau, Macau, China

Mao-hong Lin National Taipei University, Taipei, Taiwan

Xifen Lin KoGuan School of Law, Shanghai Jiaotong University, Shanghai, China

Jingwei Liu The Chinese University of Hong Kong, Shatin, Hong Kong, People's Republic of China

Yuguang Lu KoGuan School of Law, Shanghai Jiaotong University, Shanghai, China

Yu Mou School of Law, SOAS University of London, London, UK

Heng Ut Wong School of Law, University of Macau, Macau, China

Yuhao Wu Law School, Peking University, Beijing, China

Xiaoyu Yuan School of Criminal Justice, Shanghai University of Political Science and Law, Shanghai, China

Yan Zhang Department of Sociology, University of Macau, Zhuhai, China

List of Tables

Introduction

Enshen Li, Xiaoyu Yuan, and Yan Zhang

> Plea bargaining…is not some adjunct to the criminal justice system; it is the criminal justice system.
>
> –Justice Anthony Kennedy[1]

The Motivation of the Book

Over the past decades, plea bargains or mechanisms that avoid trial and result in conviction have become an essential part of criminal justice systems around the globe (Langer, 2021; Turner, 2017). Based on the idea that the defendant pleads guilty in exchange for a concession on

[1] From Missouri v. Frye, quoted in Scott and Stuntz (1992).

E. Li (✉)
School of Law, City University of Hong Kong, Hong Kong, China
e-mail: enshenli@cityu.edu.hk

X. Yuan
School of Criminal Justice, Shanghai University of Political Science and Law, Shanghai, China

Y. Zhang
Department of Sociology, University of Macau, Zhuhai, China

E. Li et al. (eds.), *Criminal Case Dispositions through Pleas in Greater China*, https://doi.org/10.1007/978-981-97-1856-6_1

criminal charges and/or sentences (Alschuler, 1979), plea bargaining and related mechanisms work to resolve the case quickly by skipping over trials, hence reducing costs associated with prosecution and court proceedings (Galanter, 2004; McConville & Mirsky, 2005; Soubise, 2018). As many have asserted (Bushway et al., 2014; Feeley, 2017; Lynch, 1998; Mather, 1978), plea bargaining and related mechanisms are vital to today's criminal justice system because they help to alleviate pressure on prosecutors who often handle overwhelming caseloads in 'an era of overcriminalisation' (Husak, 2023, p. 271). The United States is a towering county in this trend. In 1839, around 25% of all felony convictions in New York involved plea bargaining (Moley, 1928), and this figure skyrocketed to 75% one and half century later alongside 'tough on crime' policies that prevailed the administration of criminal justice (McConville & Mirsky, 1995). Now, more than 95% of criminal cases are handled through plea bargaining in the US over-burdened criminal justice system (Cohen & Kyckelhahn, 2012). Likewise, plea-based initiatives have emerged in many civil law jurisdictions (Ma, 2002). The apparent influence of the 'Americanisation' of legal systems has arguably driven this development (Langer, 2004). However, the introduction of plea bargaining or comparable trial-avoiding mechanisms in countries such as Germany, Italy, and France reveals a very different path of prosecutor-defendant interactions that aligns with local circumstances of inquisitorial criminal proceedings (Langer, 2021).

The plea-based system of criminal justice is, of course, not without criticism. Plea bargaining, for example, while streamlining the criminal procedure, is seen as compromising the integrity of the criminal justice system. It requires defendants to waive their fundamental rights enshrined in the constitutional law, including the right to a fair trial, the privilege against self-incrimination, and the presumption of innocence, among many others (Alkon, 2010; Cheng, 2023; Heumann, 1981). In that, defendants—including innocent defendants—can be induced or coerced to take pleas for various reasons, some of which have little or nothing to do with factual and legal guilt (Lynch, 1994; Nash et al., 2023; O'Hear, 2008). More markedly, the overreliance on plea bargaining as a primary way to resolve criminal cases gives rise to the strong leverage the prosecution wields in pursuing confessions and guilty pleas. Understanding and exploiting the defendants' fears of facing more severe consequences if the case goes to trial, the prosecution enjoys a paramount role in the determination of one's guilt, which renders wrongful convictions not only possible but also inevitable (Bibas, 2004; Hamin et al., 2019; O'Hear, 2008; Stemen & Escobar, 2018).

Although plea bargaining and related mechanisms have been criticised on various grounds, they have over time morphed into 'a necessary evil' in the criminal justice system (McDonough, 1979). Reflecting what Máximo Langer (2021, p. 378) calls the 'administratisation of criminal convictions', the advent of plea bargaining and related mechanisms has seemingly turned criminal convictions into an object in assembly-line justice dominated by nonjudicature officials as opposed to a product of a fair (contested) legal hearing (Langer, 2021; Lynch, 1998; Matheny, 1980; Soubise, 2018). According to the US-based criminal lawyer, such transformation has taken place 'in many corners of the world' (Langer, 2021, p. 386). This edited book is therefore motivated by an emerging global research interest in plea-based programs and schemes and their implications for the criminal justice system. While the majority of such scholarship is Euro and Anglo-centric, this volume is prepared to offer fresh and cutting-edge perspectives on plea-driven case dispositions in a non-Western context, namely Greater China. One particular objective of this book is to foster our understanding of the cultural distinctiveness of plea-based case dispositions in relation to their idiosyncratic theories and practices across societies that are less familiar to global audiences engaged in comparative criminal justice and criminology.

It is generally assumed that the criminal justice system is not only a legal process whereby violators of the criminal law are tried and sanctioned in accordance with specified legal categories and procedures, but also a social process whereby criminal justice ideologies and practices are informed by indigenous social development and cultural dimension (Garland, 2000). Plea bargaining and related mechanisms are no exception. In propositioning this thesis of a universal 'administratisation of criminal convictions', Langer (2021) acknowledges that there is incongruity in the form and manifestation of plea-based dispositional measures in different jurisdictions, considering the divergence in the way the criminal justice system plays out across varied legal and social conditions. While this cultural significance has been looked at in the US, European and Latin American context, there is a lack of cross-cultural inquiries into how plea-based case dispositions have arisen and unfurled in Greater China, a region that has yet to pique enough scholarly attention in sociolegal and comparative criminology studies.

To be sure, 'Greater China' is a term not without controversy. Despite being widely applied to narrate the system of interactions among Chinese-speaking societies, the concept of Greater China has been laden with the criticism on lacking an unequivocal and uniformly accepted conceptual framework. There are indeed powerful drivers for regional interaction and integration: mostly a common ethnic heritage that links Chinese communities across the Taiwan Strait, and a natural economic complementarity among the four economies (Shambaugh, 1993). What makes 'Greater China' a contentious lexicon perhaps lies in the fact that each entity of this Eastern region tends to encompass different systems, dimensions, and processes. Not only are there are variances in the choice of polity, the model of the economic system, and in the recognition of cultural identity, but each entity strives to maintain its local ethos of social control and governance, which has enabled different groups of Chinese people to approach Greater China with different views, attitudes, and emotions. Absent a better terminology to categorise Chinese-speaking societies, 'Greater China' in this book hence refers to a geographical area sharing cultural and economic ties with the Chinese people, including Mainland China, Taiwan, Hong Kong, and Macau.

The idea of this book emanates from Mainland China implementing the 'Admission of Guilt and Acceptance of Punishment' system (known as 'plea leniency') in 2016 as part of its ongoing criminal justice reform. Following this, all four entities of the Greater China region have adopted certain forms of trial-avoiding mechanisms in their criminal proceedings. One explicit purpose of this book, therefore, is to clearly map out the trajectories, models, and characteristics of plea-based cased dispositions as they are rationalised, conceptualised, and operationalised in the local criminal justice system of Greater China. Our chapters will attempt to answer questions relevant to legal scholars, criminologists, sociologists, and the like, using methods and approaches from a wide range of disciplines. Topics covered in this book will represent an array of important issues to highlight the discursive and practical traits of plea-based case dispositions based on a diverse range of first-hand or secondary empirical data. In particular, analysis will explore, *inter alia*, how law enforcement agencies carry out plea-driven practices on the ground, how judges act upon plea deals in the sentencing stage, how defendants interact with the prosecution when negotiating pleas, and how lawyers perform their legal work in this compressed process. To this end, the edited volume gathers scholars with different perspectives that work at different levels of analysis:

from practitioners unfolding the way in which plea-based justice administration is (re)produced in daily interactions to policy watchers explaining the extent to which guilty pleas are shaped by institutional reforms in alignment with the government's discourse of crime control. With these multiangle viewpoints and insights, this book would as well attract interest as a preliminary collection of materials that can gain new knowledge about and prompt further research on the system of plea-based case dispositions in Chinese-speaking societies, and more broadly, between the Eastern and the Western worlds.

Contours of the Book

The book is structured around the four Chinese-speaking jurisdictions to reveal the cultural distinctiveness of their approaches to criminal case dispositions through pleas. It will include an introduction and conclusion with other chapters covering Mainland China, Taiwan, Hong Kong, and Macau, respectively. To categorise the chapters according to the geographic region as opposed to the research theme is to enable a high degree of intellectual creativity and to advance the broadest spectrum of perspectives from the contributors in their area of expertise.

Mainland China: Plea Leniency and the Institutional Power Shifts

In Mainland China, the past decades have witnessed this socialist regime striving to optimise the court process (Papagianneas, 2022). Such attempt has ebbed and flowed, yet it reached new heights when the plea leniency system was formulated in 2016. The tenet of plea leniency is clear: it calls for the imposition of lighter punishment on those accused who voluntarily confess, admit the alleged criminal facts, and accept the sentence recommended by the procuratorate (Li, 2022b).[2] To distinguish from the Western plea bargain process where justice is accused of 'being malleable and negotiable' (Schulhofer, 1984), plea leniency is adapted to 'stick to finding the objective truth' by refraining the accused from negotiating with procuratorates (He, 2023). At its core, plea leniency entails not only the accused's acknowledgement of guilt and criminal facts, but also the accused's consent to the recommended sentencing

[2] *The CPL (2018)*, Article 15.

range, type of punishment, or even the means of implementation (Li, 2022a). Following two rounds of the pilot project in 18 localities, plea leniency was formally established by the 2018 Criminal Procedure Law as a fundamental principle and practice of criminal justice.

Yuguang Lu, Xifen Lin, and Enshen Li's chapter draws an overarching picture of the plea leniency system in Mainland China. This chapter teases out a theoretical and practical trajectory of plea leniency and how this dispositional measure has become the norm of seeking convictions in today's criminal justice system. The authors submit that the large-scale implementation of plea leniency is by and large attributed to the urgency to address an intensive concern for efficiency in criminal proceedings. However, a particular concern is raised over the increasing concentration of power in the hands of procurators over the course of the plea leniency practice. As they maintain, the emergence of plea leniency has enabled procuratorates to function as the de facto arbitrator of conviction with police and courts playing a passive role in the process. The chapter concludes that the supervisory power should be reserved for the judiciary which is capable of preventing the abuse of power by prosecutors through routinely questioning the guilty pleas, setting up procedures for evaluating the procurators' offers of unofficial immunity to defendants, and demanding criteria for judicial oversight of the procurators' decision-making.

The chapter contributed by Xin He further addresses the issue of a prosecutor-led plea leniency system dominating the Chinese criminal justice system. He characterises such domination as 'prosecution centeredness', which has replaced the 'investigation centeredness' that once shaped and underpinned the administration of criminal justice in China for decades (Mou, 2020). This chapter explores the operations and consequences of plea leniency and reveals that the procuratorates have outshone the police and further sidelined the courts in the process of plea leniency. In addition, defendants have little hope of being acquitted and legal representatives can offer little defence. It is contended that this paradigm shift indicates more leniency in the criminal justice system, albeit at the expense of rights protection in exchange for efficiency and crime control.

Yu Mou and Hui Chen's chapter turns to an empirical account of plea leniency by examining the role of criminal defence lawyers in China's new plea leniency system. Drawing from first-hand resources in 15 plea leniency defence cases, their chapter unravels the obstacles that have emerged in plea leniency, designed without incorporating the defence voice. They delineate defence lawyers' initial struggles, their gradual adaptation to the fast-paced, increasingly opaque process of handling criminal cases, and the uncertainties associated with prosecutorial and judicial practices that have made them more vulnerable. These difficulties highlight the systematic disadvantages and state-induced coercion that further undermine the criminal defence under this new scheme, largely driven by cost-effectiveness and increasingly punitive measures.

By investigating the decision-making process and its impact on case outcomes in plea leniency, Yuhao Wu's chapter advances our empirical comprehension of the inner workings of plea leniency from the perspective of defendants. Wu's study aims to address two questions: what factors influence the choice between pleading guilty and going to trial, and how does pleading guilty affect the sentencing results. The author analysed the data on DUI (driving under the influence) cases handled by the courts in six cities where the plea leniency program has been implemented. By exploring the legal and extralegal factors affecting the disposition of cases by plea or trial, the results indicate that the defendants who tended to plead guilty were those who had no previous criminal record, a lower Blood Alcohol Concentrations (BACs) level, or had admitted their guilt. The findings also suggest that the defendants who did not pay the victims were more inclined to plead guilty. The findings further provide that in Mainland China where the conviction rate at trial is almost 100% (Liang & Hu, 2023), a guilty plea could still lead to relatively better case outcomes from judges' sentencing decisions.

Taiwan: The Bargaining Process and Judicial Domination

The approach to plea-based case dispositions in Taiwan shows a rather different (somewhat 'deviant') landscape. *Taiwan* implemented the *plea bargain* system in 2004 with a view to optimise judicial resources and alleviate pressure from heavy workloads in the criminal justice system. It is reported that in 2008 there were 12,132 cases finalised without trial but instead by means of a bargaining agreement between the prosecution and defendants (Wang, 2011). Although this number only represented a small fraction of the handled criminal cases in that year, there has been a slow but sure decline in the use of plea bargaining ever since. As of 2019, the application rate of plea bargaining dropped to the lowest level at 2.9% (Lin, Chapter 7). Mong-hwa Chin's and Mao-hong Lin's chapters are aimed at expounding on the legal, social, and cultural factors that have engendered the stagnation of plea bargaining in Taiwan.

Chin's chapter probes into why Taiwanese prosecutors are discouraged from launching the plea bargaining process. Three reasons stand out. First, the judiciary still plays a dominate role in Taiwan's criminal justice system, which controls the narrative of case management. Second, there is a cultural resistance to plea bargains. Third, there has been various summary procedures at work in Taiwan, which appear to be less resource-demanding than plea bargaining. The author goes on to point out that the general public's lack of trust in the judiciary has impeded a widespread use of plea bargaining as judges are seen as lacking sufficient legitimacy. This is particularly the case when the new citizen judge system was recently introduced to include lay people as the decision-makers in the trial process. It is concluded that consensus among legal practitioners should be reached before plea bargaining can gain traction in Taiwan's criminal proceedings.

Lin's chapter continues to tease out the structural imbalance between the prosecution and the judiciary in the application of plea bargaining. In particular, prosecutors in Taiwan are not keen to finalise cases through guilty pleas because they perceive plea bargaining as poorly designed, cost-ineffective, and procedurally illegitimate. While judges have a different view, Lin argues that the reluctance of prosecutors to employ plea bargaining stems from the court-centric logic of criminal justice in Taiwan. This long-standing legal culture enables the judiciary to adopt a paternalistic approach, allowing judges to interfere in the plea bargaining process with little regard to the defendant-prosecutor agreement. This chapter also describes two types of the court's paternalistic role in Taiwan's plea bargaining system: the court as a protector of the defendant and the court as a promoter of moral discipline. The former is meant to safeguard defendants' rights despite their willingness to relinquish these procedural protections for entering in the plea agreement. The latter is to ensure that defendants accept their criminal responsibility and show remorse over their actions. Lastly, this chapter traces the origin of judicial paternalism to the inquisitorial legacy and civilising function of criminal courts in Taiwan's century-long civil law system.

Hong Kong and Macau: Plea Bargaining and Colonial Legal Heritage

Hong Kong and Macau are the two special administrative regions (SARs) of the People's Republic of China, which follow the principle of 'one country, two systems'. For more than a century, their special colonial legacy, cultural histories, and political conditions have shaped a unique framework of local criminal justice; hence the divergent way cases are disposed of through guilty pleas in criminal proceedings. The legal system of Hong Kong was inherited from British colonial rule, which has remained largely intact since its return to China. This distinguishes Hong Kong from its neighbouring regimes, making it the only common law jurisdiction in Greater China. Kevin Kwok-yin Cheng's chapter argues that despite the emphasis on the presumption of innocence and adversarialism, guilty pleas are significant in Hong Kong's criminal justice system. Despite twenty-five years after the handover, Hong Kong has continued to follow, although not entirely, developments of plea-based case dispositions in England and Wales. With only minor variations in practice, Hong Kong's plea bargaining system is laden with a set of general challenges as facing its common law counterparts. In a nutshell, plea bargaining gives the courts, the prosecution, and defence lawyers leverage over defendants to plead guilty and to plead guilty as early as possible, despite the law's protection on the voluntariness of plea decisions. Although it may seem to speed up the legal process, plea bargaining tends to undermine the presumption of innocence and the adversarial system that Hong Kong upholds.

Chengchen He and Jingwei Liu's chapter conducts a comparative analysis of plea-based justice in Mainland China and Hong Kong. Through a legal and policy analysis, the chapter argues that although there are different rationales behind plea bargaining in Hong Kong and plea leniency in Mainland China, the norms of due process and fairness are comprised and the punitive nature of criminal justice in effect pressures defendants to admit guilt in both jurisdictions. The authors also contend that achieving judicial efficiency and protecting defendants' rights are conflicting values and cannot be properly balanced in the plea-seeking processes.

Like Hong Kong, Macau also returned to China from the Portuguese rule only 20 years ago. However, Macau stands out as an anomaly in the prevalent adoption of plea-based case dispositions around the globe.

Rather than establishing a particular plea bargaining mechanism, Macau sticks to its entrenched simplified procedures as a main way of handling criminal cases with lesser culpability and damage. In their chapter, Zhe Li, Xueke Fan, and Heng Ut Wong introduce reconciliation as part of trial-avoiding case dispositions in Macau. They focus particularly on the suspension of criminal proceedings and complaint withdrawal by examining their legislative settings, discursive dimensions, and practical features. Their analysis revolves around the challenges facing the process of perpetrator-victim reconciliation in these programs. It indicates that among the identifiable issues, the lack of communication channels is most detrimental to meaningful and effective negotiation between the parties affected by the offence. The authors suggest that a formal mediation system presided over by prosecutors be constructed in Macau to widen the scope of criminal cases settled through reconciliation. It is because doing so would likely improve judicial efficiency and better assist the accused with their acceptance of fault and reparation of harm, as well as reintegration into society.

References

Alkon, C. (2010). Plea Bargaining as a Legal Transplant: A Good Idea for Troubled Criminal Justice Systems? *Transnational Law and Contemporary Problems, 19*, 355–419.

Alschuler, A. W. (1979). Plea Bargaining and Its History. *Law & Society Review, 13*(2), 211–245.

Bibas, S. (2004). Plea Bargaining Outside the Shadow of Trial. *Harvard Law Review, 117*(8), 2463–2547.

Bushway, S. D., Redlich, A. D., & Norris, R. J. (2014). An Explicit Test of Plea Bargaining in the "Shadow of the Trial." *Criminology, 52*(4), 723–754.

Cheng, K. K. Y. (2023). *The Timing of Guilty Pleas: Lessons from Common Law Jurisdictions*. Cambridge University Press.

Cohen, T. H., & Kyckelhahn, T. (2012). *Felony Defendants in Large Urban Counties, 2006*. Bureau of Justice Statistics.

Feeley, M. (2017). *Crime, Law and Society*. Routledge.

Galanter, M. (2004). The Vanishing Trial: An Examination of Trials and Related Matters in Federal and State Courts. *Journal of Empirical Legal Studies, 1*(3), 459–570.

Garland, D. (2000). The Culture of High Crime Societies: Some Preconditions of Recent 'Law and Order' Policies. *British Journal of Criminology, 40*(3), 347–375.

Hamin, Z., Othman, M. B., & Rani, A. R. A. (2019). When Law and Practice Collide: The Implementation of the Plea-Bargaining Process in Malaysia. *Asian Journal of Criminology, 14*(3), 223–240.

He, X. (2023). Plea Leniency and Prosecution Centredness in China's Criminal Process. *China Quarterly, 254*, 448–465.

Heumann, M. (1981). *Plea Bargaining: The Experiences of Prosecutors, Judges, and Defense Attorneys*. The University of Chicago Press.

Husak, D. (2023). Six Questions about Overcriminalization. *Annual Review of Criminology, 6*, 265–284.

Langer, M. (2004). From Legal Transplants to Legal Translations: The Globalization of Plea Bargaining and the Americanization Thesis in Criminal Procedure. *Harvard International Law Journal, 45*(1), 1–64.

Langer, M. (2021). Plea Bargaining, Conviction Without Trial, and the Global Administratization of Criminal Convictions. *Annual Review of Criminology, 4*(1), 377–411.

Li, E. (2022a). Chinese Courts' New Plea Leniency System: Scrutinizing the Efficacy of Mandatory Defense Counsel. *The China Journal, 88*(1), 78–99.

Li, E. (2022b). Haste Makes Waste: Why China's New Plea Leniency System is Doomed to Fail. *Asian Journal of Comparative Law, 17*(1), 76–105.

Liang, B., & Hu, M. (2023). 'Not-guilty' Verdicts in China: An Empirical Examination of Legal Defense and Judicial Rationales. *International Journal of Law, Crime and Justice, 74*. https://doi.org/10.1016/j.ijlcj.2023.100611

Lynch, D. (1994). The Impropriety of Plea Agreements: A Tale of Two Counties. *Law & Social Inquiry, 19*(1), 115–134.

Lynch, G. E. (1998). Our Administrative System of Criminal Justice. *Fordham Law Review, 66*, 2117–2151.

Ma, Y. (2002). Prosecutorial Discretion and Plea Bargaining the United States, France, Germany, and Italy. *International Criminal Justice Review, 12*(1), 22–52.

Matheny, A. (1980). Negotiation and Plea Bargaining Models: An Organizational Perspective. *Law & Policy, 2*(3), 267–284.

Mather, M. (1978). Comments on the History of Plea Bargaining. *Law & Society Review, 13*(2), 281–285.

McConville, M., & Mirsky, C. (1995). The Rise of Guilty Pleas: New York, 1800–1865. *Journal of Law and Society, 22*(4), 443–474.

McConville, M., & Mirsky, C. L. (2005). *Jury Trials and Plea Bargaining: A True History*. Hart Publishing.

McDonough, N. (1979). Plea Bargaining: A Necessary Evil. *University of Arkansas at Little Rock Law Review, 2*, 381–401.

Moley, R. (1928). The Vanishing Jury. *Southern California Law Review, 22*(2), 97–127.

Mou, Y. (2020). *The Construction of Guilt in China: An Empirical Account of Routine Chinese Injustice*. Hart.

Nash, C., Gravatt, M., Dioso-villa, R., & Porter, L. (2023). Efficiency Over Accuracy?: Exploring Front-Line Practitioners' Experiences and Opinions on the "Guilty Plea System." *Social & Legal Studies*, 1–23. https://doi.org/10.1177/09646639231197778

O'Hear, M. M. (2008). Plea Bargaining and Procedural Justice. *Georgia Law Review, 42*, 407–469.

Papagianneas, S. (2022). Towards Smarter and Fairer Justice? A Review of the Chinese Scholarship on Building Smart Courts and Automating Justice. *Journal of Current Chinese Affairs, 51*(2), 327–347.

Scott, R. E., & Stuntz, W. J. (1992). Plea Bargaining as Contract. *The Yale Law Journal, 101*(8), 1909–1968.

Shambaugh, D. (1993). Introduction: The Emergence of "Greater China." *The China Quarterly, 136*, 653–659.

Soubise, L. (2018). Guilty Pleas in an Inquisitorial Setting—An Empirical Study of France. *Journal of Law and Society, 45*(3), 398–426.

Stemen, D., & Escobar, G. (2018). Whither the Prosecutor? Prosecutor and County Effects on Guilty Plea Outcomes in Wisconsin. *Justice Quarterly, 35*(7), 1166–1194.

Schulhofer, S. (1984). Is Plea Bargaining Inevitable? *Harvard Law Review, 97*(5), 1037–1107.

Turner, J. I. (2017). Plea Bargaining and International Criminal Justice. *University of the Pacific Law Review, 48*(2), 219–246.

Wang, J. P. (2011). The Evolution and Revolution of Taiwan's Criminal Justice. *Taiwan in Comparative Perspective, 3*, 8–29.

Plea Leniency in Mainland China: Legislation, Characteristics and Effects

Yuguang Lu, Xifen Lin, and Enshen Li

Introduction

The criminal procedure of Plea Leniency was formally legalized in the People's Republic of China (China) in 2018. It is aimed at encouraging the defendant to admit guilt and accept the punishment recommended by the procuratorate in exchange for procedural and substantive leniency. Here, procedural leniency refers to the use of simplified criminal proceedings to finalize guilty plea cases, whereas substantive leniency refers to the imposition of a lenient sentence for consenting to enter into the plea agreement. As of 2022, Plea Leniency has reached an application rate of around 90% nationwide.[1] In addition, across all Plea Leniency cases, the courts' approval rate of sentencing recommendations by procuratorates

[1] The Supreme People's Procuratorate, 'The Application of Plea Leniency at the Prosecutorial Stage is over 90%'. Available at https://www.spp.gov.cn/spp/2023qglh/202303/t20230308_606847.shtml.

Y. Lu · X. Lin (✉)
KoGuan School of Law, Shanghai Jiaotong University, Shanghai, China
e-mail: linxifen1982@sjtu.edu.cn

E. Li
School of Law, City University of Hong Kong, Hong Kong, China
e-mail: enshenli@cityu.edu.hk

E. Li et al. (eds.), *Criminal Case Dispositions through Pleas in Greater China*, https://doi.org/10.1007/978-981-97-1856-6_2

reached 98.3%.[2] Of particular note is the rate of appeals in Plea Leniency cases being recorded as low as 3%, compared to 68% of non-Plea Leniency cases.[3] Official government data have indicated that Plea Leniency applies predominately to minor criminal offences (punishable by a sentence of imprisonment for 3 years or less).[4] This seems to be consistent with the recent trend of criminality in China as there has been a spike in minor criminal offences. The annual report of the Supreme People's Procuratorate (SPP) showed that minor crimes took up 78.7% of all criminal cases in 2019 (Han, 2021). It increased to 85.5% in 2022 and slightly dropped to 82.8% in 2023 (Jan. to Sep.) (Han, 2021; Jin et al., 2023). On the contrary, serious criminal offences have flown under the radar of this new criminal justice scheme (Jiang, 2023).

The advent of Plea Leniency is no surprise. It represents an example of China's ongoing law reform to improve efficiency, quality and accountability of criminal justice in line with the country's call for 'Ruling the Country according to Law with Chinese Characteristics'. As such, the official rationales of Plea Leniency are clear. It seeks, *inter alia*, to reduce the judicial expenditure on processing criminal cases; to offer better protection of the defendants' rights in the criminal procedure; to rebuild the relationship between procuratorates and defendants; and to reinforce China's transformed culture of penality toward softness and humanity (Shi & Li, 2016). While making significant changes to the administration of criminal justice, Plea Leniency is exposed to challenges and criticisms. Many suggest that the Plea Leniency is discursively, legally and procedurally flawed. Among those identifiable problems appears to be the lack of procedural justice in the application of this new dispositional measure (Li, 2022a; Shi & Li, 2016); the absence of professional practice guidelines to inform its principled and consistent use; the conflict of power

[2] Ibid.

[3] The Supreme People's Procuratorate, 'For the year of 2022, the rate of appeals in Plea Leniency cases was 3%, while the rate of non-Plea Leniency cases was 31.2%'. Available at https://www.spp.gov.cn/zdgz/202302/t20230209_600560.shtml, Publish date 02-09-2023.

[4] The Supreme People's Procuratorate detailed that the proportion of heavier criminal offences (more than 3 years of imprisonment) in January to September 2023 has dropped to 17.2%, compared to 1999's proportion of 45.4%. Meanwhile, Plea Leniency has been applied in more than 90% of all criminal cases. Average case duration has dropped from 47.8 days (2022) to 44.6 days (January to September 2023). Available at https://baijiahao.baidu.com/s?id=1780694622859057807&wfr=spider&for=pc.

between procuratorates and courts in terms of conviction and sentencing (He, 2023; Long, 2020); and the disconnection between guilty pleas and lenient sentences (Wu, 2020). This chapter does not intend to engage in a comprehensive critical analysis of Plea Leniency. As an opening chapter, it aims to provide an introductory and descriptive account of Plea Leniency praxis to understand its structure, form and spirit. One particular purpose of this chapter is to shed light on how Plea Leniency has come to acquire its characteristics in China, with an examination of its benefits and drawbacks within the country's broader criminal justice system.

The Legislative Formation of the Plea Leniency Procedure in China

In comparison with plea bargaining or other comparable initiatives in the West (especially the US), Plea Leniency in China is still a relatively recent product of China's criminal justice reform. Some core ideas that give rise to plea bargaining, such as interest swap, consensus, negotiations of charges and legal adversarialism, are largely absent from Chinese legal culture and policy (Zhang, 2005). In particular, criminal justice in this socialist regime originated from an ideology based on a completely *ex-officio* principle (Sun, 2002, p. 45).[5] This essentially inhibited the plea-base criminal process from finding its footing in China. Until the early 2000s, the concerns of judicial efficiency and expenditure control that became prominent in the 1970s across many Anglo-Saxon and European countries had yet to loom large in the Chinese criminal process.

Still, criminal justice in China had long been trial oriented. Often referred to as the 'Iron Triangle' (Liang et al., 2014), the criminal process is played out in an operational framework where the relationship among police, procuratorates and courts is coordinative for the collective purpose of combating crime. During this process, police are empowered to investigate the case, before handing inculpatory evidence over to procuratorates who then prepare a formal criminal charge, with the person on trial being finally convicted by courts. In 2002, there was a case which marked a

[5] *Ex-officio* principle mainly reflects in Civil Law countries' criminal procedure. During the investigation stage, police and procurators exercise their powers by strictly following legal rules. During the trial stage, judges play the role as the interrogator. Across the whole procedure, the defendants' litigation capabilities are relatively restricted, and they play a passive role on most occasions. *See* Sun (2002).

turning point and paved the way for officials to seriously contemplate the likelihood of introducing plea-based proceedings into the criminal justice system. In that case, the local procuratorate and the defense reached for the first time a 'plea agreement'.[6] The defendant admitted his guilt while showing a strong willingness to compensate the victim. It followed that the defense lawyer abstained from challenging the prosecution's case which seemed weak and tenuous. Instead, the defendant requested that his offending behavior be dealt with leniently. The procurator agreed and suggested that probation be imposed as the sentence. Upon receiving the case, the court organized a collegial panel to examine the legitimacy of the plea agreement and ultimately accepted it on the basis that the agreement was entered by the defendant voluntarily and freely. This was accompanied by a compensation agreement signed by the defendant and the victim in the view of repairing the harm caused by the crime. Following the negotiation, the court hearing only lasted 25 minutes (Ma, 2003).

This first ever 'plea negotiation' case provoked a hot debate as to whether China should introduce an American-style plea bargaining process. Although the SPC subsequently disapproved of the use of plea bargaining in criminal cases, the idea of forming a certain type of plea mechanism has begun to take root (Ma, 2003, p. 68). The legal community at the time was divided. Opponents argued that plea bargaining does not conform to a socialist concept of the rule of law, calling for the rejection of the word 'bargain' or 'trade' in the context of criminal justice. More specifically, it is contended that plea bargaining is at odds with core judicial principles, including the concept of *due process* (Sun, 2002, p. 45)

[6] In Heilongjiang, a gang of people severely injured a man by beating him up. The case was prosecuted as intentional injury, but the police only arrested the principal criminal, Meng. According to Meng's defense counsel, it could not be ascertained as to which person made the specific blows that caused the victim's serious injury and thus, the facts were unclear. The handling procurator held the view that the principal offender, Meng, should be held responsible. The defense attorney, with the oral consent of Meng, the accused criminal, negotiated with the procurator. Meng admitted his guilt and showed his willingness to compensate the victim. The defense lawyer gave up his claim that the facts were unclear and that there was insufficient evidence and requested the case to be dealt leniently. The procurator proposed leniency and probation to the court. After receiving the proposal, the court organized a collegial panel to examine the procedural legitimacy of the plea negotiation and agreement, then the court decided to sanction the agreement. Meng received a relatively light sentence, and probation was imposed as the sentence. In addition, through a process of civil mediation, the compensation agreement was entered by the offender and the victim.

and the principles of *legality* and *suiting responsibility and punishment to crime* (Sun, 2002, p. 48). Therefore, the defendant is deemed in no position to 'bargain' or 'negotiate' with the procurator under the *ex-officio* doctrine (Sun, 2002). Contrarily, supporters of plea bargaining held that the plea-based practice can be incorporated into the Chinese criminal justice system, albeit in a limited way (Chen, 2002). This is mainly because the discourse around plea bargaining tends to be conducive to the State's deep-rooted practice of 'leniency to those who confess, severity to those who resist' (*Tanbai Congkuan, Kangju Congyan* 坦白从宽，抗拒从严). Sanctioned as the 'golden thread' running through the criminal process, it has cultivated a culture which encourages defendants to confess to a crime in exchange for sentencing concessions (Li, 2022b).

Yet, like many Western counterparts, efficiency has over time morphed into a primary concern of Chinese criminal justice authorities. Two contributing reasons stand out. First, China is arguably following the road of 'overcriminalization' as a new mode of social governance (Wang, 2019b). Since the Second Amendment to the Criminal Law (CL) in 1997, about every two years there has been a new amendment introduced by the government to extend the reach of criminal jurisdiction. Consequently, the number of criminal offences increased from 412 in the Second Amendment to 483 in the Eleventh Amendment as of 2020 and the overwhelming majority of the newly prescribed crimes are *non-violent* in nature. The annual reports of the Supreme People's Procuratorate (SPP) revealed almost a twofold increase in the number of individuals charged in 2014 and 2023 (139 million v 210 million) (Cao, 2015; Zhang, 2023). With caseloads skyrocketing as a result of state resources being more thinly spread across a larger number of cases, judicial capacity to diligently handle every single case is seriously impaired.

Second, the number of judges has increased moderately but has lagged behind a drastic increase in reported criminal cases. This expansion of personnel within the judiciary may be attributed generally to the State's relatively slow pace of institutional development, but the introduction of the Judge Quota Scheme has also impacted the proportion of judges to other court personnel across the country (He, 2021). Formally implemented in 2015, the Judge Quota Scheme is driven by the vision that 'unqualified and incompetent judges' should be removed from courts. In doing so, it re-calculates the ratio of judges to judicial assistants and administrative staff to ensure that the position of judge is filled by those who are professionally trained and competent as opposed to court administrative staff who may be awarded a judge's title (Sun & Fu, 2022). One corollary of this personnel arrangement is that a considerable number of judges deemed 'unqualified and incompetent' have gone on furloughs. The remaining judges are then excessively burdened with facing the increase in the court's workload. In this light, a heavy backlog of cases from procuratorates to courts has begun to accumulate, and the time spent on each case has perceptibly increased (Zhang, 2017). Exacerbated by the enforcement of the 'lifelong responsibility mechanism', Chinese procurators and judges have been under mounting pressure, both physically and psychologically, to deal with fast-growing criminal cases with extra care and caution in seeking 'desirable' case outcomes that satisfy all parties involved.

As such, over the past decade, disquiet about heavy workloads and lengthy trial processes have been commonplace across the judiciary (He, 2021; Zhang, 2017). In June 2014, the Standing Committee of the National People's Committee (NPC) approved the proposal of utilizing plea-based case dispositions as an approach to criminal cases. Two years later, a two-year trial of 'Plea Leniency' commenced in 18 major cities across the country. It was not until 2018 that Plea Leniency was codified in the CPL as a fundamental principle and practice of criminal justice.

There are multiple provisions set out in the 2018 Criminal Procedure Law (CPL) which characterize this new criminal justice initiative. Notionally, Article 15 of the 2018 CPL defines Plea Leniency as a process wherein the defendant voluntarily and truthfully confesses to criminal conduct, admits criminal behavior as charged, accepts the final punishment and has an opportunity to receive a lenient sentence. In that, the accused has a right to legal representation. Particularly, Article 36 states that legal aid lawyers should be stationed at courts, procuratorates and detention houses to provide timely legal assistance services. It is stipulated that legal aid lawyers, when performing their duties, should be allowed to raise opinions, either orally or in writing, on issues relative to the plea process (Article 173).

To initiate Plea Leniency, Article 120 requires that procurators inform defendants of their rights to plead guilty for leniency. In the meantime, while processing the case through Plea Leniency, procuratorates ought to pay attention to the time limit (Article 172), prepare the plea agreement (Article 174) and make the sentencing recommendation to the court (Article 176). Once the case proceeds to a court hearing upon a guilty plea, it is mandated that the judge inform the defendant about their rights during the trial proceedings (Article 90). The judge is, however, empowered to rule out, as much as possible, the defendant's confession obtained through illegal means or the plea deal unlawfully entered by the defendant and the procurator (Article 226).[7] In hearing a Plea Leniency case, only one judge is required—the adjudicative panel is not needed.[8] The trial should be held within 15 days from the time that the procurator submits the case to the court.[9] At the end of the hearing, the judge should immediately announce the verdict.[10]

[7] Article 226 of the CPL: Where people's courts discover in the course of trial that defendants conduct does not constitute a crime or should not be pursued for criminal responsibility, that they admitted guilt and accepted punishment against their will, that the defendant denies the alleged facts of the crime, or that there are other circumstances making application of the expedited procedures inappropriate, a new trial shall be held in accordance with Section 1 or Section 3 of this Chapter (of the CPL). Article 190: Where defendants admit guilt and accept punishment, the chief judge shall inform the defendant of the procedural rights they enjoy and the legal provisions on admitting guilt and accepting punishment, and review the voluntariness of the admission of guilt and acceptance of punishment and the truthfulness and lawfulness of the written plea affidavit. Article 201: When the people's court lawfully makes a judgement in a plea case, the charges and sentencing recommendation of the people's procuratorate are usually adopted, except in the following circumstances:

1. The defendant has not constituted a crime or should not be pursued for criminal responsibility;
2. The defendant admitted guilt and accepted punishment against his wishes;
3. The defendant denies the alleged criminal facts;
4. The charge in the indictment and the charge verified at trial are not the same;
5. Other situations that might impact the fairness of trial.

Where through trial people's courts find that the sentencing recommendation is clearly improper, or where the defendant or defender raises objections to the sentencing recommendation, people's procuratorate may adjust its sentencing recommendation. Where the people's procuratorate does not adjust the sentencing recommendation, or where after adjusting the sentencing recommendation, it is still clearly improper, the people's court shall make a judgement in accordance with law.

[8] A summary trial deals with crimes punishable by more than 3 years of fixed-term imprisonment and requires a panel of at least 3 judges. The expedited procedure trial deals with crimes punishable by a sentence of up to a three-year fixed-term imprisonment within the jurisdiction of the basic level of the people's courts.

[9] Article 225 of the CPL.

[10] Article 224 of the CPL.

Plea Leniency—A System with Chinese Characteristics

In many respects, Plea Leniency departs significantly from plea bargaining (or charge negotiation) which is widely employed in the US and other similar jurisdictions. This is particularly the case when Plea Leniency cases are enjoined to go through a simplified trial as the requisite step toward case finalization. This may sound at odds with the idea of advancing the speed of case disposition, but it is aimed at providing a certain degree of control over the outcome of Plea Leniency cases, which shows that the officials are unwilling to put Plea Leniency into action as an unsupervised criminal justice practice that can take place behind closed doors.

Defendants get to negotiate, more or less, for lesser charges or lighter sentences under plea bargaining, whereas defendants under Plea Leniency enjoy little to no right to 'negotiate a plea bargain' with procuratorates in terms of their charges and sentences. Just like the traditional tenet of 'leniency to those who confess, severity to those who resist', Plea Leniency exhibits no elements of a 'bargain', but rather a form of 'one-sided consensus' imposed solely by procuratorates. More specifically, defendants are given only the option to choose between a summary trial and an expediated trial as a dispositional approach to their cases.[11] Expediated trials can be regarded as an exclusive derivative of Plea Leniency legislation.

Still, the type of the trial procedure is subject to the approval of the handling procurator and later endorsement by the court. When the defendant agrees to plead guilty for leniency, they must give up on their right to a regular trial. Although Chinese defendants are not afforded a constitutional right to a (fair) trial, a regular trial entails the judge's due diligence in reviewing the case presented by the procurator and the defense, with the latter having proper opportunity (in theory) to challenge the State's case at court. Therefore, a regular trial is believed to secure 'absolute substantive justice' as opposed to 'relative substantive justice' which Plea Leniency has arguably brought in its wake.[12] In other words, from a utilitarian perspective, Plea Leniency can be more appropriately seen as a program achieving 'timely justice'. While it processes criminal cases in a

[11] Article 214 of the CPL.

[12] In a general sense, 'relative substantive justice' refers to a rapid sentencing process, while 'absolute substantive justice' focuses on strictly and rightfully '*suiting punishment to criminal offense*'.

speedier fashion, there is a possibility that Plea Leniency does not produce results that fit the defendant's criminal malice and responsibility.

Regardless, the court is legally obligated to examine the voluntariness of the defendant's guilty plea before acting upon it. Specifically, judges ought to pay special heed to the evidential rule established in Article 56 of the CPL as grounds for ruling out illegally obtained evidence.[13] Matters that can be examined include police/prosecutorial records, lawyers' opinions and most crucially defendants' testimonies given during the process of Plea Leniency. It is noteworthy that in China illegally obtained (oral) evidence is not strictly excluded. For Chinese legislators, all categories of evidence have certain degrees of probative value, as they may be regarded. And as such, China has yet to adopt the fruit of the poisonous tree doctrine, which means that evidence should be inadmissible in court if it was derived from evidence that was obtained in an unlawful manner. This rule, however, now seems to apply to Plea Leniency where judges are asked to set aside the plea agreement should the defendant's guilty plea and oral consent to the plea agreement be illegally acquired. The reason is clear: oral evidence has a completely different level of significance in Plea Leniency cases as opposed to non-plea criminal cases, especially those processed through a regular trial. In Plea Leniency cases, the prosecution case relies entirely upon confessions made 'willingly' and 'voluntarily' by defendants, whereas oral evidence only forms part of the evidence chain at trial in which cross-examination is arguably at work to test the validity of confession. Differently put, if the defendant's guilty plea and consent under Plea Leniency prove to be problematic, then the defendant's free will of admitting guilt is on the line, rendering the plea agreement unsafe and unsatisfactory.

Even if the plea agreement is accepted by the court, the defendant is entitled to appeal against their conviction. In contrast to American plea

[13] Article 56 of the CPL: 'Confessions extorted from a criminal suspect or defendant by illegal means such as torture, testimony of witnesses and statements of victims collected by violent means, threat or other unlawful means shall be excluded. Physical evidence or documentary evidence that is not collected according to statutory procedures and is therefore likely to materially damage judicial justice shall be subject to correction or reasonable explanations, and shall be excluded if correction or reasonable explanations are not made. Evidence that shall be excluded as found during investigation, examination before prosecution and trial shall be excluded in accordance with the law, and shall not serve as the basis for making prosecution opinions, prosecution decisions and judgments'.

bargaining,[14] the grounds on which a defendant can appeal under Plea Leniency are much more relaxed.[15] The reason that China permits appeals in Plea Leniency cases perhaps lies in the fact that *the appellate* court will then get a proper opportunity to review the case thoroughly should the defendant regard the first trial unfair. As Plea Leniency circumvents a full-on court hearing which ordinarily involves courtroom debate and cross-examination, appeals tend to allow the higher court to revert to a trial-centered procedure, remedying issues such as the abuse of process wherein the admissibility of illegally obtained evidence appears to be of great concern (Chen, 2017).

[14] *18 U.S.C. § 3742 (a)* regulates four conditions of appealing for defendants on their initiative. But if clause (a) is combined with clause (c) (1) under the same section, only three circumstances are left in which defendants can actively appeal: if a law violation has happened; incorrect sentencing; or a harsher sentence than the maximum penalty that was agreed to in the plea agreement. 18 U.S.C. § 3742 (a): Appeal by a Defendant: A defendant may file a notice of appeal in the district court for review of an otherwise final sentence if the sentence:

1. Was imposed in violation of law;
2. Was imposed as a result of an incorrect application of the sentencing guidelines; or
3. Is greater than the sentence specified in the applicable guideline range to the extent that the sentence includes a greater fine or term of imprisonment, probation, or supervised release than the maximum established in the guideline range, or includes a more limiting condition of probation or supervised release under section 3563(b)(6) or (b)(11) [1] than the maximum established in the guideline range; or (4) was imposed for an offence for which there is no sentencing guideline and is plainly unreasonable. *18 U.S.C. § 3742 (c)*: Plea Agreements: In the case of a plea agreement that includes a specific sentence under rule 11(e)(1)(C) of the Federal Rules of Criminal Procedure:

   a. A defendant may not file a notice of appeal under paragraph (3) or (4) of subsection (a) unless the sentence imposed is greater than the sentence set forth in such agreement; and
   b. The government may not file a notice of appeal under paragraph (3) or (4) of subsection (b) unless the sentence imposed is less than the sentence set forth in such agreement.

[15] The 2018 revision of CPL did not add any extra restriction on defendants' right to appeal in Plea Leniency.

For those who are familiar with American plea bargaining, defense lawyers in the plea process are thought to play the role of 'legal counsel' who are free to provide legal services.[16] Chinese Plea Leniency, on the contrary, witnesses a different role of defense lawyers. Largely driven by the divergence between the adversarial and inquisitorial system, Chinese lawyers function more as a 'passive party' who stay outside of the plea process with the defendant facing the procurator directly. There is evidence that defense lawyers under Plea Leniency are confined to three peripheral roles—'explainer', 'persuader' and 'observer'. They are present to advise defendants about the law on Plea Leniency and the consequences of pleading (not) guilty, while impartially observing the plea process (Li, 2022b). Instead of providing sufficient legal advice, it is not uncommon that lawyers have found themselves in the position of only being able to help defendants gain a simple understanding of Plea Leniency while encouraging that they accept the proposed sentence (Li, 2022b). For example, it is nearly impossible for the defense lawyer to persuade the procurator to downgrade the charge through Plea Leniency (e.g., from organized prostitution (*Zuzhi Maiyin Zui* 组织卖淫罪) to introducing/sheltering prostitution (*Jieshao Shourong Maiyin Zui* 教唆收容卖淫罪)). The only way to have the case dealt with on a lesser charge is to plead not guilty to the procuratorate's original charge and request a regular trial to test the prosecution's case. As the defense lawyer cannot negotiate the criminal charge on behalf of the defendant, the decision to accept or reject the plea offer made by the procurator is entirely on the defendant (both orally and in writing). While the defense lawyer can assist the defendant with comprehending the circumstances of the case in order to inform the defendant's plea decision, the defendant must enter the plea in the exercise of their free will (Kong, 2017). If the lawyer suspects illegal actions from police or procurators, which the defendant cannot discern, during the investigation or interrogation, the lawyer has the right to and should raise an objection or request to pause or end the plea process, all of which must be recorded and displayed in court.

[16] The right to legal counsel is derived from the 6th Amendment of American Constitution: 'In all criminal prosecutions, the accused shall enjoy the right to a speedy and public trial, by an impartial jury of the State and district wherein the crime shall have been committed, which district shall have been previously ascertained by law, and to be informed of the nature and cause of the accusation; to be confronted with the witnesses against him; to have compulsory process for obtaining witnesses in his favor, and to have the Assistance of Counsel for his defense'.

Defense lawyers, however, may discuss the possible sentences with procurators under Plea Leniency. In the traditional criminal procedure, Chinese lawyers often encounter challenges referred to as 'three difficulties' in defense practice. They include practical difficulties of lawyers (1) in meeting criminal suspects, (2) in obtaining access to case files and (3) in collecting evidence to defend criminal defendants (Liu & Halliday, 2016). This left lawyers with only one meaningful task—striving for lesser punishments during the trial (Li, 2010). In other words, the point at which defense lawyers were able to take part in sentencing is the trial stage (Wang, 2019b). However, absent a well-prepared defense, lawyers were by no means in a position to argue for a lighter sentence, particularly when the procuratorates' options on sentencing were hardly ever rejected by courts due to the 'Iron Triangle' framework. Facing these challenges, defense lawyers in China were a far cry from an equal adversary of procurators. Plea Leniency, however, seemingly seeks to downplay the adversarial nature of lawyer-procuratorate interaction. That is, procurators are now expected to facilitate the defendant's access to legal aid lawyers; to guarantee the attendance of lawyers in Plea Leniency cases; and to listen to the opinions and suggestions offered by defense lawyers on the sentencing options (Kong, 2017; Wang, 2019a). In a sense, this paves the way for defense lawyers to participate in the penalty measuring process. It is hoped that the procurator's sentencing recommendation can be more acceptable to the defendant. However, the extent to which the lawyer's presence influences the sentencing outcome remains dubious.

Does Plea Leniency Reshape the Criminal Justice System?

To a considerable extent, the rise of Plea Leniency has restructured Chinese criminal procedure. This is mostly done by reshaping the interface between different stakeholders under the previous 'Iron Triangle' system. For one, Plea Leniency alters the relationship between the procuratorate and the defense. This is because the priority of obtaining guilty pleas has enabled procuratorates to shift their interaction with defendants from predominately confrontational to cooperative. In the plea process, the defendant is no longer a subject of coercive law enforcement, being questioned for inculpatory evidence conducive to conviction. But rather, the defendant is now engaged more actively in making pleas, accepting punishment and repairing harms to the victim among others. To a certain degree, the process of Plea Leniency speaks to a practice of restorative justice characterized by 'people's mediation' and 'victim-offender reconciliation' that have long been operational on Chinese soil (Yuan, 2017). This is due mainly to the fact that the SPP urges procurators to carry out Plea Leniency only when two conditions are satisfied at the same time: (1) the defendant has reached a criminal reconciliation agreement with the victim, and (2) the victim has forgiven the defendant. Evidence shows that disagreement between procurators and defendants becomes less likely when a compensation deal is reached under Plea Leniency. As a result, defendants are more willing to accept sentences suggested by procuratorates.[17]

On a more procedural level, Plea Leniency gives rise to a transformation by basing criminal justice on a more efficient mechanism of cross-agency coordination. In the 'Iron Triangle' framework, police transfer case dossiers including all relevant materials and evidence to procuratorates, mostly after police discharge their obligation of investigation. Here, the investigation phase could last for a maximum period of 7 months in ordinary circumstances and 17.5 months in exceptional circumstances.[18] This relay process is being altered under Plea Leniency where procuratorates reach out to police as early as when the defendant is arrested. At this juncture, procuratorates are empowered to request case information from police. As part of what is called 'early intervention', procuratorates are encouraged to 'offer opinions and suggestions on issues relating to evidence collection, fact determination, legal application and investigative activity of police in cases which are significant, difficult and complex'.[19] The primary objective is then to ensure that evidence gathered by police meets the minimum standard of admissibility and is also lawfully obtained.

All the while, procuratorates are assigned with a significant duty of submitting sentencing recommendations to courts after the plea agreement is entered by defendants. In December 2021, the SPP published a guideline aimed at helping procurators better exercise their 'sentencing powers' in Plea Leniency cases. In the traditional 'Iron Triangle' process,

[17] In 2021, the application rate of Plea Leniency was 89.4%. Among these cases, the rate of appeals was 3.5%. Available at https://baijiahao.baidu.com/s?id=1726922734544179452&wfr=spider&for=pc. Publish date 03-10-2022.

[18] Article 138, 154, 156, 157, 158, 178, 199, 202, 232.

[19] Article 85 of the CPL.

procurators are seen as playing a similar role to a 'chef'. Police provide ingredients (case dossiers) to procurators who then 'do the cooking' (building the case based on evidence), and bring dishes to the table (trials) for judges to 'taste and remark upon' (judgements). However, under Plea Leniency, Chinese procurators must not only be capable of 'cooking', they have to prepare for 'feedback on dishes'. Therefore, judges have turned into 'reviewers of the feedback' instead of simply tasting the 'food' as customers (He, 2023).

That said, the procurators' power has been magnified to become the core actor who determines final penalties, even though judges are legally the approvers of sentencing recommendations. This is demonstrated by the fact that in the overwhelming majority of Plea Leniency cases judges do not raise objection to the procuratorates' sentencing proposals.[20] It is no secret, though, that the way Chinese procurators assess the appropriate sentence varies from case to case, just like in any other jurisdiction where *inconsistency* in penalty *has been* one of the foremost *problems* of the *sentencing* system (Lin et al., 2022; Mitchell, 2005). Under Plea Leniency, some procurators are inclined toward making sentencing recommendations with specific options, whereas others tend to recommend a range of possible sentences for judges to choose from. In the official '2020 Report' (Zhang, 2020), the SPP formally established that procurators should reach an agreement with defendants in terms of their sentencing outcomes before handing the case over to courts. Of significant importance is that procurators should always present specific sentencing recommendations whenever reasonably practicable.

Substantially, a sentencing recommendation can be perceived as a legal 'promise' offered by the procurator to the defendant and their defense lawyer. A specific sentencing recommendation with a certain level of precision renders this 'promise' more explicit and appealing, laying grounds for better communication between the defendant and the procurator in seeking a clearer expectation of sentence reduction following the guilty plea. Relatedly, from the perspective of courts, specific sentencing recommendations are likely to improve judicial efficiency (compared to a range

[20] It is reported that from January to June 2023 the acceptance rate of sentencing recommendation in Plea Leniency (that procurators raised to courts) had surpassed 99%. Available at https://www.spp.gov.cn/spp/zhuanlan/202309/t20230905_627274.shtml.

of sentences) not least because the judges get to spend less time on exercising 'instinctive synthesis' in making the proper sentencing decision in every single Plea Leniency case.

Therefore, while it might be true that the efficiency of case processing has more or less improved, the workload of Chinese procuratorates does not seem to be lessened. In practice, to secure the defendant's guilty plea, procurators must collaborate with police during the investigation phase, must meet regularly with the defendant and their defense lawyer to discuss the plea agreement, and then prepare the sentencing recommendation for courts to consider. According to the author's empirical research of procurators from a Municipality in China, it is shown that more procedural chores have been created to meet the new requirements of paperwork and advancing the processing of guilty pleas (Lin, 2020). This is compounded by the SPP declaring the expectation of an average of 85% application rate of Plea Leniency across all criminal cases (Wang, 2023; Zhang, 2020). Needless to say, it has generated more pressure on procurators to persuade defendants into pleading guilty, which turns Plea Leniency into a one-sided process wherein procurators get to push the plea process with defendants having little power to say no. On the other hand, the expanded duty of procuratorates appears to have assisted courts in easing court backlogs. This is because judges, after receiving the case submitted by procurators, no longer need to thoroughly review the evidence of the case. Instead, they only need to focus on the validity of the plea agreement, approve the recommended sentence and make the final verdict. As the application rate of Plea Leniency has exceeded 90%, the number of regular trials for judges to preside at has significantly dwindled. Just like police, courts are able to focus their resources on more serious, significant and complicated cases.

Of course, from the perspective of defendants, procedural efficiency of Plea Leniency is of little salience to them, unless it also leads to penalty reduction. Therefore, substantive leniency appears to be a much stronger incentive than procedural leniency for defendants to admit guilt in a timely manner. The reality, however, is that while Plea Leniency has occupied a central place in China's criminal justice system, the incarceration population keeps expanding.[21] The advent of Plea Leniency seems to

[21] From 2000 to 2018, the number of incarcerated defendants increased from around 1,428,000 to 1,710,000 (19.8%).

have failed to downsize the prison population regardless of the program's promise to reduce sentences in exchange for confessions.

What the Future Holds for Plea Leniency?

Operationally, Plea Leniency happens to target criminal offences punishable by less than 3 years imprisonment (Shi, 2023). Following Plea Leniency's codification in 2018, debate among Chinese legal scholars has intensified as to whether the purview of Plea Leniency should be extended to cover more serious offences. While such debate has yet to bear fruits, China's hesitation to make such a move is not difficult to understand. Primarily, Civil Law jurisdictions have a long history of clinging to rigorous trial proceedings as a means of 'seeking truth' in serious crimes. Italy, for example, strictly forbids the application of plea bargaining to crimes that can trigger a prison term of more than 7.5 years.[22] In addition, Italy purposefully removes some specific crimes punishable by a prison term of less than 7.5 years from the orbit of plea bargaining, including juvenile offending and cases involving Mafia. Another major continental country, France, has an even more conservative attitude toward plea bargaining. It prohibits the use of plea bargaining on criminal offences punishable by a maximum period of 5 years imprisonment.[23] In contrast, common law countries are vastly divergent—the US, for example, has an array of rather relaxed rules about plea bargaining being applied to felonies. Plea agreements are excluded in only very exceptional circumstances (Shi, 2007, p. 114).[24]

While, in China, many have voiced their support for an expanded application of Plea Leniency to serious offences (Chen, 2016), such propositions may lack adequate jurisprudential grounds. For a long time, the Chinese criminal procedure has operated, at least on paper, under the principle of *legality* and the principle of *suiting responsibility and*

[22] See Codice di Procedura Penale, Article 444, Clause 1. It provides that plea bargaining only applies to crimes punishable by less than 5 years of imprisonment, with a maximum of 1/3 sentence discount being given.

[23] See Code de Procedure Penale, Clause 495–497, 16.

[24] Generally, three types of crimes are ineligible for the application of plea bargaining in the United States: juvenile cases, minimal offences (that merit no prison term, only fines or community service, etc.), and special categories of felony—mainly treason and espionage.

punishment to crime. This means that once the individual's perpetration meets the legal thresholds of criminalization, procuratorates would have to charge the person with a particular crime as per the criminal law with no compromise being made on the level of the charge. To a large extent, this underlying principle prevents procurators from downgrading the charge from a serious offence to a lesser offence at their will in order to induce the defendant's guilty plea, unlike their US counterparts. This also casts a pall over the procurator's power to reduce the number of changes, as frequently seen in US plea bargaining practices.

Indeed, the current application rate hovering around 90% has already indicated that a high proportion of criminal cases are being dealt with through Plea Leniency in China. Allowing Plea Leniency to include serious offences is likely to see this figure skyrocket up to more than 95% (provided that some accused refuse to plead guilty). In a country where the public still holds a plain vision of justice—namely seeing 'bad people' receiving proportional, if not overly harsh, punishment—adopting an all-inclusive approach of Plea Leniency may stand in the way of pursuing retribution and a populist version of punishment (Sun, 2002). Even if Plea Leniency is gradually expanded to criminal offences with a sentencing range of 3–7 years, the possibility of the accused being awarded a lenient penalty for pleading guilty would remain high and hence has the potential to damage the public confidence in the integrity of the criminal justice system, considering that the whole process of Plea Leniency takes place in private without judicial oversight (Wang, 2020). That said, public skepticism is likely to serve as an equally powerful impediment as the legal deficiency to the expansion of Plea Leniency in today's China.

Similarly, the defendant's right to appeal in Plea Leniency cases has prompted discussion around the direction this dispositional measure is heading in. On the one hand, from the perspectives of judicial efficiency and *consensus ad idem*, defendants who pled guilty are taken as giving up on their procedural rights to trade for procedural simplification and substantive penalty discounts. Seen in this light, the plea agreement is deemed virtually a 'contract' between defendants and procuratorates, and its revocation would need to be justified on 'substantial reasons' and approved by the judiciary in the interests of justice. On the other hand, the long-standing custom of trial-basedness in China requires that defendants are afforded the right of appeal for error correction as well as a process of clarifying and interpreting law. This tension seemed to reach its peak in a high-profile Plea Leniency case where the court imposed a harsher penalty on the defendant who appealed the sentence after entering the plea. In this widely reported case, the defendant pled guilty and received a 9-month prison term as his punishment. The defendant however appealed the sentence on the ground that the penalty was manifestly excessive. The court of appeal varied the sentence. Instead of giving a shorter sentence, it handed down a prison sentence of 15 months. The court of appeal justified its decision on the basis that the defendant was 'trading a lower penalty by pleading guilty, then appealing by using the principle of no additional penalty on appeal' (Wang, 2019c).[25] This decision suggests that the defendant's intent of pleading and appealing was 'impure', violating the *consensus ad idem* of the plea agreement which warrants additional punishment.

The ruling of this Chinese case shows great resemblances with a landmark case in US plea bargaining—the Erwin case.[26] In the Erwin case, the defendant appealed the sentence on the ground that the district court should reduce the penalty from a level 38 felony from a level 39 felony.[27] The appellate court's decision was nevertheless to set aside the penalty, allowing the prosecution to suggest a harsher sentence. According to the appellate court, the appeal made by the defendant represents an act that breaches the 'contract' (the plea agreement) between the defendant and the prosecution, despite the fact that this 'contract' is a product of coercive law enforcement in the criminal justice system. It is held that 'a classic rule of contract law is that a party should be prevented from benefitting from its own breach'.[28] As such, the appellant court's decision is deemed not only warranted but also necessary to 'punish the breach of the contract'. Otherwise, the plea agreement, as the judge views it, will turn into a 'legal fiction'.[29]

Another issue with Plea Leniency is whether procuratorates should still be encouraged to submit *specific* sentencing recommendations. In some Western plea bargaining jurisdictions (e.g., Australia), prosecutors are mandated—under both statutory and common law—to refrain themselves

[25] Such circumstances have been named "Technical Appeal" in China.

[26] United States v. Erwin, 765 F. 3d 219 (3d Cir. 2014).

[27] Id. See also U.S.S.G. § 2D 1.1(c), Drug Quantity Table.

[28] See Assaf v. Trinity Med. Ctr., 696 F.3d 681, 686 (7th Cir. 2012).

[29] See United States v. Erwin, 765 F. 3d 219 (3d Cir. 2014). "… rendering the concept of a binding agreement a legal fiction," Referring U.S. v. Williams, 510 F.3d at 422, 423.

from making sentencing recommendations at all to courts (Flynn, 2016). Notwithstanding efficiency concerns, a strongly *judge*-centered approach to sentencing is retained. While this does not take place in Chinese Plea Leniency, it begs the question whether a *range* of sentencing recommendations works better than specific sentencing recommendations in terms of approaching an appropriate sentence. Specific sentencing recommendation has its merits. Yet, concerns have been raised over its procedural legitimacy. Opponents argue that the power of holding a 'substantial trial' (including the power to hand down the sentence) should not be stripped from judges, as Plea Leniency already undermines the court's authority as an exclusive arbiter of criminal proceedings (Chen, 2017; Xiong, 2019a, 2019b). Specific sentencing recommendations invade the space of judicial independence and discretion. In particular, it has yet to provide leeway for the court to adjust the sentence should the specific penalty submitted by the procuratorate be inaccurate or inappropriate (Wei, 2021; Yu & Lu, 2021). Absent the intervention of the judiciary, there is little leverage that defendants and their lawyers can wield in the face of the procuratorates' mighty position, leading to involuntary acceptance of proposed sentences by the accused being not only possible but almost inevitable (Xiong, 2019a, 2019b). This, in turn, significantly increases the procurators' workload. The burden on procuratorates to make specific sentencing recommendations means that prosecuting officers would have to invest more time, energy and resources in the determination of punishment which was previously beyond their job descriptions (Lin, 2020).

On a more practical note, opting for either a range of or specific sentencing recommendations may depend on—or is at least relative to—the category of trial to which Plea Leniency is applied. In an expediated trial, it would be less problematic for the procurator to submit a specific sentencing recommendation given that the simple facts of the case can readily be agreed upon by the defendant. For summary trials involving Plea Leniency, however, it is not uncommon that the case may contain disputed factual issues, particularly related to the mitigating or aggravating circumstances that are likely to affect the judge's sentencing decision. If a compromise can be made, a 'semi-specific' sentencing recommendation could be an alternate option. Instead of putting forth a clear-cut sentence length, procurators may make submissions as to a maximum penalty. As the minimum penalty of a particular crime is established by the CL, the judge would only need to consider an appropriate sentence between the minimum penalty in law and the maximum penalty as proposed by the procurator. This arrangement should be, of course, first consented to by the defendant insomuch as the defendant has already formed a clear expectation of the worst result of sentencing. At the same time, the procurator gets to retain the monopoly over the outcome of the Plea Leniency case, whereas the judge gets to keep the sentencing discretion to a reasonable degree to decide what the final penalty should be.

Conclusion

Since its inception, Plea Leniency as a new case dispositional measure has become the norm in China's criminal justice system. Multiple factors have contributed to the popularity of Plea Leniency; yet the urgency to address an intensive concern for efficiency in criminal proceedings has seemingly topped the list. Although Plea Leniency is said to optimize case processing as well as to save costs associated with trials, its enforcement has been met with normative, legal and procedural challenges. Of particular concern appears to be the increasing concentration of power in the hands of procuratorates over the course of the Plea Leniency practice.

There is little doubt that Plea Leniency has elevated procuratorates to be the de facto arbitrators of conviction with police and courts taking a back seat in the process. Not only are procuratorates able to lay their hands on police investigations through early intervention, but they have also begun to take over the sentencing power from courts, leaving judges with the administrative task of merely verifying the 'voluntary nature, authenticity and legality of the guilty plea' (He, 2023, p. 454). At trial, however, what the judge sees is only what the procurator offers. This largely undermines the judge's function as an impartial adjudicator seeking 'substantive justice'. Without sufficient knowledge about evidence, guilty pleas and the facts of the case, the judge does nothing but rubber stamp the prosecutorial decision. There is every reason to believe that the court's role as the final line of defense against miscarriage of justice is diminished not least because judges are virtually left in the cold during the Plea Leniency procedure. Worse, evidence indicates that Chinese judges have been voicing frustration about this imbalance of power, and in some Plea Leniency cases judges even raised questions about the prosecution's case in relation to the defendant's plea, the gathering of evidence and the inappropriate sentencing proposal submitted by the procurator, among other concerns (Yu & Lu, 2021; Wei, 2021; Zhan & Li, 2021; Zhang & Pan, 2021; Zhou, 2021).

Unfortunately, a viable solution to this power asymmetry between procuratorates and courts seems lacking. How to impose checks and balances on prosecutorial discretion while the court's role is reduced to symbolic significance presents a challenge for the future of Plea Leniency. This may readily lead to either 'judicial inertia' or 'judicial corruption', if not both. To prevent the prosecutorial power from running on autopilot and generating unsustainable consequences, it is important that, as suggested in the SPP's '2020 Operation Guide of Plea Leniency', defense lawyers' procedural capabilities be improved in Plea Leniency. Also, the government disciplinary department may enter the arena to oversee the plea process if complaints are made. Alternatively, it is recommended that a supervisory branch be established within procuratorates to monitor the performance of legal duties by individual procurators under Plea Leniency (Lu, 2021). Either way, the process lacks functioning external oversight to minimize the occurrence of wrongful convictions through guilty pleas and an effective redress procedure which allows defendants to settle their disputes with procurators before an independent, competent and impartial tribunal. Surely, this issue is not unique to China. Across plea bargaining jurisdictions, the exclusive authority of the prosecution to initiate, dismiss or reduce criminal charges, as well as their dominant role in plea bargaining has made prosecutors nearly autonomous. It has been demonstrated, however, that self-regulation, self-supervision and self-control have had little bearing on prosecutorial discretion. That being said, the burden of curtailing the abuse of power by procuratorates will still have to rest on courts—namely judges routinely inquiring into guilty pleas, establishing procedures for considering procurators' promises of informal immunity to defendants and pressing for standards regarding judicial review of procurators' actions.

References

Cao, J. (2015). Work Report of the Supreme People's Procuratorate. *The Supreme People's Procuratorate of the People's Republic of China*. https://www.spp.gov.cn/spp/gzbg/201503/t20150324_93812.shtml

Chen, R. (2016). Theoretical Rethink of the Revolution of "Plea Leniency"—Based on the Examination of Criminal Expedite Procedure's Operation. *Contemporary Law Review, 30*(4), 3–13.

Chen, R. (2017). Several Disputed Issues of Plea Leniency. *China Legal Science, 1*, 35–52.

Chen, W. (2002). From Establishing the System of Plea of Guilt for Defendants to Introducing Plea Bargaining-On the Significance of Using American System of Plea Bargaining as Reference. *Tribune of Political Science and Law, 6*, 8–13.

Flynn, A. (2016). Plea-negotiations, prosecutors and discretion: An argument for legal reform. *Australian & New Zealand Journal of Criminology, 49*(4), 564–582.

Han, Q. (2021). With the Proportion of Felony Cases Declining and the Rate of Non-Arrest and Non-Prosecution Increasing, what are the Challenges and Opportunities for Criminal Defense? *Southern Weekly*. http://www.infzm.com/contents/216545

He, X. (2021). Pressures on Chinese Judges Under XI. *The China Journal*, 49–74.

He, X. (2023). Plea Leniency and Prosecution Centeredness in China's Criminal Process. *The China Quarterly, 254*, 448–465.

Jiang, A. (2023). Fewer Arrests, Cautious Litigation, Cautious Punishment! SPP Releases Strong Signal. *Shanghai Observer*. https://export.shobserver.com/baijiahao/html/415508.html

Jin, G. et al. (2023). The Analyse and Prediction of China's Criminal Offenses 2022–2023. *Journal of People's Public Security University of China (Social Science Education), 39*(2), 1–11.

Kong, G. (2017). The Logical Expansion of the Leniency System of Guilty Plea. *Journal of National Prosecutors College, 25*(1), 20–30.

Li, E. (2010). The Li Zhuang Case: Examining the Challenges Facing Criminal Defense Lawyers in China. *Columbia Journal of Asian Law, 24*(1), 129–169.

Li, E. (2022a). Haste Makes Waste: Why China's New Plea Leniency System is Doomed to Fail. *Asian Journal of Comparative Law, 17*(1), 76–105.

Li, E. (2022b). Chinese Courts' New Plea Leniency System: Scrutinizing the Efficacy of Mandatory Defense Counsel. *The China Journal, 88*, 78–99.

Liang, B., He, N. P., & Lu, H. (2014). The Deep Divide in China's Criminal Justice System: Contrasting Perceptions of Lawyers and the Iron Triangle. *Crime, Law and Social Change, 62*, 585–601.

Lin, X. (2020). The Standardized Structure and Mode of Sentencing Recommendation. *Criminal Science, 1*, 3–16.

Lin, X., Liu, S., Li, E. et al. (2022). Sentencing Disparity and Sentencing Guidelines: the Case of China. *Asian Journal of Criminology, 17*, 127–155

Liu, S., & Halliday, T. (2016). *Criminal Defense in China: The Politics of Lawyers at Work*. Cambridge University Press.

Long, Z. (2020). The Balance between Prosecution and Defense is the Key Method to Improve Plea Leniency. *Global Law Review, 42*(2), 5–22.

Lu, Y. (2021). *Comparative Research of the Plea Leniency System of China* [S.J.D. dissertation of Indiana University, 200]. Submitted in December 2021.

Ma, M. (2003). The Prospects for the Development of Plea Bargain in China. *Chinese Journal of Criminal Law, 2*, 67–79.

Mitchell, O. (2005). A Meta-Analysis of Race and Sentencing Research: Explaining the Inconsistencies. *Journal of Quantitative Criminology, 21*, 439–466.

Shi, J., & Li, W. (2016). "Sentencing Trading" in the Criminal Justice Research in China. *Journal of Southwest University of Political Science & Law, 18*(4), 24–35.

Shi, P. (2007). Comparative Study of Plea Bargain in Italy and France. *Criminal Science, 5*, 110–120 at 114.

Shi, Z. (2023). SPP: Further Deepen the Application of the Leniency System of Guilty Plea. *The Supreme People's Procuratorate of the People's Republic of China*. https://www.spp.gov.cn/zdgz/202302/t20230209_600560.shtml

Sun, C. (2002). Appreciating Due Process Rejecting Plea Bargaining. *Tribune of Political Science and Law, 6*, 44–50.

Sun, Y., & Fu, H. (2022). Of Judge Quota and Judicial Autonomy: An Enduring Professionalization Project in China. *The China Quarterly, 251*, 866–887.

Wang, D. (2023). The Application Rate of The Leniency System for Guilty Plea Has Remained Stable at Over 85%. *The Supreme People's Procuratorate of the People's Republic of China*. https://www.spp.gov.cn/spp/zdgz/202302/t20230215_601755.shtml

Wang, H. (2019a). Triple Deviation: The Predicament of Duty Lawyer in Plea Leniency. *Law Science Magazine, 40*(12), 12–23.

Wang, Q. (2019b). The Hidden Concern about Overcriminalization in the Context of Social Management. *Contemporary Law Review, 2*(3), 3–12.

Wang, Y. (2019c). The Research of Appealing in Plea Leniency Cases. *Journal of China University of Political Science and Law, 2*, 114–126.

Wang, H. (2020). The Research of Felonies' Application of Plea Leniency Procedure. *Peking University Law Journal, 32*(5), 1187–1210.

Wei, X. (2021). Judicial Application and Problems of Plea Leniency. *People's Judicature, 26*, 26–32.

Wu, Y. (2020). Is a Plea Really a Bargain? An Empirical Study of Six Cities in China. *Asian Journal of Criminal, 15*, 237–258.

Xiong, Q. (2019a). Plea Leniency in the Perspective of Comparative Law: A Review on the "4th Paradigm" of Criminal Procedure. *Journal of Comparative Law, 5*, 80–101.

Xiong, Q. (2019b). Sentencing Recommendation under Plea Leniency. *Peking University Law Journal, 32*(5), 1168–1186.

Yu, J., & Lu, Z. (2021). The Court Shall Make Judgement According to Law if The Sentencing Suggestion is Obviously Improper. *People's Judicature, 26*, 8–11.

Yuan, X. (2017). *Restorative Justice in China: Comparing Theory and Practice*. Springer.

Zhan, X., & Li, L. (2021). Disposal Procedures and Sentencing Regulations in Case of Guilty Pleading in Court. *People's Judicature, 26*, 12–15.

Zhang, J. (2005). *Legal Adversarialism: Common Law Traditions and Chinese Trial Methods*. Peking University Press.

Zhang, J. (2020). Report Of the SPP on the Application of the Plea Leniency System in the People's Procuratorates. *The Supreme People's Procuratorate of the People's Republic of China*. https://www.spp.gov.cn/spp/zdgz/202010/t20201017_482200.shtml

Zhang, J. (2023). Work report of the Supreme People's Procuratorate. *The Supreme People's Procuratorate of the People's Republic of China*. https://www.spp.gov.cn/spp/gzbg/202303/t20230317_608767.shtml

Zhang, P., & Pan, Y. (2021). Guarantee of Defendant's Litigation Right in Case of Guilty Pleading. *People's Judicature, 26*, 16–18.

Zhang, S. (2017). *Study on the Lifelong Responsibilities of Judges in China* [Dissertation of Guangxi Normal University]. Submitted in April 2017.

Zhou, F. (2021). Defendant Who Pleaded Guilty Still Enjoys Complete Right to Appeal. *People's Judicature, 23*, 2–6.

Plea Leniency and Prosecution Centredness in China's Criminal Process

Xin He

Introduction

Until recently, China's criminal proceedings have been known as 'investigation centred' (*zhencha zhongxin zhuyi* 侦查中心主义) (Chen, 2017a; McConville et al., 2011; Miao, 2021; Mou, 2020; Trevaskes, 2010a). A popular saying captures the relationship between the three criminal apparatuses: the police cook the rice, the prosecutors deliver the rice, and the judges eat the rice (Fu, 2003). In this sequential yet collective process, the cook—the police—initiates the process. Once the rice is cooked, judges will consume all of it. Although constraints occur at both the prosecution phase and the trial phase, they have little effect on the course towards conviction. A guilty verdict is all but inevitable.

Upon realizing the grave consequences of investigation centeredness—miscarriage of justice being the most conspicuous—the state called for a shift to 'trial centeredness' (*shenpan zhongxin zhuyi* 以审判为中心). In its historic Plenum Decision, China's Communist Party promoted trial centeredness in criminal justice (CCP, 2014). Academics debate what this means (Chen, 2016), but the general consensus is that the courts shall

X. He (✉)
Faculty of Law, The University of Hong Kong, Hong Kong, China
e-mail: xfhe@hku.hk

E. Li et al. (eds.), *Criminal Case Dispositions through Pleas in Greater China*, https://doi.org/10.1007/978-981-97-1856-6_3

play a prominent role and evidence other than oral confession is key to conviction.

However, almost a decade after the call, trial centeredness has not taken shape. Rather, it has been subsumed by the role of confessions, which has gained new momentum. The Plea Leniency System (*renzui renfa congkuan zhidu* 认罪认罚从宽制度, literally, 'acknowledging guilt and accepting penalties for leniency') has dominated criminal trial reforms and official discourse. Under the slogan of efficiency, the implementation of plea leniency has been breakneck. Less than two years after a 2016 pilot program, it was enacted into the Criminal Procedural Law (CPL). As an overarching principle of the 'mini-constitution', it has since gripped the whole criminal process. It covers an array of crimes from minor offences causing personal injury, to property damage, to drug trafficking, to rape and murder. Moreover, it is applied at all phases of the process from the police investigation to public prosecution, and then to court trial. Two years into its enactment, the System has encompassed 86.8% of all criminal cases (Jiao, 2021). In this time period, the duration for handling cases has shortened and the appeal rate has dropped precipitously.

In plea leniency, the procuratorates have taken the centre stage: not only do they obtain a guilty acknowledgement from the suspects/defendants, they also secure their acceptance for specific sentences. The prosecutors also play a central role in liaising with lawyers in facilitating the consent. After all the details regarding the crime and the punishment have been sealed, the trial is nothing more than a procedural formality: the court merely rubber-stamps the confession affidavit.

Few studies in the English have regarded this as paradigm shifting. In Jeremy Daum's (2021) comprehensive introduction, he merely suggests that the reforms 'have the potential to undermine the already limited protections afforded to China's criminal defendants and risk encouraging false confessions'. Yuguang Lu (2021, p. 69) argues that with plea leniency, China's criminal procedure has 'entered a new stage'. He then shifts to detailed comparisons between plea leniency and plea bargaining, indicating that he does not regard the change as systemic. Similarly, Wu (2020a, 2020b) plunges into measuring the duration of the process and the amount of leniency afforded, but pays little attention to the changing roles of the three apparatuses in the system. Enshen Li focuses on the role of the mandatory lawyers (2022b) and whether the system can boost legitimacy (2022a).

By contrast, papers in Chinese are replete with discussions on this topic, not least because it is a topical political conversation. For obvious reasons, the leading authorities in China's criminal system unanimously hail the System with fanfare (Zheng, 2020). Fan Chongyi 樊崇义 calls it 'a historic transition in China's criminal process'. Hu Yunteng 胡云腾, then a vice president of the Supreme People's Court (SPC), asserts that the System will benefit all litigation participants. A Xinhua report acclaims it as 'monumental' (Jiao, 2021). As one can imagine, propaganda has outweighed proper analysis. Most of them embrace the central authorities' positions with open arms. Some do suggest that the procuratorates have become dominant, or have shouldered the bulk of the responsibility in the criminal process. However, they often adopt a doctrinal or comparative perspective, without offering actual evidence (Wan, 2019; Xiong, 2019; Yan, 2020).

This article analyses the developments, operations, and consequences of the Plea Leniency System. I argue that the rise of plea leniency has led to 'prosecution centredness' in China's criminal process. The power of police has declined while the power of procuratorates has expanded considerably. While police may still dominate the investigatory period, the procuratorate has acquired increasing power in the investigatory period and clearly dominate the post-investigatory period. This change has further marginalized the role of the courts. I will also demonstrate that plea leniency fundamentally differs from plea bargaining. While it signals further leniency in criminal justice, rights protections make way to efficiency and crime control in its stead. Conceived in this way, plea leniency has profound implications on the operations of the criminal justice apparatuses, defendants, defence lawyers, and the mode of crime control in China.

Investigation Centredness and Its Discontents

Criminal justice in China is conducted by three state apparatuses: the police, the procuratorates, and the courts. Their relationship in administering the system is depicted as a relay race, or a conveyor belt, which turns criminal suspects into convicted prisoners (Chen, 2006; Miao, 2021, p. 246). The CPL defines their relationship as 'division of responsibility, mutual coordination, mutual constraint' (*fengong fuze, huxiang peihe, huxiang zhiyue* 分工负责, 互相配合, 互相制约). Nicknamed the 'iron triangle', there is more coordination than constraint operating in their relationship. Rather than forming a triangular framework to keep each other in check, the three apparatuses collaborate to ensure criminal convictions. Few mechanisms exist which enable them to correct each other. The courts have not been regarded as independent institutions for fact-finding or decision-making.

Traditionally, of the three apparatuses, the police have occupied a dominant role. While they are originally only responsible for the preliminary investigation, they have gained ascendency over the entire criminal justice process. The police have enormous formal and informal power to deprive suspects of personal liberty for a significant amount of time and dispose of relevant property (Chen, 2017a). Only in some formal situations such as arrests do they need the procuratorates' endorsement, which has never fallen below 80% (Li, 2022a, p. 96; Zalman, 2017, p. 153 & p. 166). Despite China's commitment in international treaties, in no situation was *habeas corpus* needed (Kaiser, 2021).

The evidence collected by the police has an overwhelming impact on court decisions. The criminal trial has long been centred on dossiers (Chen, 2006; Mou, 2020), with the courts confirming the written evidence prepared by the police. Although the CPL stipulates exclusion rules for illegally obtained evidence, the hurdle is too high to overcome. To exclude evidence, defendants or their lawyers have to prove that the evidence was obtained by force or torture. For defence lawyers not participating in the investigation process, this is a formidable undertaking. Even if there is a chance the procuratorates might adjust the charges and fix some procedural or evidential defects, the courts invariably confirm the predetermined guilty outcome. The minimum sentence has invariably been no less than the detention period they receive, so as to prevent police mistakes or state compensation (Liebman, 2015). Police investigation—the starting point of the criminal process—is often regarded as its endpoint.

One consequence of investigation centeredness is the lack of rights protection for defendants (McConville et al., 2011). Most notably, wrongful convictions or miscarriages of justice have haunted China's criminal justice system: in extreme cases, the actual murderer emerges years after the legal 'murderer' has been executed, or the 'murdered' victim returns from grave (He, 2016). Investigation centeredness is widely regarded as a leading cause of such cases (Biddulph et al., 2017). In an empirical analysis, Zhong and Dai (2019) found that the top three reasons for wrongful convictions all related to the police.

In this light, the CCP (2013) has prohibited extracting confessions through torture during the investigation stage of the criminal trial. Evidence obtained through torture or other illegal means must be excluded. Furthermore, and for the first time, instances of torture or forgery attract punishment. Judges, prosecutors, and police can be held accountable for life for negligent or wrongful acts that result in wrongful convictions.

In contrast, trial centeredness focuses on the *evidence* which forms the centre of the criminal trial. Court hearings, instead of the dossiers, are the central forum in the fact-finding process (Chen & Zhou, 2015). Evidence presented by the police and the prosecution are to be determined as factual only after it has been tested in court.

The Plea Leniency System

As trial centeredness sought to diminish investigation centeredness, it would have also diminished the procuratorates' influence in the criminal justice process. The SPP has tried to maintain their status (Yu, 2021). The Plea Leniency System, though only mentioned in passing in the Party's 2014 Decision, has been picked up as a major vehicle. Of course, efficiency, social stability, and over-crowded detention centres which cannot detain minor offenders for too long are the formal arguments.

The Plea Leniency System stipulates that if a defendant acknowledges guilt and accepts the proposed sentences (either specific sentences or a sentencing range), he or she receives lenience. Acknowledging guilt means that the defendants/suspects confess to the offence/s and do not dispute the charges. Accepting sentences means that the defendant feels contrition and is willing to accept the requisite penalty. In a Guiding Opinion jointly released by the two Supremes (the SPP and SPC) and three Ministries (Public Security, State Security and Justice, hereafter cite as Guiding Opinion, 2019), the litmus tests are their attitudes and behaviour: do they offer sincere apologies and adequate compensation to victims (Guiding Opinions, 2019, art. 6–7)?

The System originated from the Expediated Procedure on minor criminal cases. The Expediated Procedure applied to defendants subject to less than three years of imprisonment. The procedure curtailed court investigation and debate, preserving only the announcement of judgement (CPL, 2018, art. 224). The Plea Leniency System was introduced to further address concerns regarding efficiency in dealing with large caseloads. The SPP argued that given China's increasing criminal caseloads, complicated and straightforward cases ought to be channelled into different procedures. In other words, only through expediently processing minor cases can more resources be allocated to the serious and complicated ones. This argument was endorsed by Meng Jianzhu 孟建柱, then the head of the Central Political and Legal Committee: 'Leniency in substance and simplification in procedure will better allocate resources, and provide both leniency and rights protection. It reduces confrontation and facilitates the confessions of both the suspects and defendants, making them cooperate with the judicial apparatuses in lawfully handling the cases' (Xing, 2016). In 2016, a pilot scheme was implemented in eighteen cities (NPC, 2016).

However, was the concern for efficiency in criminal cases real and pressing? While overall caseloads in courts have increased, the criminal caseload has plateaued to around one million per year since the late 2010s.[1] In addition, as Zuo Weimin (2017) points out, the handling of criminal cases has already increased efficiency from the launch of the Expediated Procedure. In these circumstances, there was little necessity for further truncation. According to him, under the Expediated Procedure, an average court trial lasts only 5 minutes, 90% of cases last less than 10 minutes, and it takes 6.4 days for the court to process a case (Zou, 2017).

Queries and concerns raised about the introduction of plea leniency do not cease there. Other scholars have questioned whether plea leniency can protect human rights (Chen, 2017b). Others have expressed concern about whether plea leniency is compatible with trial centeredness (Gu & Xiao, 2017).

All of these concerns have been largely ignored, however. On the eve of the amendment of the 2018 CPL, the SPP, in an interim report, stated that the pilot scheme had achieved 'stunning' success: 'Until October 2018, about 50 per cent of the criminal cases had adopted the scheme in the pilot cities. The prosecution duration had been shortened to 26 days. 70 per cent of them were processed in the Expediated Procedure, in which 95 per cent of the court decisions were handed out instantly after the trial' (Zheng, 2020).

[1] SPC Work Reports, various years.

Backed by these numbers, the scheme was officially incorporated into the CPL (2018). However, it was not merely funnelled through an alternative channel in the legislation. Listed as one of the general provisions, it has become a fundamental principle of the criminal proceedings (CPL, 2018, art. 15). It is applied throughout all phases of the criminal process and covers all kinds of crimes. In 2019, the two Supremes (the SPP and SPC) and three Ministries jointly issued detailed regulations on its implementation.

Traditionally, Chinese criminal justice policy has followed the mantra—'leniency for those who confess; severity for those who resist' (*tanbai congkuan, kangju congyan* 坦白从宽，抗拒从严). However, this vague policy does not by itself encourage suspects to confess: many do not trust that the authorities will stay loyal to their promises of leniency. In many cases, the policy has been regarded as a hoax to entice confessions and self-incrimination. A cynical saying goes, 'one stays imprisoned forever once they confess' (*tanbai congkuan, laodi zuochuan* 坦白从宽，牢底坐穿). An empirical study (Fang & Liang, 2019) based on more than 6000 judgements on intentional injuries shows that confessions do not lead to lenient punishments because 'confession is the duty'. In theory, the Plea Leniency System is meant to overcome this mistrust (Zuo, 2017). Under the System, the type and amount of sentences are usually specified in the confessional affidavit. In addition, the Guiding Opinions (2019) stipulates that under the Plea Leniency System, those who confess receive more leniency than those who only admit guilt. In practice, the scope of leniency is within about 10–30% of the original sentence (Daum, 2018). The promises of the prosecutor, with specific sentencing terms written into the confession affidavit, and witnessed by defence lawyers, can be considered as more credible.

To address concerns on the rights of defendants, China has made it mandatory to have either a professional lawyer or a legal aid lawyer for every defendant (the lawyer-for-all scheme) (SPC & MoJ, 2018). For suspects and defendants who do not hire a lawyer, authorities assign a stand-by duty lawyer at detention centres. When prosecutors process the cases, they consult the defence lawyers. The CPL also clarifies that, *inter alia*, the authorities shall allow these lawyers to review dossiers and meet suspects or defendants (CPL, 2018, art. 173). This is to ensure that when the suspects or defendants undertake the process of plea leniency, they are able to understand its nature, processes, and consequences (Guiding Opinion, 2019, part 4).

It is remarkable how wide-ranging this system has been applied since its inception. In January 2019, the System only covered 20.9% of all criminal cases. By 2020, the rate had skyrocketed to 86%. From January 2020 to November 2021, 85% of criminal cases followed this route. By 2021, the courts confirmed 96.85% of sentences proposed by procuratorates (Dong, 2021). The appeal rate for these cases was 3.5%, 20.51% lower than before the System was implemented. The System has been touted by Zhang Jun 张军, the SPP President, as a 'modernized governance approach to control crime with Chinese characteristics' (Zheng, 2020).

Prosecution Centredness

Traditional, the procuratorates already have considerable power over the police and courts, acting as the middleman between these two units with their supervisory power. Under the Plea Leniency System, procuratorates are able to assert more power over the police and the courts. Indeed, this change is evinced in their relationships with all participants of the criminal justice system—including the police, courts, defendants, defence lawyers, and victims.

Overshadowing Police

Although plea leniency is a process covering all three phases in criminal justice, leniency promises can only be granted at the prosecutorial phase where much of the police grip has been removed. The procuratorates can invoke plea leniency or educate suspects on how to plead, whereas the Guiding Opinions (2019, art. 23) expressively prohibit the police from granting leniency or recommending sentences. If the suspects do plead, the police only record the pleas in the dossiers and transfer them to the procuratorates. Only after there is involvement of procuratorates can such leniency agreements be made.

In addition, plea leniency allows prosecutors to constrain police investigatory power. Traditionally, prosecutors intervene only after the police have finished investigation, interrogation, and evidence collection; that is, when the rice has already been cooked. Plea leniency offers prosecutors another reason to determine whether to grant arrests or not (CPL, 2018, art. 81(2)). Moreover, prosecutors can intervene earlier, usually following arrest or detention (Lu, 2021, pp. 61–62). Once the prosecutor steps in, 'the police no longer need to do further work gathering substantial evidence' (Lu, 2021). From that point onwards, collecting evidence becomes the prosecutors' job. They are not just one of the cooks; they become the head chef. On this issue, Chen Guoqing 陈国庆, a vice president of the SPP, has said that the procuratorates have assumed part of the investigatory responsibility (Zheng, 2020).

Generally understood, the Plea Leniency System allows the procuratorates to have a greater voice: 'During the arrest granting period or on influential cases, the police shall carefully listen to the opinions and suggestions of the procuratorate with regard to plea leniency and conduct relevant work accordingly' (Guiding Opinions, 2019, art. 24(3)). This is in contrast to earlier practices where procuratorates followed the request of police and assist in fixing any defects within the evidence. Now they share the power with the police to interrogate defendants/suspects.

In the post-investigatory period, the procuratorates have power and enormous discretion which the police can only envy: they rephrase, redact, and frame the elements of the crime; they communicate with the judges, defence lawyers, and victims. They have the power to initiate charges, determine detention periods and conditions, and more importantly, whether or not there is culpability. They determine whether to charge or to spare charges (Guiding Opinions, 2019, art. 8(2)). They recommend sentences. If the police have remained the initiator of the criminal justice process, the procuratorates have assumed the role of the terminator. The police, though dominant in the investigation period, have almost no say in charge initiations or adjudication outcomes. According to Yan (2020, p. 42), the police's power to initiate the process or withdraw cases is under regulatory scrutiny: 'They cannot determine the case's trajectory and outcome under plea leniency'. However, the procuratorates' power, in granting leniency, is more flexible. No longer the middleman between the police and the courts, the prosecutors have become a dominant actor. This is reinforced by the SPP's statement that the procuratorate shoulders 'the dominant responsibility' in the criminal process (SPP, 2019; Zhang, 2019, pp. 9–10). The Plea Leniency System has been cited as the leading evidence for the change (Ibid., 2019, p. 9).

This begs the question: why have the police given up so much power? Put simply, the reduction of police power is as a result of Xi's process to consolidate full control in response to the issue of wrongful convictions (Nessosi, 2017). Reducing wrongful convictions needs a more regulated police power. The police are relieved from collecting evidence once the procuratorate step in, reducing the chance of making mistakes. In this way, wrongful convictions under plea leniency ought to be rare. After all, the defendants have themselves voluntarily admitted guilt and accepted their punishment.

Marginalizing Courts

The procuratorates are not shy in asserting dominance over the courts. Chen Guoqing, vice president of the SPP, openly states that the procuratorates have replaced the courts in assuming 'much' of the judicial responsibility (Zheng, 2020). Conventionally, procuratorates enact charges. Under plea leniency, they also determine whether or not there is culpability, the type of crime, and the exact sentence. In this way, prosecutors have become the 'judges'.

Traditionally, courts reserve the power to make the final decision. Under plea leniency, the judge only verifies the voluntariness, authenticity, and legality of the plea. Has there been violence or duress? Are the defendants mentally healthy? Has there been effective communication between the defendant and the procuratorate (Guiding opinions, 2019, art. 39)? Yet the procuratorates have already done this. The CPL stipulates that except for five situations, the courts shall confirm the protectorates' recommendations (CPL, 2018, art. 201). All of the exceptions are difficult to establish. For example, one is that the defendant confessed involuntarily. However, it is hard to prove voluntariness under the threat of greater sentences. Even according to the Supreme Court in the United States, as long as one understands the pros and cons of her choices, an action is generally regarded as voluntary.[2] According to Sun and Tian (2021)'s empirical study, the trial is little more than a formality. Although only 23.73% of judges regarded the recommended sentences as accurate, 95% followed the recommendations (Sun & Tian, 2021, p. 11). The main reasons stem from the desire to maintain a good relationship with the prosecutors and to avoid protests or appeal. Moreover, Li (2022a, p. 89) finds that lawyers do not even appear in almost two-thirds of the trials.

The most crucial component of a trial is the evidence. Originally, few witnesses appear in court trials (Guo, 2021, pp. 194–196; McConville

[2] Brady vs. The United States (1970).

et al., 2011, p. 246; Mou, 2020, p. 193). Under plea leniency, there are even fewer witnesses. Since the prosecutors have reached an agreement with defendants and their lawyers, any negotiation between the lawyers and witnesses has already been incorporated into the confession affidavit. What is the point of calling more witnesses to the stand? The prosecutors' burden of proof is exempted (Sun, 2018, p. 181). All other evidence has been sifted, scrutinized, arranged, or rephrased by the prosecutors. Is there any need to challenge the prosecutorial recommendations?

With the procuratorates encroaching the courts' power, one might expect a turf war, or resistance from the courts. Yet, this is not the case. The courts soon find that plea leniency conforms to, if not maximizes, their institutional interests (He, 2021a; Ng & He, 2017a): plea leniency lowers both appeal rates from the defendants and protest rates from the procuratorates; the trial duration has been shortened; most decisions can now be handed out right after the trial, a goal long yearned by the courts; some even lay out the means of implementation; the number of closed cases for individual judges has tripled, or even quadrupled.

While the criminal caseload remains stable, there has been an explosion in civil and enforcement dockets. The average caseload per judge has been climbing ever since the judicial reforms in 2014, and especially after the Judges Quota reforms, under which only the court staff under the judge's track can adjudicate cases, nearly halving the number of judges (He, 2021b). Plea leniency does not merely deliver marvellously efficient relief from the workload, it also sets aside the most complicated or organized crimes to be channelled through the regular trial channel.

Plea leniency also spares the judge the risk of an appeal. In fact, by erasing the possibility of either factual or legal errors in the proceedings, they are exempted from much responsibility (Lu, 2021, p. 61). Since 2014, judges have been held accountable for their mistakes for life. Plea leniency provides a form of safety net to this strict accountability. Plea leniency appears to also promote the legitimacy of the system as a whole. Thus, the courts are happy to cooperate with the procuratorates in implementing it. Empirical studies have shown that the judges even urge the defendants to confess and to plead for leniency (Chen, 2017b). As long as neither the victims nor their families complain, all parties are content.

In most cases, the courts merely rubber-stamp what the procuratorates present—that is, they eat all the rice that the procuratorate has cooked. They have no reason to conduct a full-fledged cross examination of witnesses, or any serious questioning of the evidence. Excluding illegally or improperly obtained evidence and altering suggested sentences has become increasingly rare. Under plea leniency, trial times have become even shorter as the judge simply checks the boxes. The trial has become more administrative than judicial as a consequence of the limitations on judicial power as usurped by the procuratorates.

Overwhelming the Defendants

Given the plea leniency target rate set by SPP at 70%, the natural result is that the procuratorates pressure defendants to plead (Lu, 2021, p. 63). The pressure and imbalance between these players have been characterized as 'repeat players' positioned against 'one-shotters' (Galanter, 1974). Following Galanter's analysis, the prosecutors are repeat players, with repeated involvement in similar cases, and the defendants/suspects are one-shotters, most of whom are first-timers in the process. The latter have no way to compete against the former in terms of knowledge and resources.

Armed with considerable discretion, the procuratorates exert immense pressure on defendants. This is a versatile tool. In addition to the 10–30% discretion in sentences, the prosecutors can grant probation, bail, or even withdraw the charge, they can increase or shorten the duration of detention, and they can schedule an earlier or later trial date. Non-pleading defendants will likely be stuck waiting in custody at the detention centre (Li, 2022b), with no indication of how long the process will take. Pleading defendants may get bail or be tried within a few days. Their attitudes, including any hesitation, reluctance or eagerness to admit guilt, can yield a difference. In these circumstances, the pressure placed on defendants to plead is staggering. Defendants can do little to resist this pressure.

The procuratorates can also withdraw any leniency previously granted. If defendants regret and reverse their original confessions in the trial, the confession affidavit will be revoked and the case will follow the regular route. Thus, most defendants are reluctant to reverse their pleas not least because there is much to lose in making this decision.

In a guiding case issued by SPP (2020, No. 82), the suspect was found to have committed the offence of breaking, entering, and stealing. He pled to and accepted the proposed sentence of 25 months in jail, but later appealed, citing that the penalty was too heavy. This sparked a protest from the local procuratorate who stated that 'any defendant who provides neither new evidence, nor new facts reneges his commitment to the confession and the proposed sentence'. The appeal is solely based on the fact that 'the sentence was grave', without proper legal basis. This move wastes the state's resources and the original condition of leniency has vanished'. The appeal court remanded the case to the original basic-level court, revoked the original 25-month sentence, and handed out a new sentence of 31 months.

Controlling Defence Lawyers

Even though defence lawyers are required to be present, the imbalance between defence and prosecution persists. First, the skills of the lawyers, especially those of the public defenders, pale in comparison with those of the prosecutors. Duty or legal aid lawyers are usually not the cream of the profession as many of them are neophytes. They are selected and salaried by local justice bureaus (Guiding Opinion, 2019; Li, 2022a, p. 87). On the other hand, privately hired lawyers do not often specialize in crime. The prosecutors, who regularly deal with criminal charges, understand the jurisdiction comprehensively, and the novice of defence lawyers pales in comparison with their prosecutorial opponents.

Second, and perhaps more fatal, is lack of independence and professionalism. The relationship between Chinese lawyers and state officials has been termed as 'symbiotic' (Liu, 2011); private-hired lawyers rely on state officials for case referral and favourable decisions, let alone duty and legal aid lawyers. There might be a small group of rights advocating lawyers, but most are pragmatic deal brokers. Originally, the judges were in a better position to control the lawyers, since they monopolized the decision-making power and controlled the case sources. Under plea leniency, it is the prosecutors who control the case sources and make decisions that are nearly impossible to refute. The lawyers have to rely on the prosecutors to make a living. Any belligerent, confrontative, or uncooperative behaviour will only harm their interests, or even sabotage their careers. On the contrary, cooperation or showing kindness earns extra discounts on charges and sentences for their clients (Li, 2022b).

This tendency is also illustrated by the SPP's guiding cases, which are required to be followed by the procuratorates across the country in similar cases. These cases are intended to exemplify plea leniency's superiority in terms of fairness and rights protection. However, one of the four guiding cases fails to even mention the presence of lawyers (SPP Guiding Cases,

2020, Nos. 81–84); maybe it did not have (Ibid, No. 84). In another, their role was limited to that of a notary public witnessing the hearing (Ibid, No. 81). In another, the lawyer helped convince the defendant to accept the deal proposed (Ibid, No. 83).

One case in particular demonstrates their minimal role (Ibid, No. 83). The defendant had injured his friend, leading to death, and the prosecutors had consulted the defence lawyer on whether the defendant had turned himself in (自首), whether it was self-defence, and whether the victim's family had forgiven the defendant. The defence lawyer suggested that there had been self-defence. The procuratorate then explained that the evidence showed that the defendant, after being hit on his head with a wine glass, had taken a knife from the kitchen to stab the victim, stating: 'This is an instigated response, instead of self-defence'.

The legal analysis in the guiding case is not problematic. The point, instead, is that the procuratorate dominates each stage throughout the process. The guiding case also showed that the lawyer immediately accepted the procuratorate's narrative without challenge. The case states, 'after communicating with, and seeking the opinion of the lawyer on duty, the prosecutor, under the presence of the lawyer on duty, explicated the detailed elements and the legal basis of the sentences'. The lawyer cast no doubt on whether any evidence ought to have been excluded and made no submissions on an alternative interpretation to the evidence or the propose sentence.

Traditionally, there have been 'three difficulties' for criminal lawyers (Li, 2014; Liu & Halliday, 2016). In plea leniency, two can been alleviated in theory—the difficulties in accessing case files and in meeting suspects/defendants. However, the situation remains largely unchanged due to the control of the procuratorates. When the procuratorates have only a few weeks to complete a plea leniency case, the pressure turns on defence lawyers. Although these lawyers may access the dossiers or meet the suspects, they are often reminded to be expedient as defendants have already been informed about their rights (Li, 2022b). In many cases, the confession affidavit is prepared before the lawyers are even notified. Faced with these circumstances, many help the procuratorate by urging the defendants to plead. Thus, instead of defending clients, the lawyer becomes an 'explainer', 'persuader', or 'observer' (Li, 2022b). Some are there only to witness the 'signing ceremony', being downgraded to a notary public. One survey found that 89% of lawyers admitted that their role was confined to seeking 'lenient sentencing outcomes' (Hu, 2018,

p. 115). Li (2022a, pp. 89–90) found that in 99.67% of his surveyed cases, lawyers raised no objection to the prosecution's case. Their presence is merely a formality, as it constitutes the best evidence that plea leniency has been 'voluntary'. In most situations, their presence is ceremonial and symbolic, serving the purpose of fulfilling the procedural requirement.

As a natural extension, legal representation has little effect on case outcomes. According to Wu's (2020c) empirical study, even after representation in plea leniency cases increased from less than 10% to nearly 50%, overall case outcomes did not change. The positive effect from court-appointed lawyers even disappeared after the lawyers-for-all program was implemented.

Pacifying Victims

For the most part, granting leniency to defendants breeds discontent among victims. They not only want to see the murders, rapists, thieves, burglars, etc., duly punished by the law, but also, in many circumstances, they want financial compensation. Relevantly, defendants may receive leniency if they financially compensate the victim and are forgiven (Ng & He, 2017b). Usually, more leniency is awarded where more compensation is offered. The role of the procuratorate has therefore assumed an aspect of pacifying victims.

Under the Plea Leniency System, prosecutors have been equipped with more resources. The prosecutorial relief fund, a scheme to help victims who cannot get proper compensation from defendants, tripled during plea leniency's installation from 2018 to 2021 (China News, 2022).

In the aforementioned Guiding Case (SPP Guiding Cases, 2020, No. 82), the prosecutor learnt that the compensation provided to the victim's family was insufficient to cover the family's losses. The prosecutor then paid several visits to the family, offering not just condolences, but also judicial remedies. Following the prosecutor's intervention, the family promised that they would not take their hatred any further.

In this case, the prosecutor effectively ended the dispute by providing funds as a gesture of goodwill. Ensuring that the defendant does not appeal is one matter; ensuring that the victim's family does not complain or petition is another. Thus, the judicial relief fund under plea leniency further empowers the remit of procuratorate power.

Differences from Plea Bargaining

Plea bargaining involves a process of negotiation between the prosecution and the defendant, usually via their lawyers where the prosecutors may 'drop some charges or accept a plea to a lesser crime' if the defendant admits to others (Fisher, 2000, p. 864; Hessick, 2021, p. 23). In theory, this facilitates the criminal trial process. Once a deal is made, a jury or judge trial is unnecessary, thus contributing to the vanishing trial in many jurisdictions. In the federal courts of the United States, for example, the plea bargaining rate was more than 97% in 2018 (Ibid, 2021, p. 32). In explaining the 'triumph' of plea bargaining, Fisher (2000, p. 859) believes that prosecutors have the strongest incentives and power to make it happen, and judges 'see it as in their interests'. Legislators then allocate more sentencing authority to prosecutors, which has 'tilted the terms of battle'. Although defendants have a 'nominal' right not to plead, they are hopelessly undefended in this system.

The development of plea bargaining and plea leniency has been strikingly similar. There are, however, two crucial differences, however. First, the reference point in front of the choice is different. Defendants who choose not to bargain are subject to a jury trial, or in rarer instances, a judge trial (Friedman, 1998). Going to trial is a gamble: one might win big or lose big; plea bargaining is only a means to hedge the bets (Hessick, 2021). Acquittal is a possible and foreseeable outcome. For example, in the United States, juries acquit one-third to 16% of defendants (Friedman, 1998, p. 192). However, these rates do not count cases where the prosecution drops the charges completely. In other words, if the defendant is determined to pursue a jury trial, acquittal is likely. For the prosecutors, going to trial also means that the jury could 'spurn their painstakingly assembled cases' (Fisher, 2000, p. 865). Thus, the defendants, with their lawyers behind them, can wedge a meaningful battle against the prosecutors at jury trial.

By contrast, in Chinese criminal trials, conviction rates have been astronomical, even after recent emphasis on trial centeredness. Official statistics state that of the 1.1 million criminal cases closed in 2020, only 1040 cases were the verdict not guilty (SPC, 2021). Of the 1040 cases, 384, or almost 40%, were private-charged cases. These were minor crimes which do involve the procuratorates. In other words, it is extremely rare for a defendant to walk free after being charged by the procuratorates. The choice to not undergo plead leniency is neither a gamble nor a hedge; the choice is destined to result in a conviction.

In plea bargaining, if the judge detects any duress, ignorance, defence lawyer absence, or complaints from the victim, he or she will reject the deal. The court process allows the defendants another opportunity at 'arraignment' (Chen, 2017b, p. 38). However, even if Chinese judges find evidential or procedural discrepancies at trial, an acquittal is not within contemplation. In China, an acquittal means that the procuratorates have blundered (Miao, 2021). Due to the mutual supervisory relationship between the courts and the procuratorates, both institutions have to tolerate each other's shortcomings and find a way to avoid the undesirable outcomes. According to Mou (2020, p. 183), upon learning that the court is about to issue an acquittal, the procuratorate often proposes an exchange: to drop some potential protests for the purposes of replacing the acquittal with a conviction. In this way, both institutions maintain a cooperative relationship.

Another related difference between plea bargaining and plea leniency is that the former is preconditioned on professional and independent lawyering. While defence lawyers may not be able to truly represent their clients' interests in plea bargaining, as shown in Alschuler's (1975) classic study their mere presence serves as a form of resistance for defendants to plead. Fisher (2000, pp. 970–977) demonstrates that in Massachusetts in the eighteenth century when poor defendants had more legal representation, plea bargaining rates dropped precipitously. He calls this 'the power of representation'. Yet in plea leniency, defence lawyers often side with the prosecution in persuading, if not coercing, defendants to acknowledge guilt and to accept the suggested sentences. The reality is that they are not in a position to negotiate with the prosecution on the sanction. Under rare circumstances, the best they can achieve is to find faults in the evidence prepared by the police or other prosecutorial recommendations. But they cannot reverse the destined course towards conviction. If there is room for negotiations at all, the positions for the parties to do so are never level.

In summary, plea leniency is dominated by the procuratorates. In essence, plea leniency allows for discounted sentences for an early guilty plea. Unlike plea bargaining, the procedure does not allow dropping or changing charges. Indeed, plea leniency clarifies its difference from plea bargaining in the way it is worded. Plea leniency is no *bargaining*, but rather a ‘plea for leniency’. The defendant is to earn leniency by acknowledging guilt, showing contrition, and providing clues for cracking cases (Zheng, 2020). The officials may, or may not, show mercy. Wu’s (2020a) empirical study shows that in felonies, there is no leniency, regardless of whether or not plea leniency is chosen; it is one-sided pleading instead of two-way bargaining. The procuratorates are not the negotiator, they are the arbitrator, or, to put it bluntly, the ‘judge’. They grant leniency according to their discretion set by the law. In doing so, the confession affidavit with sentencing recommendations is not a contract, but rather, a pending judgement for punishment. Sun and Tian (2021, p. 5) found that prosecutor’s recommended sentences are effectively a Hobson’s choice. The ‘negotiation’ time of duty lawyers has never exceeded 10 minutes (Sun & Tian, 2021, p. 9). Therefore, if justice is negotiated in plea bargaining (Baldwin & McConville, 1978), justice is imposed and coerced in plea leniency. Despite that the CCP has tried to reduce the role of confession in the criminal process (Biddulph et al., 2017, p. 99), the rise of plea leniency suggests that confession remains a gene of the system (Belkin, 2013).

Consequences

The rise of plea leniency is likely to have an immense impact on the operation of China’s criminal justice. According to official rhetoric, both social stability and efficiency have been achieved with the shortening of the case process and diminished appeal rates. However, there are consequences beyond the official rhetoric which come at the expense of other matters, including the rights of defendants.

Since the procuratorate has now become the crux of the three apparatuses, they enjoy enormous yet almost unconstrained discretion. Under the current arrangement, the courts have lost any meaningful supervision over them. If, in plea bargaining, the prosecutor’s constrained discretion may pose a source of unfairness (Hessick, 2021), there are greater ramifications in plea leniency with the procuratorates’ unbridled discretion. The procuratorates can easily strike an agreement with defendants by manipulating the evidence. For example, they can do this by only disclosing unfavourable evidence to urge defendants to confess and accept the suggested sentence. Neither the CPL nor the Guiding Opinions stipulate mechanisms to guarantee full disclosure, let alone a penalty should they fail to fully disclose. The procuratorates can intentionally conceal or subconsciously impair any evidence unfavourable for the defendants. They can also manipulate the timing: favourable evidence may only become known after striking a plea deal (Liang & He, 2014). The procuratorates can also drop charges, in part or in full, due to the suspects' 'meritorious service'. The determination of the 'merits' of this service is by and large subject to their interpretation (Guiding Opinions, 2019, part III), and a favourable finding can terminate the criminal process, even before the courts have become involved.

Concerningly, plea leniency creates incentives for over-confession. Given information asymmetry between parties, inhospitable conditions of detention and interrogation, and the lack of any mechanisms to shield defendants from these issues, guilty pleas are unlikely to be the product of considerable deliberation on the strength of evidence. As Biddulph et al., (2017, p. 110) question, there are no mechanisms to verify whether the acknowledgement of guilt is accurate or reliable in cases in which the defendant has confessed.

In the absence of robust lawyers, the role of courts in countervailing police or prosecutorial defects has diminished with the rise of plea leniency. Traditionally, if there was defective evidence, the courts would ask the procuratorates to fix them. Similarly, the procuratorates also required the police to clear defects. The mutual supervisory relationship between the three constituted a certain balance of power which offered defendants some protection from abuse of power by officials. However, under plea leniency, proposed charges are rarely rejected and incentives for further investigation have diminished. Reliance is placed on achieving a confession to the exclusion of the rest of the investigation. After all, it is the confession which determines the case outcome. In this way, the police and prosecutors spend less time gathering evidence (Lu, 2021, pp. 61–62), marginalizing the role of evidence and witnesses in the process despite the focus on 'trial centredness'.

Furthermore, confessions 'voluntarily' made mean that convictions are accepted as correct and assumed to be without error. Without a fully developed factual record, it is hard to determine what went wrong when an innocent person is wrongfully convicted. Conceived in this way, plea leniency has de facto abolished the appeal system. In the No. 82 guiding case, the defendant was bestowed six extra months for appealing after plea leniency. The jail time increased by 24% despite the entrenched legal principle in Chinese criminal procedural law that there is 'no added penalty for appealing'. Arguably, the practice may still be compatible with the principle: the original sentence imposed was as a result of lenient treatment so the penalty added reflects considerations of the matter without the leniency aspect. In any event, the practice belittles the safeguard which protects a defendant's right to appeal. For the procuratorates, the first instance trial is the final event. To be fair, there is also a trial penalty in plea bargaining. However as shown, when a conviction is imminent in China's criminal process, few defendants appeal. This is why across the country, the appeal rate has fallen as low as 2.3%. In Lu's (2021) study of 388 plea leniency cases, only four appealed and no decisions were changed on appeal. It therefore appears that as long as confessions remain at the core of the system, appeals are dispensed with in practice.

Plea leniency marks a further type of leniency in China's criminal justice policy. Since Xiao Yang became the president of the SPC, 'balancing severity and leniency' has replaced 'swift and severity' (Trevaskes, 2010b). The thrust of this principle is to treat serious crimes with severity while treating minor crimes with lenience. Since then, there has been a trend towards leniency: most crimes have been treated with lenience with the exception of crimes against state interests where the defendants span from rights lawyers, terrorists, and separatists (Li, 2014; Liebman, 2015). Executions have plummeted (Johnson & Miao, 2016). With plea leniency constituting nearly 90% of all criminal cases, the trend towards leniency is clear.

Although leniency for confessions has long been China's criminal justice policy, plea leniency has taken this policy one step further. The Guiding Opinions (2019) stipulates 'additional' reductions beyond what is covered under the 'confession for leniency policy'. The trend towards leniency is illustrated not just in substantive laws, but also in criminal procedures. Originally, criminal reconciliation was the major vehicle towards leniency and this was largely driven by private forces (Liebman, 2015). With the advent of plea leniency, this has become more systematic as it is driven through state power. Under statutory guidelines, criminal reconciliation is only supposed to be applied in minor cases (CPL, 2018, art. 288), but plea leniency covers all types of crimes, broadening the scope of application for criminal reconciliation. In contrast to the 'swift and severe' policy before Xiao Yang, one may even argue that the criminal justice policy has evolved into 'swift and lenient'.

Conclusions and Implications

If it is accepted that China's criminal justice process has remained a conveyor belt turning suspects into convicts, it has become apparent that players on this conveyer belt have changed. With the rise of plea leniency, the procuratorates have superseded police in their determination of most final outcomes. They are the only apparatus which is involved in all investigatory, prosecutorial, and judicial phases. In this process, 'the police take notes, the prosecutors make recommendations, and the judges review the recommendations' (Yan, 2020). There is no resistance to the prosecutor's recommendations as it is almost always accepted in full. Even for cases outside the Plea Leniency System, the procuratorates can also recommend sentences in a similar manner (CPL, 2018, art. 282). In this way, trial centeredness and the role of courts have been supplanted by prosecution centeredness, and the sequential process of the conveyor belt has been condensed. In addition to cooking, prosecutors now also submit 'Michelin' stars. Judges lose the opportunity to eat; they are turned into the 'editors', if not 'readers', of the Michelin stars (Lu, 2021, p. 85).

The ideology underlying China's criminal justice system had long been to locate the 'objective truth' and officials 'are expected to bring their knowledge to bear in reaching the unique factual truth' (Mou, 2020, p. 13). Under plea leniency, the ultimate point to be reached has become the 'consented truth'. As long as the procuratorates and the defendant reach a consensus, the process is deemed to be over. As a natural extension, this ideological change will affect how China defines 'wrongful convictions', as the consensus reached may serve to suppress any miscarriages of justice. With prosecution centeredness replacing investigation centeredness, the role of the confession has only become strengthened. In other words, where these confessions are recorded to be reached 'consensually', miscarriages of justice through prosecutorial errors or wrongful convictions will naturally continue.

The sweeping triumph of plea leniency—breaking the narrow hold of minor crimes in the Expediated Procedure and conquering the whole penal territory within a few years—shows that of the two functions of criminal justice (Packer, 1964), China prioritizes crime control rather than rights protection. While both fairness and efficiency are listed as the justice system's paramount goals, efficiency has been favoured and prioritized almost in ignorance of these principles. The regime's not unfamiliar emphasis on crime control and legitimacy leaves little room for procedural justice and rights protection; the presumption of innocence remains a principle on paper.

Throughout this plea leniency process, it is apparent that the regime has achieved its goal for efficiency whilst at the same time maintaining its legitimacy. And it appears that this will continue as there is little contest on the system's legitimacy. Under plea leniency and consented to confessions, wrongful convictions are hard to detect. Petitions and appeals are fewer. Citizens are therefore punished with little resistance through a ruthlessly efficient machinery which finalizes in an administrative process before the judge with no further recourse.

References

Alschuler, A. W. (1975). The Defense Attorney's Role in Plea Bargaining. *The Yale Law Journal, 84*(6), 1179–1314.

Baldwin, J., & McConville, M. (1978). Plea Bargaining and Plea Negotiation in England. *Law & Society Review, 13*, 287–307.

Belkin, I. (2013). China's Tortuous Path Towards Ending Torture in Criminal Investigations. In M. McConville & E. Pils (Eds.), *Comparative Perspectives on Criminal Justice in China* (pp. 91–117). Edward Elgar.

Biddulph, S., Nesossi, E., & Trevaskes, S. (2017). Criminal Justice Reform in the Xi Jinping Era. *China Law and Society Review, 2*(1), 63–128.

Brady vs. the United States. (1970).

CCP. (2013). *Zhongyang zhengfawei guanyu qieshi fangzhi yuanjiacuo'an de guiding (zhongzhengwei (2013) 27 hao)* [Provisions on Preventing Miscarriage of Justice]. Political-Legal Committee of the CPC. https://www.pkulaw.com/

CCP. (2014). *Zhonggong zhongyang guanyu quanmian tuijin yifa zhiguo ruogan zhongda wenti de jueding* [Decision of the CPC Central Committee on Several Major Issues Concerning Comprehensively Advancing the Rule of Law]. Central Committee of the Communist Party of China. https://www.pkulaw.com/

Chen, G., & Zhou, Y. (2015). *'Yi shenpan wei zhongxin' yu jiancha gongzuo* [Making the Trial Central to the Process and Prosecution Work]. In National Prosecutors College (ed.), *Yi shenpan wei zhongxin yu shenpan gongzuo fazhan—di shiyi jie guojia gaoji jianchaguan luntan lunwen ji* [Symposium of the Eleventh National Forum for Senior Prosecutors: Trial as the Center and Trial Work Development] (pp. 557–569).

Chen, R. (2006). Anjuan bilu zhongxin zhuyi——dui zhongguo xingshi shenpan fangshi de chongxin kaocha [File-Transcript Centralism: The Reinspection of Chinese Criminal Trial]. *Faxue Yanjiu, 4*, 63–79.

Chen, R. (2017a). Lun zhencha zhongxin zhuyi [The Investigation Centralism]. *Zhongguo Jianchaguan, 35*(2), 3–19.

Chen, R. (2017b). Renzui renfa congkuan zhidu de ruogan zhengyi wenti [Several Issues on the System of Leniency on Admission of Guilty and Acceptance of Punishment]. *Zhongguo Faxue, 1*, 35–52.

Chen, W. (2016). Yi shenpan wei zhongxin: Jiedu, shixian yu zhanwang [Making the Trial Central to the Process: Interpretation, Realization, and Development]. *Dangdai Faxue, 30*(4), 14–21.

Chinanews. (2022, March 6). *2021 nian jiacha jiguan gong fafang sifa jiuzhujin 6.1 yi yu* [The Procuratorates Delivered Judicial Relief Funds for More Than 610 Millions in 2021]. https://www.chinanews.com.cn/gn/2022/03-06/9693803.shtml. Accessed 24 June 2022.

CPL. (2018). *Criminal Procedure Law*, China.

Daum, J. (2018, April 25). Plea Leniency Pilot Overview. *China Law Translate.* https://www.chinalawtranslate.com/en/plea-leniency-pilot-overview/. Accessed 27 June 2022.

Daum, J. (2021, June 28). A Plea for Greater Reform and Engagement. *China Law Translate.* https://www.chinalawtranslate.com/en/a-plea-for-greater-reform-and-engagement/. Accessed 24 June 2022.

Dong, L. (2021). Zuigaojian: qian 11 ge yue fayuan dui jiancha jiguan renzui renfa liangxing jianyi cainalv wei 96.85% [96.85% of Prosecutorial Suggested Sentences Confirmed by Courts for the First 11 Months]. *Guangzhou Daily.* http://news.ycwb.com/2021-12/20/content_40463829.htm. Accessed 25 February 2022.

Fang, W., & Liang, G. (2019). Do Confessions Contribute to Lenient Punishments in China: An Empirical Study Based on Crimes-of-Intentional-Injury Trials. *Tsinghua China Law Review, 12*(1), 57–85.

Fisher, G. (2000). Plea Bargaining's Triumph. *The Yale Law Journal, 109*(5), 857–1086.

Friedman, L. M. (1998). *American Law: An Introduction* (2nd ed.). W.W. Norton.

Fu, H. (2003). Putting China's Judiciary into Perspective: Is It Independent, Competent and Fair? In E. G. Jensen & T. C. Heller (Eds.), *Beyond Common Knowledge: Empirical Approaches to the Rule of Law* (pp. 193–219). Standard University Press.

Galanter, M. (1974). Why the Haves Come Out Ahead? Speculations on the Limits of Legal Change. *Law & Society Review, 9*, 95–160.

Gu, Y., & Xiao, P. (2017). 'Wanshan renzui renfa congkuan zhidu' de qinli guancha yu sikao, jianyi [Observations in Person, Thoughts and Suggestions for 'Perfecting Plea Leniency']. *Fazhi Yanjiu, 1*, 56–70.

Guo, Z. (2021). Live Witness Testimony in the Chinese Criminal Courts. In B. Ahl (Ed.), *Chinese Courts and Criminal Procedure: Post-2013 Reforms* (pp. 183–207). Cambridge University Press.

He, J. (2016). *Back from the Dead: Wrongful Convictions and Criminal Justice in China*. University of Hawaii Press.

He, X. (2021a). *Divorce in China: Institutional Constraints and Gendered Outcomes*. New York University Press.

He, X. (2021b). Pressures on Chinese Judges Under XI. *The China Journal, 85*(1), 49–74.

Hessick, C. B. (2021). *Punishment without Trial: Why Plea Bargaining Is a Bad Deal*. Abrams Press.

Hu, M. (2018). Lvshi zai renzui renfa congkuan zhidu zhong de dingwei jiqi wanshan—yi Z sheng H shi weili de shizheng fenxi [The Role of Lawyers and Its Perfection in the System of Plea Leniency—An Empirical Analysis of City H in Z Province). *Zhongguo Xingshifa Zazhi, 5*, 115–126. https://doi.org/10.19430/j.cnki.3891.2018.05.008

Jiao, P. (2021, February 1). Renzui renfa congkuan, yixiang lishi zuobiaoshi de sifa zhidu gaige [The System of Leniency on Admission of Guilty and Acceptance of Punishment, a Legal System Reform as a Historical Coordinate]. *Xinhua News*. http://www.xinhuanet.com/politics/2021-02/01/c_1127047715.htm. Accessed 7 August 2022.

Johnson, D.T., & Miao M. (2016). Chinese Capital Punishment in Comparative Perspective. In B. Liang & H. Lu (Eds.), *The Death Penalty in China: Policy, Practice, and Reform* (pp. 300–326). Columbia University Press.

Kaiser, A. (2021). A New Model of Habeas Corpus in China? Procuratorial Necessity Examination of Pretrial Custody. In B. Ahl (Ed.), *Chinese Courts and Criminal Procedure: Post-2013 Reforms* (pp. 144–182). Cambridge University Press.

Li, E. (2022a). Haste Makes Waste: Why China's New Plea Leniency System is Doomed to Fail. *Asian Journal of Comparative Law, 17*, 76–105.

Li, E. (2022b). Chinese Courts' New Plea Leniency System: Scrutinizing the Efficacy of Mandatory Defense Counsel. *China Journal, 88*, 78–99.

Li, Y. (2014). *The Judicial System and Reform in Post-Mao China*. Ashgate.

Liang, B., & He, N. (2014). Criminal Defense in Chinese Courtrooms: An Empirical Inquiry. *International Journal of Offender Therapy and Comparative Criminology, 58*(10), 1230–1252.

Liebman, B. L. (2015). Leniency in Chinese Criminal Law? Everyday Justice in Henan. *Berkeley Journal of International Law, 33*(1), 153–222.

Liu, S. (2011). Lawyers, State Officials and Significant Others: Symbiotic Exchange in the Chinese Legal Services Market. *The China Quarterly, 206*, 276–293.

Liu, S., & Halliday, T. C. (2016). *Criminal Defense in China: The Politics of Lawyers at Work*. Cambridge University Press.

Lu, Y. (2021). *Comparative Research of the Plea Leniency System of China*. Indiana University.

McConville, M. et al. (2011). *Criminal Justice in China: An Empirical Inquiry*. Edward Elgar Publishing.

Miao, M. (2021). Performance Evaluation in the Context of Criminal Justice Reform: A Critical Analysis. In B. Ahl (Ed.), *Chinese Courts and Criminal Procedure: Post-2013 Reforms* (pp. 235–257). Cambridge University Press.

Mou, Y. (2020). *The Construction of Guilt in China: An Empirical Account of Routine Chinese Injustice*. Hart Publishing.

Nesossi, E. (2017). Wrongful Convictions: The Useful Injustice?" In F. Sapio, S. Trevaskes, S. Biddulph, & E. Nesossi (eds.), *Justice: The China Experience* (pp. 141–167). Cambridge University Press.

Ng, K. H., & He, X. (2017a). *Embedded Courts: Judicial Decision-Making in China*. Cambridge University Press.

Ng, K. H., & He, X. (2017b). The Institutional and Cultural Logics of Legal Commensuration: Blood Money and Negotiated Justice in China. *American Journal of Sociology, 122*(4), 1104–1143.

NPC. (2016, September 3). Guanyu shouquan zuigao renmin fayuan, zuigao renmin jianchayuan zai bufen diqu kaizhan xingshi anjian renzui renfa congkuan zhidu shidian gongzuo de jueding [The Decision to Authorize the Implementation of the Pilot Scheme for Plea Leniency in Some Regions]. *Standing Committee of the National People's Congress*. https://www.pkulaw.com/

Packer, H. L. (1964). Two Models of the Criminal Process. *University of Pennsylvania Law Review, 113*(1), 1–68.

SPC Annual Work Reports. (2021). *Various Years*. SPC's Official Website. http://gongbao.court.gov.cn/ArticleList.html?serial_no=wx. Accessed 25 February 2022.

SPC & MoJ. (2018). Zuigao renmin fayuan, sifabu guanyu kuoda xingshi anjian lvshi bianhu quanfugai shidian fanwei de tongzhi [The Notice on Expanding the Pilot Work in Full Coverage of Lawyers' Defense in Criminal Cases]. *Supreme People's Court and Ministry of Justice*. https://www.pkulaw.com/

SPC, SPP, MPS, MSS, & MoJ. (2019, October 24). Guanyu shiyong renzui renfa congkuan zhidu de zhidao yijian [Guiding Opinions on Implementing Plea Leniency]. *Supreme People's Court, Supreme People's Procuratorate, Ministry of Public Security, Ministry of State Security, and Ministry of Justice*. https://www.pkulaw.com/

SPP. (2020, December 8). Zuigao renmin jiancha yuan di er shi er pi zhidaoxing anli [SPP Guiding Cases: The 22nd Batch]. *Supreme People's Procuratorate*. https://www.spp.gov.cn/spp/xwfbh/wsfbt/202012/t20201208_488360.shtml#2. Accessed 15 February 2022.

SPP. (2019). 2019 Annual Work Report. *Supreme People's Procuratorate*. https://www.spp.gov.cn/spp/gzbg/201903/t20190319_412293.shtml. Accessed 25 June 2022.

Sun, C. (2018). Renzui renfa anjian de zhengming biaozhun [The Standard of Proof in the Pleading Guilty and Accepting Punishments Cases). *Faxue Yanjiu, 40*(1), 167–187.

Sun, C., & Tian, W. (2021). Renzui renfa anjian liangxing jianyi jizhi shizheng yanjiu (An Empirical Study on the Sentencing Recommendations in Plea Leniency). *Xibei Zhengfa Daxue Xuebao, 23*(5), 3–16.

Trevaskes, S. (2010a). *Policing Serious Crime in China: From Strike Hard to Kill Fewer*. Routledge.

Trevaskes, S. (2010b). The Shifting Sands of Punishment in China in the Era of 'Harmonious Society.' *Law & Policy, 32*(3), 332–361.

Wan, Y. (2019). "un jianchaguan zai xingshi chengxu zhong de zhudao diwei jiqi xiandu [A Review of the Procurator's Predominance in Criminal Trial and Its Boundary]. *Zhongguo xingshifa zazhi, 6*, 42–50.

Wu, Y. (2020a). Is a Plea Really a Bargain? An Empirical Study of Six Cities in China. *Asian Journal of Criminology, 15*(3), 237–258.

Wu, Y. (2020b). On the Effect of the Chinese Version of Speedy Trial and Plea Bargaining Pilot Programs: Observation from Dui Cases in Fujian Province. *Crime, Law, and Social Change, 74*(4), 457–484.

Wu, Y. (2020c). *Empirical Studies of The Effects of Legal Reforms on The Criminal Justice System in China*. University of Pennsylvania.

Xing, S. (2016, January 1). Zhongyang zhengfawei shuji: shidian renzui renfa congkuan zhidu [Secretary of the Central Political and Legal Commission: Conducting the Pilot of the System of Leniency on Admission of Guilty and Acceptance of Punishment]. *Sina News*. http://news.sina.com.cn/c/2016-01-22/doc-ifxnuvxc1651648.shtml. Accessed on 7 August 2022.

Xiong, Q. (2019). Bijiaofa shiye xia de renzui renfa congkuan zhidu—jianlun xingshi susong 'disi fanshi' [System of Pleading Guilty and Accepting Punishments with Leniency in the Perspective of Comparative Law: A Review on the 'Fourth Paradigm' of Criminal Procedure]. *Bijiaofa Yanjiu, 5*, 80–101.

Yan, Z. (2020). Jiancha zhudao: Renzui renfa congkuan chengxu moshi de goujian [Procuratorial Organs' Dominant Status: The Rational Construction of Procedure Mode of Giving Leniency for Pleading Guilty and Accepting Penalty]. *Xiandai Faxue, 42*(4), 37–51.

Yu, X. (2021). The Meandering Path of Judicial Reform with Chinese Characteristics. In B. Ahl (Ed.), *Chinese Courts and Criminal Procedure: Post-2013 Reforms* (pp. 29–58). Cambridge University Press.

Zalman, M. (2017). False Convictions: A Systemic Concern in China and the World. *China Review, 17*(1), 153–177.

Zhang, J. (2019). Guanyu jiancha gongzuo de ruogan wenti [Several Issues on the Prosecutorial Work]. *Renmin Jiacha, 13*, 5–11.

Zheng, B. (2020, October 13). Renzui renfa congkuan zhidu: shixian gongzheng gaoxiao sifa de 'Zhongguo fang'an' [The System of Leniency on Admission of Guilty and Acceptance of Punishment: 'Chinese Approach' to Realize Impartial and Efficient Justice]. *Supreme People's Procuratorate*. https://www.spp.gov.cn/spp/zdgz/202010/t20201013_481731.shtml. Accessed 15 February 2022.

Zhong, L. Y., & Dai, M. (2019). The Politics of Wrongful Convictions in China. *Journal of Contemporary China, 28*(116), 260–276.

Zuo, W. (2017). Renzui renfa heyi congkuan: Wuqu yu zhengjie [How to be Lenient on Admission of Guilty and Acceptance of Punishment: Misunderstanding and Rectification]. *Faxue Yanjiu, 39*(3), 160–175.

Guilty Pleas and New Challenges to Criminal Defence Practices in China

Yu Mou and *Hui Chen*

Introduction

Criminal trials in China have never been exemplary in any sense. The contested court hearing has often been criticised for its lack of substance: witnesses rarely come to courts to testify and what happens at trial is largely incidental to the verdict, occasionally functioning to serve a wider social or political purpose (McConville et al., 2011; Mou, 2020). Senior state officials who work within the system have been alive to these long-standing problems in trial procedures. As a result, several rounds of trial-centred criminal justice reform have taken place since the criminal procedure reform in 1996. The effort was renewed in 2017 when the Supreme People's Court (SPC) announced its commitment to improving evidence examination at trial, emphasising the importance of preventing miscarriages of justice (SPC, 2017). Just as these hopes for the criminal trial in China were rekindled, a new principle known as Leniency for Pleading Guilty and Accepting Punishment (*renzui renfa congkuan*

Y. Mou (✉)
School of Law, SOAS University of London, London, UK
e-mail: ym19@soas.ac.uk

H. Chen
SGLA (Sino-Global Legal Alliance) Law Firm, Shanghai, China

E. Li et al. (eds.), *Criminal Case Dispositions through Pleas in Greater China*, https://doi.org/10.1007/978-981-97-1856-6_4

zhidu, hereinafter 'Plea Leniency') was formally launched by the Criminal Procedure Law 2018 (CPL, 2018), diminishing the trial-centred criminal process in lieu of a procedure which encouraged and even, demanded for guilty pleas.

The introduction of Plea Leniency has profoundly changed the landscape of criminal justice in China. The immediate effect of its initiation was the drastic decline in formal adjudications, replaced by an abbreviated judicial verification process following the accused's guilty plea and the sentence proposal suggested by the prosecutor. Five years on since its implementation, over 90% of criminal cases are now disposed of by this fresh way of administering criminal justice (SPP, 2023a, 2023b). The contested trial is making way for a different power shift within the criminal justice system. Studies on Plea Leniency have delineated the expanded power of the prosecutor, which now takes the centre stage, and the diminished safeguards for the accused in the criminal process (He, 2023; Li, 2022b). A new measure introduced by Plea Leniency is the mandatory requirement of legal advice for the accused, which can be provided either by a defence lawyer retained by the accused, or by a duty lawyer pursuant to Article 174 of CPL 2018. A large body of literature has hence been devoted to the recently developed duty lawyer scheme and the Legal Aid Law 2021 (Chen, 2021; Chen & An, 2020; Han, 2021; Li, 2022a; Min, 2017). While these issues are worth investigating, to date scant research has been directed to the impact that Plea Leniency has had on criminal defence lawyers, who are key players in the criminal justice arena. Aside from the duty lawyer scheme, little is known about the defence challenges that have been brought about by the transformed power structure under the Plea Leniency regime. Multiple issues follow from this line of investigation. To what extent has Plea Leniency changed criminal defence practices and had an impact on the role of defence lawyers? How have defence lawyers adapted to the new reality and formulated strategies to overcome the obstacles?

To pursue these enquiries, this paper proceeds in three main sections. Section "The Rise of Plea Leniency and the Diminished Room for Criminal Defence" explains how and why Plea Leniency was created as a new system to substitute the traditional criminal proceedings. It explains that, at the outset of invention, Plea Leniency was designed to reflect the interests of criminal justice institutions, the procuratorate and the courts in particular; with the voice of defence parties largely ignored. The purpose of the new system to offer an expeditious and cost-effective way of dealing with large volumes of cases stands antithetical and indeed constrains defence rights. The system has made it difficult for an accused to withdraw a guilty plea after recognisance is signed and any exercise of the right to appeal is likely to be threatened with a harsh sentence. Section "The Unprepared and Slowly Adapted: Plea Leniency's Impact on the Criminal Defence Community" reviews the way in which defence lawyers have responded to the changed reality in practice. In exploring their newly-added responsibilities now encumbered by the fast-paced, ever more opaque, criminal process, this section outlines the initial struggles of defence lawyers and how they have gradually adapted to the novel system. Section "Uncertainties in the Rules and the Exercise of Judicial Power" moves on to explore two particular uncertainties that defence lawyers face in processing Plea Leniency cases. One is related to the delicate boundary between advancing a defence case and the retraction of a guilty plea; the other is concerned with the phenomenon of judicial decision-making which overrides the Plea Leniency agreement. These difficulties highlight the systematic disadvantages and the state-induced coercion that defence lawyers face in their practice under this new regime. However, defence lawyers are not alone in their grievances against this system as the efficiency demanded from this process extends also to their prosecutorial opponents.

This chapter draws from empirical data on criminal defence lawyers' experiences based on 15 Plea Leniency cases. We collected all the information of these defence cases, consisting of the case dossiers, criminal judgments, defence counsels' account of their interactions with the legal actors involved (especially prosecutors and judges) and their observations of criminal justice administration. Drawing from these first-hand resources, we have compiled 15 case studies which represent variegated features and challenges of criminal defence practices. To be sure, these cases by no means represent the general status quo of the concerns in defending Plea Leniency cases in China. These detailed, professional experience, nevertheless, allows us to appreciate the particular challenges raised by the new regime of Plea Leniency and the injustice that has followed, as identified by legal professionals. The case studies were based on cases mainly from three major cities in East China.[1] The types of cases consist

[1] Shanghai ($n = 8$), Shuzou city, Jiangsu ($n = 3$); Wuxi ($n = 3$) and Yunhe county, Zhejiang ($n = 1$).

of cases ranging from financial crimes and mafia-style gang crimes to relatively minor drug offences and obstructing the administration of public order.[2] Of the 15 cases, judgments of six of them can be viewed on the China Judgments Online.[3] To protect the identities of the people (not least the prosecutor and the judges) involved, we decided to anonymise these cases to protect the private information of the individuals. The empirical data is organised in the form of case studies and each case is given a code that begins with *PL_A*. Despite the proliferation in Plea Leniency studies in recent years, the impact of this new regime in legal practice, and particularly on defence practice, has not been addressed by academic researchers both inside China and beyond. This chapter therefore aims to remedy that gap by investigating these issues in practice, exploring the impact that Plea Leniency has on defence practices in the Chinese context.

The Rise of Plea Leniency and the Diminished Room for Criminal Defence

The Creation of Plea Leniency

There is little doubt that the guilty plea system as structured under the principle of Plea Leniency is an adopted version of plea bargaining. Differing from the practice in the US, where plea bargaining was organically developed by the 'vast, unregulated power of prosecutors', Plea Leniency, from the very outset, was designed and engineered by top-down policy and legislation (Stuntz, 2004). The idea that plea bargaining enables a formal or informal agreement to be entered into, usually by the prosecutor and defence lawyer, under which a lesser sentence can be entertained as a 'reward' for a plea of guilty for the defendant's

[2] The crimes involved in these cases encompass selling counterfeit registered trademark ($n = 1$); selling toxic and harmful food ($n = 2$); illegally taking in public deposits ($n = 1$); fraud ($n = 4$); falsely making out special invoices for value-added tax ($n = 1$); illegally opening a casino ($n = 1$); organising prostitution ($n = 2$); extortion of property ($n = 1$); harbouring prostitution ($n = 1$); defrauding a government compensation fund for relocation ($n = 1$); and picking quarrels and provoking troubles ($n = 3$). In certain cases, the defendants were charged with multiple offences.

[3] The China Judgments Online (https://wenshu.court.gov.cn/) is a centralised judicial platform to publish a proportion of judicial documents, especially judgements, in China. It has been a major resource of judicial data for Chinese legal studies.

waiving a full trial, has long been acquainted with and debated by Chinese scholars (Chen & Liu, 2002; Ji, 2007; Wang, 2002). Plea bargaining as a mechanism to dispose of cases on a mass scale can be traced back to the early 2000s. Through judicial interpretations, the Chinese courts allowed a simplified trial procedure and a lesser sentence to be considered in exchange for the defendant's admission of guilt.[4] Since then, guilty pleas have gained greater prominence in each ensuing criminal procedure law reform. Notably, the Criminal Procedure Law 2012 (CPL, 2012) extended procedures on a guilty plea to most of the criminal cases tried by the basic courts.

Although guilty pleas and abbreviated trial procedures were introduced to Chinese criminal justice two decades ago, Plea Leniency is saliently different from guilty plea procedures in the traditional sense. The term, Plea Leniency (*renzui renfa*), first emerged in the pilot scheme of the expediated criminal procedure proposed by the Standing Committee of the National People's Congress (SCNPC). Following a flurry of judicial decisions, the pilot scheme on the expediated trial procedure was soon turned into an experiment project of Plea Leniency, seeking to maximise the effect of plea negotiations between the prosecution and the defence in efficiently addressing backlogs at court.[5] In his speech addressed to the SCNPC on 29 August 2016, the former President of the Supreme People's Court (SPC), Zhou Qiang stressed the urgency to overcome the caseload pressure for petty crimes. His speech appealed to a solution to

[4] The first guilty plea procedure was introduced by a judicial interpretation titled 'Several Conditions of the application of the guilty plea proceeding by the Supreme Court, the Supreme Procuratorate and the Department of Central Justice in China in 2003' issued by the Supreme People's Court.

[5] These decisions are *The Decision on Delegating the Supreme People's Court and the Supreme People's Procuratorate to Implement Expedited Procedures to Process Criminal Cases in Certain Areas* (promulgated by the Standing Committee of the National People's Congress, 27/06/2014); *Measures on Implementing the Pilot Work of Expedited Procedures* (Jointly promulgated by the Supreme People's Court, the Supreme People's Procuratorate, the Ministry of Public Security and the Ministry of Justice, 22/08/2014); *Several Important Decisions on Promoting Rule of Law by the Central Committee of the Communist Party of China* (Promulgated by the Fourth Plenary Session of the Eighteenth Communist Party Conference, 20-23/10/2014); *Notice on Implementing the Pilot Work of Expedited Procedures in Criminal Cases* (Promulgated by Ministry of Public Security; 20/22/2014).

alleviate the heavy burden beset by low-level criminal cases and encumbered by unnecessary trial procedures (SPC & SPP).[6] In response to the call, efficiency and managerialism were prioritised in the pilot project of the expediated trial procedure, and Plea Leniency was suggested in the criminal justice reform.

New ways to dispose of criminal cases in a cost-efficient manner became the focus of criminal justice institutions during the pilot scheme. Thus, Plea Leniency carried different meanings for different institutions. For the police, Plea Leniency was there to strengthen their ability to acquire the evidence of confession and to enhance smoother cooperation with the procuratorate and the judiciary.[7] For the prosecutor, Plea Leniency was a way to secure the accused's guilty pleas and to redeem the recommended sentence at court (SPC & SPP).[8] As far as the courts were concerned, Plea Leniency was considered to be the ultimate solution to ease caseload and to resolve and finalise minor cases expeditiously. After two years of experimentation to accommodate these needs advanced by the criminal justice institutions, it was eventually codified through the Criminal Procedure Law 2018 (CPL, 2018).

Plea Leniency is therefore a reflection of the efficiency demanded by the police, the procuratorate, and the courts. Unlike the previous guilty plea policies that merely encouraged all suspects to plead guilty, Plea Leniency under CPL 2018 is an overarching principle designed to offer a formalised system to systematically substitute the existing criminal process (CPL, 2018).[9] Allowing a lesser sentence to be considered in exchange for the accused's admission of guilt, Plea Leniency is applicable to all types of crimes and criminal procedures, regardless of the stage of the

[6] See explanation on *The Decision on Delegating the Supreme People's Court and the Supreme People's Procuratorate to Implement Expedited Procedures to Process Criminal Cases in Certain Areas (Draft)*.

[7] *Notice on Implementing Pilot Work of Plea Leniency by the General Office of the Ministry of Public Security*, Issued on 8/12/2016.

[8] *The Decision on Delegating the Supreme People's Court and the Supreme People's Procuratorate to Implement Expedited Procedures to Process Criminal Cases in Certain Areas.*

[9] There is no separate section of Plea Leniency in CPL 2018. Instead, as a criminal justice principle, it is scattered throughout the law. The relevant articles are Articles 15; 36; 81; 120; 162; 173; 176; 182; 190; 201, 222–226 in CPL 2018.

criminal proceedings or the instance of the trial (Hu, 2020).[10] From the official reports published during the pilot process, Plea Leniency was predominantly designed and orchestrated by criminal justice institutions to the exclusion of defence lawyers, whose voices were not paid attention to and whose concerns were largely ignored.[11] An explanation to this perhaps lies in the fact that Plea Leniency is not, and ought not to be, interpreted as a level playing field where negotiations between the prosecution and the accused (and their representatives) can be held on equal terms. Thus, in the official speech in 2019, the then SPC Vice President, Li Shaoping, emphasised that Plea Leniency is distinguished from US-style plea bargaining in that the accused and her defence lawyers have no right to 'negotiate' or 'bargain' with their potential sentences: they are merely offered an opportunity to appeal to a degree of leniency subject to the discretion of the courts and the prosecution (SPC, 2019).[12] In this regard, Plea Leniency is fundamentally different from plea bargaining. Chinese defendants have a different legal status compared to their Western counterparts and are merely granted a form of leniency from the benevolent state based on guilty admissions.

Early on, concerns were raised about the impact of retracting guilty pleas entered during pre-trial, which may lead to a reversed procedure and render the earlier effort a fruitless journey, thereby incurring greater operational resources (Wei, 2021). It was on this ground that the duty lawyer scheme was set up and integrated into Plea Leniency. Duty lawyers are tasked to help the accused appreciate the legal consequence of entering into a guilty plea.[13] Their participation was to validate and secure the guilty plea by explaining the consequences of entering the guilty plea by

[10] In practice the application of Plea Leniency is often associated with one of two fast-tracked trial procedures, namely the simplified procedure or the expedited trial.

[11] See *The Method on How to Implement Plea Leniency in the Criminal Process in Certain Areas*, jointly published by the SPC, SPP, Ministry of Public Security, Ministry of National Security, Ministry of Justice on 11/11/2016 (Fa Ban [2016] no. 386); *The Mid-Term Report on the Implementation of Plea Leniency on Certain Areas by the SPC and SPP*, delivered by the President of the SPC, Zhou Qiang, on 23/12/2017; and *The Final Summary Report of the Pilot of Plea Leniency*, published by the SPC in 2018.

[12] SPC, *The Notice on Issuing and Circulating the Speech Delivered by the Vice President Li Shaoping on Promoting and Implementing the Work of Plea Leniency* (SPC, Doc. Fa Ban 2019, no 49; 27/02/2019).

[13] This information is also notified by 'the Information Notice of Plea Leniency' (*Renzui renfa congkuan zhidu gaozhishu*) delivered by the procuratorate.

signing the recognisance (*jujieshu*), which is a pro forma written statement used to acknowledge their decision to admit guilt and accept the sentence proposed by the prosecution (Han, 2021; Law Daily, 2019). Signing the recognisance hence has the *conclusive* legal effect that the entry of a guilty plea is a truly voluntary act of the defendant, witnessed by the suspect's defence lawyer or a duty lawyer.[14] Once the terms on the recognisance are accepted, contrary indications from the accused are not conventionally expected in a later phase of the process. The signature on recognisance signifies the relinquishment of any challenge to the prosecution case in the contested trial.[15] The significance of entering into a guilty plea is therefore material to decision-making, necessitating the presence of legal representatives even in these minor and non-serious matters. In the event that the defendant withdraws the plea after signing the recognisance, he or she runs the risk of being imposed a heavier sentence (Wang, 2021). However, of all the rights forgone under such circumstances, the right to appeal is perhaps one of the most impactful.

The Punitive Approach to the Right to Appeal

Attaching a waiver of the right to appeal to the plea agreement is nothing new in jurisdictions where plea bargaining is part of the criminal justice system (Borman, 1975; Dyer & Judge, 1989; Reimelt, 2010). However, appeal waivers in plea bargains are not without problems. Research has highlighted that adverse consequences derive from appeal waivers, as it undermines the due process principle and the state's legitimate interest in providing appellate review of criminal cases (Ivsan, 2017; Teeter, 2005; Zachary, 2003). In China, Plea Leniency does not explicitly prohibit defendants from appealing to the higher court if they plead guilty. Since Plea Leniency cannot be understood as a negotiation between the prosecution and the defence, no such waiver clauses can be validly attached to the recognisance. This nevertheless does not stop the procuratorate from finding alternative ways to discourage appeals against the Plea Leniency

[14] According to Article 190 of CPL 2018, the validity and lawfulness of the recognisance must be ascertained by the court before the sentence discount is decided.

[15] Legitimate reasons to withdrawals of previous recognisances include the lack of factual foundation of the guilty plea and if the procuratorate unilaterally changes the sentence agreement (Wang, 2021).

arrangement. The whole purpose of Plea Leniency is to relieve prosecutors and judges from the burden of conducting full trials for the criminal cases. Allowing a trial in the second instance to ascertain the facts and evaluate the sentence undoubtedly defies the purpose of a reduced workload (Wang, 2021). To prevent the defendant from appealing to the higher court, the procuratorate normally takes a vindictive reaction against the defendant. Hence, when an appeal is made against the Plea Leniency arrangement, a threat of graver sentence often occurs in the second instance.[16]

Judicial practices in the last few years for Plea Leniency have given a shape to a baneful effect when the defendant exercises her right to appeal. On 9 April 2019, the Supreme People's Procuratorate (SPP) posted a case comment on its official WeChat website, with a striking title 'Fancying to Use Appeal to Get a Sentence Reduction? Outsmarting the System with a Devious Plan Only to Fall into one's Own Trap!'. In this case commentary, the procuratorate lambasted a defendant, Jiang, who was not pleased with his Plea Leniency arrangement and appealed for a lighter punishment after receiving a custodial term of 9 months and a fine of 2000 RMB. The case commentary caricatured Jiang as a 'trickster' of the system (*dongji buchun*) who tried his luck by appealing to the higher court, but ended up with a heavier punishment. Jiang was 'duly' meted out a sentence of a 15-month imprisonment and a fine of 10,000 RMB due to the procuratorate's counter-appeal protest (*kangsu*) in the court of appeal (SPP, 2019). A similar situation was reported in 2021 when a defendant, Luo, charged with theft, appealed against the sentence of eight-month imprisonment as provided for on the Plea Leniency terms. He received a doubled jail term after the procuratorate sought retribution for his bad faith (Guangzhou Daily, 2021).

Reports like this send a chilling effect on defendants and defence lawyers alike who must now think twice when considering an appeal against the Plea Leniency arrangement. To be sure, the procuratorate's counter-appeal protest is not always supported by the appellant courts. In

[16] According to Article 237 of CPL 2018, when the defendant exercises her right to appeal, the second instance court (either a higher court or the original court that retries the case) must not aggravate the punishment on the defendant unless there is any new crime and/or the procuratorate initiates a supplementary prosecution or a counter-appeal protest. This procedural safeguard is often undermined by the procuratorate's counter-appeal protests.

Xie's (2023) research on prosecutor's retaliatory counter-appeal protests, he found that the procuratorate's retributive suggestions were approved in only 81 out of 232 cases (34.9%). Indeed, the courts are currently divided as to whether or not the defendant retains the right to appeal in Plea Leniency cases (Xie, 2023). In the meantime, empirical research found that defendants' motives to appeal were mixed. Apparently, a number of defendants appealed for practical reasons other than merely seeking a lighter sentence (Lan & Zhao, 2020). For example, some defendants who have already been remanded in custody for a period of time and wanted to prolong their time in the same detention centre may appeal strategically. In making an appeal, they effect their case to be held in abeyance pending the final judgement while the custodial time is still running, thereby preventing themselves from being relocated to a different detention centre, especially when the custodial sentence is relatively short (Yuan & Yuan, 2021).

Nevertheless, the practice that the prosecutor should robustly and emphatically respond to the defendant's appeal against the Plea Leniency decision is publicly endorsed by the SPP. In an official interview with the SPP Chief Representative in 2022, the SPP made it clear that prosecutors must initiate a vindictive counter-appeal protest to pre-empt an unnecessary second instance trial (SPP, 2022). Their decision was based on the ground that the defendant's earlier indication of a guilty plea was not a true reflection of their remorse, and therefore, they should be divested from the entitlement of a lenient sentence (SPP, 2022). The flaw in this justification is clear: it is one thing that the prosecution has the power to recommend a lighter sentence based on the defendant's guilty pleas; it is quite another to propose a retaliatory sentence where an appeal is lodged to deter a defendant from retracting a prior guilty plea and exercising her right to appeal. For the latter, the law certainly did not grant the power to the prosecution. Nonetheless, prudent defence lawyers must advise their clients cautiously, mindful of the procuratorate's determination to reinforce this iron-fisted policy. Given the diminution of defence rights in Plea Leniency, the question of how to react strategically to protect their clients' best interest is ever more pressing. Given the reality that Plea Leniency cases are less likely to be reviewed and without running the risk of an appeal penalty, any defence advice that is not circumspect enough can tread the danger of ruining the defence case completely. As such, defence lawyers are faced with greater pressure in carrying out their roles with all the above complexities in mind from the outset.

The Unprepared and Slowly Adapted: Plea Leniency's Impact on the Criminal Defence Community

The Delayed Response from the Defence

With hindsight, the criminal defence community in China did not respond promptly enough to the changed reality brought about by Plea Leniency process. As noted, defence lawyers were not amongst the legal actors who laid the foundation for Plea Leniency. They were excluded from the consultation process and have never been an active participant in Plea Leniency since its inception. The news on the efficacy of Plea Leniency in disposing of large volumes of low-level crimes circulated shortly after its implementation (NPC, 2020). This, however, was thought to be a minor tinkering with the old guilty plea system as far as many defence lawyers were concerned (*PL_A1, A2 and A4*). Even when Plea Leniency was in full swing and became heavily utilised to substitute the traditional criminal process in the majority of instances, defence lawyers' reaction on the sea change remained lukewarm. Up until 2021, hardly any practitioners' seminars, exchange papers, lawyers' blogs, or public lectures inside the defence community touched upon issues surrounding Plea Leniency (Zhou, 2021). In fact, many defence lawyers were oblivious to the advent of Plea Leniency, its seismic shift in criminal justice and its far-reaching impact on criminal defence practices (*PL_A1*). It was only until 2022 when Plea Leniency already dominated and became completely cemented into the system, had its impact on criminal justice been appreciated by the defence professionals. As if suddenly awakened to the issues, the defence community started seriously to consider Plea Leniency. Seminars, publications, and internal discussions on Plea Leniency burgeoned on various professional platforms, exploring strategies on how to overcome the challenges raised in the new regime (*PL_A3 and A4*).

The delayed response from the defence community was caused by several reasons. To begin with, discussions on defence strategies within the community were often led by eminent defence lawyers, whose attention at the time was drawn elsewhere (*PL_A1*). As previously mentioned, the SPC inaugurated a wave of judicial reform in 2017 to strengthen evidence examination procedures at trial and to prevent miscarriages of justice (SPC, 2018). Defence lawyers formed an impression that the due process principle was being embraced by the criminal justice system and as a result, their focus diverted to improving their advocacy skills in cross-examinations (*PL_A1; A7*). The judicial reform agenda in 2017 stroked the inner resonance of leading defence lawyers, many of whom held an obstinate, wishful, belief that 'guilty pleas are merely applicable to petty little crimes; but when it comes to serious, complicated criminal cases, lawyers are expected to win the case by their guns-blazing courtroom advocacy skills' (*PL_A12*). Such a dismissive attitude towards Plea Leniency was not without reason. For many, pleading guilty is considered a matter of their client's own business (*PL_A3; A4*). As legal professionals who represent their rights, lawyers are not supposed to influence their decision-making (*PL_A3; A4*). This *laissez-faire* attitude made many defence lawyers reluctant to engage with their clients in the decision-making process. In addition, the success of a defence lawyer is measured by their track record of defending complex and serious cases, and legal fees charged by defence lawyers are based on their professional profiles. Plea Leniency cases, due to the less intensive court advocacy skills required, produce limited financial incentives to ambitious lawyers, who are keen to build up their professional reputations.

New Obstacles Arising Out of Plea Leniency

The landscape of criminal justice nevertheless transformed to the obliviousness of defence lawyers. When defence lawyers caught up with the new rules, they came to face challenges compelling them to change their defence practices. The first obstacle was the fast-paced criminal process. A large number of Plea Leniency cases are eligible to be processed by the expediated procedure according to Article 222 of CPL 2018.[17] The expediated procedure greatly accelerates the turnaround of cases by imposing a tight deadline on both the prosecutor and the courts: the prosecutor is given a maximum of ten days to review and to propose a sentence; the court has no more than ten days to finally resolve the case (CPL 2018,

[17] Article 222 of CPL 2018 states that the expediated procedure applies to a case where the defendant may be sentenced to fixed-term imprisonment of not more than three years, provided that the facts of the case are clear, the evidence is definitive and sufficient, and the defendant admits guilt, accepts punishment, and agrees with the application of the fast-track sentencing procedure; the case shall be tried by a sole judge.

Art.172 & 225). Efficient as it is in enhancing the administration of criminal justice in this way, the condensed criminal process creates significant difficulties for defence.

Since the introduction of the Criminal Procedure Law 1996 (CPL 1996), defence lawyers first point of contact with their clients in the vast majority of instances has been during the prosecution review, i.e. after the completion of the police investigation and when the criminal case dossier is formally transferred to the procuratorate (CPL 1996, Art.33; CPL 2012; CPL 2018, Art.34).[18] For ordinary criminal procedures, this point of defence entry poses no particular problem, as defence lawyers are able to prepare the case at a manageable pace, particularly due to common delays caused by supplementary investigations during the prosecution review. The timeline of the expediated procedure, however, has completely changed the rhythm that defence lawyers engage with cases. The expediated procedure has not taken account of the time for defence preparation, neglecting the fact that the defence lawyer needs time to review the case and to formulate defence strategies. The situation is particularly tense if there are multiple defendants involved in a case and the facts in question are complicated. Take *PL_A1* as an example, a case concerning selling counterfeit registered trademarks. Although being processed with the expediated procedure, the case was a complex one, with large volumes of evidence and four co-defendants involved. The case arrived at the procuratorate in site A on Thursday 18 November 2021; on the next day (Friday 19 November) the defence lawyer requested a copy of the case dossiers containing all the prosecution evidence. Immediately after the weekend (Monday 22 November), the suspect was informed to sign the recognisance. Upon receiving the short notice, the defence lawyer filed a complaint for the limited time available to read through and digest all the evidence and to prepare an opinion. However, the protest was disregarded by the prosecutor, who, apparently under the time constraint, threatened that if the suspects did not sign the recognisance on that particular day and accept the proposed sentence of the 39-month imprisonment, the

[18] Although the accused can retain defence lawyers during the police investigation, their assistance is limited at this stage, subject to their lack of case information: they can only access the criminal investigative dossier after the case was passed on to the procuratorate (CPL 2018, Art.34). The main reason to retain a defence lawyer during the police investigation is to visit the suspect in the detention centre. For minor crimes where the suspect is not remanded in custody, getting a legal advisor during police investigations is often regarded as unnecessary.

minimum sentence that the accused shall receive would be a jail term of four or five years. Facing the threat from the prosecution, the suspect and the defence lawyer had no choice but to accept the sentence proposal.

Timing is of paramount importance to defending a Plea Leniency case. The tight turnaround means that any delay on the part of the defence (no matter the suspect's initial contact with a defence lawyer, the defence lawyer's decision to get involved, or her access to the case dossier and her communication with the client) may result in the loss of an opportunity in challenging the prosecution case. In *PL_A2*, a case concerning selling toxic and harmful food, the defence lawyer was retained on the same day when the suspect was asked to sign the recognisance by the prosecutor. Due to the late intervention, the defence lawyer had no time to go through the details of the case, not to mention advising his client. Under this time pressure, he advised his client to enter the guilty plea agreement and accept the prosecutor's suggestion of a six-month imprisonment which appeared reasonable for such type of cases. After studying the case in greater detail later on, the defence lawyer reflected regretfully on the advice, as the facts of the case presented a realistic opportunity that the suspect may have got a non-custodial sentence had he been given more time to prepare the defence case.

Literature on Plea Leniency has acknowledged the prevalent phenomena that defence counsel chiefly operate as a witness to the suspect's signing of the recognisance (Chen, 2021; Han, 2021; Li, 2022a). Li's (2022a, 2022b) empirical study based on 34 interviews with duty lawyers in Shanghai found that the lawyer-suspect consultation is 'no more than providing emotional support' and that duty lawyers identify themselves as observers, explainers, and persuaders. Our case study confirms that duty lawyers are overall more compliant than privately retained defence lawyers. The passive role playing is, however, not limited to duty lawyers, as the service of some retained defence lawyers is also restricted to informing their clients of the alleged offence and its legal basis. The extraordinarily high conviction rates in China mean that a criminal case resulting in an acquittal is highly unlikely if not entirely impossible (China Law Year Book, 2022).[19] Identifying the grounds to challenge the prosecution case and endeavouring to mitigate the sentence as much as practically possible is the principal task for criminal defence

[19] China's conviction rates have been over 99.9% for over two decades. China Law Year Book (2010–2022).

professionals. Under the Plea Leniency regime, the room to do so has substantially shrunk. On the one hand, defence lawyers are under the obligation to discern the weakness of the prosecution case in the hope that the sentence can be reduced for their client. On the other hand, they must be careful enough not to leave a wrong impression that their client refuses to cooperate, which may prompt the prosecutor to drop the Plea Leniency proposal altogether and recommend a draconian sentence as retribution. The best defence strategy for guilty plea cases is to tread a delicate line between cajoling the prosecutor into realising the flaws of the prosecution case and losing the benefit of sentence reduction under Plea Leniency. The success of achieving this goal hinges on effective communications with the prosecutor, which is considered to be one of the most difficult tasks for many defence lawyers (*PL_A2; A4*).

Defence lawyers are a marginalised group within the Chinese criminal justice system who suffer from antagonistic relationships with state officials (McConville et al., 2011, pp. 349–350; Mou, 2020, pp. 163–165; Liu & Halliday, 2016, pp. 73–79). While they can manage to reduce their private contact with the prosecutor to the minimum in ordinary cases, this can no longer be the case when it comes to dealing with Plea Leniency. According *to The Guidance on Sentence Recommendations in Handling Guilty Plea Cases* (hereinafter Sentence Guidance) published by the SPP in 2021, defence lawyers are obliged to be an active source of consultation for the prosecutor's decision-making. As the power of the procuratorate has expanded under Plea Leniency, prosecutors have taken on the roles of case manager, adjudicator, and sentencer (Mou, 2022). Since a contested trial is rarely available, effective communication with the prosecutor becomes the main avenue to present the defence case, through which defence issues surrounding guilty pleas can, to a certain extent, be incorporated into the Plea Leniency arrangement, reflecting the interest of the accused. However, drawing from conversations with the defence lawyers in our case study, we can easily perceive their vulnerability when engaging with prosecutors. The power imbalance ensures that defence lawyers constantly feel they are at the mercy of prosecutors' capricious decision-making (*PL_A11*).

To be specific, a defence lawyer's plight manifests in three aspects. First, meeting with prosecutors is often described as a 'depressing' and 'disagreeable' experience. The disparity in power and standing between lawyers and state officials is the status quo in the Chinese criminal justice system (Liu & Halliday, 2016). This unequal status can lead to unpleasant interactions between the two legal actors in the course of communications (*PL_A7*). Thus, defence lawyers often complain about prosecutors' impatience and their condescending attitude when they submit their defence views (*PL_A8*). Prosecutors' lack of respect towards defence lawyers may be attributed to the fact that they are under no legal obligation to consider their views and factor them in in their decision-making, other than merely offering them an opportunity to express their opinions in compliance with the Sentence Guidance (Article 25). The timing to reach out to the prosecutor is crucial. If the defence lawyer fails to take initiative and discuss the defence case with the prosecution in good time, the opportunity to persuade them to downgrade the charge and/or recommend a lighter sentence will disappear. As the defence lawyer in *PL_A3* revealed, once the prosecutor has reached a decision and showed his card, it is an uphill challenge to change their mind.

This is in connection with the second predicament for defence lawyers. To effectively engage with the prosecution, defence lawyers are required to know their work routine and synchronise their own work pace with the prosecutor's in the Plea Leniency process. This poses significant challenges for defence lawyers, as many of them are not familiar with the inner workings of the procuratorate, its bureaucratic constraints and the specific pressures to which prosecutors are subject. Also, prosecution practices may vary from region to region and each prosecutor may have an individualised work style. Thus, defence lawyers have revealed that they were without the knowledge of prosecutor work routines, which rendered them not being able to take advantage of prosecutors' weak spot (such as their pressure to fulfil certain performance indicators) and to advance their defence strategically (*PL_A 12; A 13*). The defence lawyer in *PL_A1*, for example, lamented that had she been aware that the prosecutor was anxious about the 'end of year appraisal evaluation' (***niandi kaohe***) when processing the Plea Leniency case, she would have adjusted their defence strategy and engage with the prosecutor in a very different manner.

Finally, some defence lawyers are reluctant or lacking in confidence to robustly confront misconduct of the prosecutor in handling Plea Leniency matters. Defence lawyers are perceptive of the ways in which guilty plea are given, whether procured or facilitated through malpractice carried out by state officials. Yet concerns about the potential retaliatory actions may have implications on future cases in their career which may discourage many defence lawyers from reporting the misconduct, quietly tolerating the unfair treatment. Defence lawyers have revealed to us that in some cases, prosecutors demanded the suspect to replace his own defence counsel, who was prepared to challenge the prosecution case, with an obedient duty lawyer to ensure that the suspect 'signed the cognisance without any drama' (*PL_A5*). Similarly, in *PL_A15* the prosecutor asked the accused to substitute his lawyer who insisted that he should plead not guilty with a duty lawyer who would have advised in support of a plea of guilty. In the face of prosecutorial misconduct, many defence lawyers choose to acquiesce rather than filing a complaint for a protest. Indeed, the present Plea Leniency framework offers no substantial remedies to which that they can seek recourse for oppressive prosecutorial power and to address the power abuse. As such, they are unable to protect their own legal rights, let alone the rights of their clients.

Uncertainties in the Rules and the Exercise of Judicial Power

Aside from the challenges in adapting to Plea Leniency as a new system, two plights were particularly highlighted by defence lawyers in our case studies. The 'predicament (***kunjin***)', as referred by to some of the defence lawyers, is related to the uncertainties they face in preparing defence cases in Plea Leniency. Compared to the traditional criminal process, where the reactions from the prosecution and the courts are relatively predictable after many years' experience, defence lawyers indicated that there are two new factors in the consensual justice which may render the defence effort futile. On the one hand, there is an ambiguity between effectively advancing the defence case in pleading a lenient treatment and an interpretation of insincerity in remorse that amounts to a retraction of guilty plea. On the other hand, judicial review of the Plea Leniency agreement is a variable that may lead to unexpected outcomes. Both uncertainties derive from the exercise of discretionary power from these criminal justice institutions. They pose special challenges for the defence because the motives that underpin those decisions are driven by the institutional interest under the given circumstances, rather than a rule-based consideration that can be anticipated.

The Binding Effect of the Recognisance and the Power to Withdraw

As mentioned earlier, the main distinction between US plea bargaining and Plea Leniency in China lies in the unequal status of the parties, namely the accused and her defence lawyer, whose legal standing disqualifies them from negotiating with the prosecution on an equal footing (SPC, 2019).[20] This inequality embodied in the guilty plea agreement is reflected in the power relations and legal consequences: the agreement is binding on the accused, but not on the prosecution. As a result, when the suspect retracts the guilty plea, she will be punished with a heavier sentence for breaching the guilty plea agreement, whereas the prosecution is given the freedom to withdraw the cognisance if necessary.

There are three ways of retracting guilty pleas in the context of Plea Leniency, which, as many scholars have suggested, should be treated differently. The first one is the withdrawal of the facts of the case. Section 6 of the Sentence Guidance distinguishes the material facts of the case (*zhuyao fanzui shishi*) from facts associated with certain isolated circumstances (*gebie qingjie*), stipulating that only the denial of the former amounts to withdrawing guilty pleas. The second type is related to the withdrawal of the charged offence to which the defendant pleaded guilty. The general view on this kind of retraction is that any challenge to the charge on the part of the defendant would be regarded as a formal cancellation of the guilty plea (Wang, 2021). Nevertheless, Liang (2022) argues that the principle to deal with this form of retraction should be the same as the withdrawal of the material facts of the case, as the prosecution and the courts need to identify the main charge(s) from minor charge(s); if the defendant denies the minor charge(s) and admits the guilt as indicated in the main charge(s), his guilty plea is still valid and is entitled to the sentence discount. The last category of retraction is related to recanting the agreed sentence proposed by the prosecution. There is a dispute as to whether the agreement in sentencing represents the core of guilty pleas (Liang, 2022). But Article 201 (2) of CPL 2018 has clearly stated that the prosecution can adjust the sentence proposal if the defendant objects to the recommended sentence. If the proposed sentence can be revised subject to the opinion on the authority of law, later withdrawal of the sentence agreement, as an expression of the defendant's choice, should be allowed without incurring any penalties. In keeping with this legal principle, any challenge of the suggested sentence should not represent any retraction of the guilty plea entered into.

[20] This inequality is also embodied in the Plea Leniency rules, see *Guiding Opinions on the Application of Plea Leniency* published by the SPC, SPP, Ministry of National Security, Ministry of Public Security, and Ministry of Justice on 24/10/2019.

Despite the nuanced academic analysis of retractions, both the prosecution and the courts have taken a hard line in practice. Min (2021) found that any dispute with the charged offence and the sentence arrangement submitted by the defence is currently recognised as a formal retraction, which will revoke the Plea Leniency agreement and the sentence discount. Studies have also noticed that the demarcation between the material facts and isolated circumstances is rather fluid; the uncertainty has led to the practice that *any* contentious issues raised by the defence are currently interpreted as a challenge to the material facts by the prosecutor (Liang, 2022). The expansive approach to retractions seems to have applied to sentence arrangements too, despite the explicit law in CPL 2018. In *PL_A4*, a case concerned with falsely making out special invoices for value-added tax, the defendant pleaded guilty and agreed upon a sentence proposal of three years and four months' imprisonment. Regretting that the accepted sentence proposal was too harsh for his crime, the defendant retained a defence lawyer afterwards to test out whether there was any latitude to reduce his sentence. During the pre-trial conference with the judge, the defence lawyer expressed a view that the proposed sentence was out of proportion, as these types of cases were normally sentenced with non-custodial sentences based on statistic surveys of published judgments. In response to the challenge, the prosecutor increased the sentence proposal to a term of five years and eight months at trial, with an intention to penalise the defendant's insincere acceptance of the guilty plea agreement, despite that the defendant maintained his guilty plea and showed his remorse by indicating his willingness to hand in all the criminal proceeds. Controversially, the court in this case also concurred with the prosecution and declared that challenging the accepted sentencing arrangement was a retraction of guilty plea. The case ended up with the court meting out a jail term of three years and five months, taking into account his remorse and effort in remedying the situation financially.

While it is clear that defendants attempting to amend the recognisance will result in a vindicative penalty, prosecutors enjoy the liberty to withdraw the guilty plea proposal without incurring any adverse implication for the prosecution case. In fact, some of the prosecutors have sometimes retracted the signed recognisance tactically to enable a more serious sentence to be imposed. For instance, the prosecutor in *PL_A15* unilaterally withdrew the Plea Leniency proposal after the suspect signed the recognisance with a suggested sentence of a two-year imprisonment. The purpose of withdrawing the guilty plea agreement in this case was to ensure that the defendant could be punished without any discount. Defence are powerless in situations such as this, where the rule on Plea Leniency is clearly on the prosecution's side. Article 52 of the Sentence Guidance explicitly states that retraction by the prosecution will render the recognisance void, allowing the prosecutor to bring a fresh charge against the defendant and recommend a new sentence commensurate with it.

The rationale of the regulation is hence a reflection of the power relations in Plea Leniency, which is commandeered by the prosecution (He & Peng, 2020). Such regulations appear to be based on the assumption that since the prosecution initiates the guilty plea agreement and determines the final decision, they have the absolute power to adjourn or cancel the process, without heeding the potential impact the decision has on defence. Rules like this cast doubt on the promulgated values of the criminal process by compounding the power disparity between the two parties rather than respecting procedural rights of the individual.

The Legitimate Power to Override?

The defence's predicament in Plea Leniency, however, is not limited to the prosecutor's tough stance and capricious decisions. Courts may also take a punitive approach in processing Plea Leniency cases to ensure that they can exert their judicial authority. Literature has shown the intricate power dynamics between the procuratorate and the courts with the advent of Plea Leniency (Long, 2020; Zeng, 2021). It is well acknowledged that the procuratorate has greatly profited from the newly acquired power of sentence recommendations in Plea Leniency, resulting in the judicial power being reduced to the official ascertainment of the guilty plea and approval of the sentence recommendation (Sun, 2021). While prior research indicates that judges generally endorse the sentence proposals advanced by the prosecution, this is not always the case (Sun & Tian, 2021). Although mutual cooperation between the courts and the procuratorate are standard, discord erupts sporadically. High-profile cases such as *Yu Jinping*[21] have showcased the court's ability to override the

[21] The case involved an incident of drink-driving, occasioning the death of the victim. The defendant signed the recognisance and agreed a proposed sentence of three years' imprisonment with a reprieve of four years. However, the court rejected the sentence suggestion and imposed a term of two years' imprisonment with no reprieve, a sentence

arranged Plea Leniency arrangements and impose more serious sentences if they see fit (Long, 2020; Sun, 2021).

A similar instance is *PL_A3*, a case concerning the financial crime of illegally taking in public deposits, in which the defendant pleaded guilty and consented to be punished with a proposed sentence of three years' imprisonment with a reprieve of three years. Despite the recognisance agreed upon by both the prosecution and the defendant, the court issued an objection and requested the procuratorate to amend the sentence and re-propose with a more serious sentence. The prosecutor in this case disregarded the judicial suggestion, without notifying the defence. Throughout the process, the defendant and the defence lawyer were kept in the dark about the court's disapproval of the agreement. When the judgment was handled down, they were shocked to find out that the court imposed a jail term of seven years with no reprieve, a draconian sentence departing significantly from the sentence agreed upon by the accused and the prosecution. A similar instance occurred in *PL_A4*, a case related to defrauding a government compensation fund for relocation. The defendant was investigated and prosecuted for defrauding 400,000 yuan in a public-funded relocation scheme. The defendant pleaded guilty and agreed to disgorge all the criminal proceeds as well as paying extra compensation of one million yuan. Based on the defendant's remorseful suggestion, the prosecutor recommended a sentence of four years and six months' imprisonment. During the course of the trial, the court did not raise any objection as to the guilty plea agreement. Unexpectedly, shortly before the judgment was due to be delivered, the court notified the defendant that the recognisance could only be approved if he was willing to pay an extra million yuan. The defendant was unable to afford such a large sum of money at the time and turned down the court's condition. Upon receiving the rejection, the court handed down a judgment and sentenced the defendant to a jail term of six years and three months.[22]

Judicial practices such as these are deeply worrying to the defence community. Indeed, the courts have the power to impose the final

that is legally deemed to be substantially harsher than the prosecutorial recommendation, given the reprieve component of the sentence. When the case was appealed to the intermediate court, the sentence was replaced by a harsher custodial sentence of three years and six months without reprieve. For more details of this case see Long (2020).

[22] Interestingly, the prosecution in this case also refused to revise the agreed proposal on receiving the request from the court.

sentences regardless of the parties' prior arrangement as specified by the law. Be that as it may, one may wonder what purpose judicial control aims to achieve under such circumstances other than exerting their power. The courts may have concerns on perceived leniency following the guilty plea agreement and decide to take an action to re-balance the outcome. Even so, the sentencing proceedings in these instances are fundamentally flawed. The court hearing concerning Plea Leniency is pro forma only. The defence in these instances are not expected to adduce the defence case or attack the prosecution case, based on the conventional understanding that the court operates to approve the recognisance. In consequence, the facts affirmed on such an occasion may be compromised on the part of the defendant, having relinquished the right to contest the prosecution case as an exchange for discount on sentence. Without hearing the defence case or fully investigating and ascertaining the overall facts impartially, the basis on which the final sentence is meted out can be fallible; and that in return makes the sentence incommensurate with the defendant's culpability. The defence counsel in *PL_A3* expressed his frustration:

> The defendant and I are both shocked at the court's decision since we completely trusted the expected validity and legal effect of recognisance. We gave up any substantial defence right at trial. We cannot believe that our trust and acceptance was returned by the sentence ambush from the court, whose role is supposed to provide us with remedies rather than divesting them from us.

It is trite to say that Chinese criminal justice is not truly an adversarial system. Yet completely dismissing individual autonomy by overruling considered negotiations between the parties is highly problematic. This research is not in a position to investigate the extent to which such judicial practice exists, although the defence lawyers who participated in this study had explicitly raised the issue and expressed their deep concern on the role the courts play in those instances. Indeed, the judiciary, being widely perceived as the last bastion against injustice, is expected to be impartial and to safeguard the procedural rights of the defendant and to proffer remedies to those unfairly treated. For all that, what has manifested in these cases has been nothing but blatant state-induced coercion, which is punitive in nature. When a court makes the controversial decision to supersede the Plea Leniency sentence arrangement, they pay no heed to defence rights, especially their right to information, nor take notice of its detrimental consequence on the defendant. How the decision was made and how messages were communicated between judges and prosecutors are opaque and dubious.

The Margin of Negotiation

Given the above, does that mean defence lawyers can do nothing but to passively submit to the powers of the prosecution and the courts in Plea Leniency? The answer is quite the opposite, as our case study suggests. In fact, most of the lawyers with whom we had conversations emphasised the importance of a well-planned defence strategy and active confrontation and engagement with the state officials (*PL_A1, A3 and A4*). They declared that their role is not, and should never be, a mouthpiece of their clients, or a facilitator of Plea Leniency on behalf of the State. Some of them were gravely concerned about the widespread application of Plea Leniency in criminal justice, which, in their view, may lead to a mass production of miscarriages of justice (*PL_A14*). It has long been noted in the Western literature that plea bargaining poses serious risks to the innocent due to the state-induced coercion (Baldwin & McConville, 1977; Bottoms & McClean, 1976; McConville & Marsh, 2014). Such risk seems to be magnified in China. The Chinese criminal justice system has been dominated by the criminal justice institutions marginalising defence lawyers; the coercive police interrogations give raise to a remarkably high confession rate (McConville et al., 2011, pp. 122–124; Mou, 2020). As a result, the pressure to which suspects are exposed is significantly greater.

In the meanwhile, the phenomenon of overcriminalisation in China exacerbates these concerns (Cai et al., 2020). Defence lawyers in our case study reported that a good proportion of their clients are victimised by the expansion of criminal law in the last few years, as their conduct would not have been considered as crimes a decade ago (*PL_A9; A11*). The problem was particularly acute during the Sweeping Away Black and Eradicating Evil Force (SABEEF) Campaign between 2018 and 2020. During that time, the judicially invented concept of evil force crime (*e'shili fanzui*) widened the net of criminalisation to encompass certain tort feasances, breaches of contract, and administrative violations (Yin & Mou, 2022). These cases were prosecuted due to the top-down demand to fulfil political campaign targets. Due to the campaign-style law enforcement, some of the prosecuted cases were weak in nature and should not have been investigated or prosecuted in the first place (*PL_A9; A11*). Prosecutors in charge were aware of the deficiencies of these cases and there was a general tendency to dispose of them through the Plea Leniency route. Knowing the weaknesses of the prosecution case, defence lawyers have occasionally identified a realistic scope for negotiation with the prosecutor. *PL_A11* is one of such cases. The defendant was involved in a peer-to-peer online lending platform which was cracked down during the SABEEF campaign. The accused was charged with five offences, including black society gang crime, fraud, extortion of properties, picking quarrels and provoking troubles, and infringement of citizens' personal information. Through a painstaking analysis of a multitude of evidence contained in 420 case dossiers, dissecting and taking issue with the charged offences, defence counsel successfully persuaded the prosecution and the courts to acknowledge the weaknesses of the case. On that account, the prosecution decided to drop four out of the five intended charges. The case ended with a Plea Leniency agreement with a much lighter sentence. Another successful defence case is *PL_A12,* where the defendant was originally charged with organising prostitution, with criminal proceeds of 500,000 yuan. After a thorough analysis of the evidence, defence counsel vigorously disputed with the prosecution's claim of the prostitute organisation. Through several rounds of communication with the prosecution and intense negotiations, the prosecution finally agreed to adopt the defence proposal and downgraded the charge to the offence of harbouring prostitution, with 500-yuan criminal proceeds. Based on this, the defendant pleaded guilty and received a non-custodial sentence.

Compared to defending traditional criminal cases in a contested trial, Plea Leniency cases are more demanding to the defence in the sense that they have a tight timeframe available to identify the flaws of the prosecution case and to develop a sound defence strategy. Despite this, the defence lawyers in our case study have observed that the quick turnaround in Plea Leniency cases are equally unfavourable to the prosecution. Prosecutors are subjected to regimented and taxing managerial performance targets which require them to process large volumes of cases in an expeditious manner (Yu, 2015). To prioritise efficiency, prosecutors may need to compromise the strength of the prosecution case and quite often may not be able to effectively check the reliability and sufficiency of the prosecution evidence. This may be damaging to the prosecution case especially when the investigation was poorly executed. Meanwhile, prosecutors have to cope with a heavy caseload, meaning that the time and energy they can invest on each case is limited. By taking advantage of these weaknesses, defence lawyers can indeed avail themselves to discuss terms in favour of their client and to secure their best interests.

Conclusion

There is no doubt that Plea Leniency has ushered in a new era in Chinese criminal justice. Drawing from 15 case studies on criminal defence practices, this chapter has examined the new hurdles that confront defence lawyers when defending guilty plea cases. As a new form of criminal justice administration, Plea Leniency was set up to substitute the traditional criminal procedure and to facilitate the needs of the criminal justice institutions, especially the procuratorate and the courts. The system was therefore created to meet the prosecutorial and judicial demands of procedural efficiency, while the interests of defence were largely ignored. Defence lawyers found themselves in a profound predicament given the diminished room to defend criminal cases under this process. The punitive approach underlying the process has made it difficult to withdraw a guilty plea after the accused has signed the recognisance and her exercise of the right to appeal is likely to be threatened with a harsh sentence. The tight timeframes to prepare defence cases and the challenges in communicating with prosecutors have made the defence job tougher and unpalatable. The uncertainties they face in advancing defence views without triggering an adverse inference of retracting the guilty plea and the judicial ambush that overrides the prior Plea Leniency agreement also showcase the continued perpetuation of criminal defence marginalisation. In light of the changed reality of Chinese criminal justice, there is no surprise that defence lawyers are deeply concerned about the mass production of miscarriages of justice in the Plea Leniency era. It is true that criminal defence lawyers can take advantage of the sentence discount and protect their clients' best interest in certain cases. But the rules in relation to Plea Leniency and the professional interactions between state officials and defence lawyers have certainly compounded defence lawyers' disadvantaged status in China's criminal justice system.

References

Baldwin, J., & McConville, M. (1977). *Negotiated Justice*. Martin Robertson.

Borman, P. D. (1975). Chilled Right to Appeal from a Plea Bargain Conviction: A Due Process Cure. *Northwestern University Law Review, 69*(5), 663–715.

Bottoms, A., & McClean, J. (1976). *Defendants in the Criminal Process*. Routledge.

Cai, S., Gao, Q., & Fan, X. (2020). "Saohei chue" zhuanxiang douzheng fazhi baozhang yanjiu: yi X shi W qu weili (Research on the Legal Protection in the SABEEF Campaign). Vol. 4. *Nanfang Lunkan* (*The Southern Forum*), 44–49.

Chen, S. (2021). The Legitimacy of Duty Lawyers. *Zhongguo Jianchaguan (The Chinese Procuratorate), 10*, 43–45.

Chen, W., & An, N. (2020). The Roles and Functions of Lawyers in Leniency for Guilty Pleas: A Perspective of Three Stages. *Zhejianggongshang Daxuexuebao (journal of Zhejiang Gongshang University), 6*, 71–85.

Chen, W., & Liu, J. (2002). Cong jianli beigaoren youzuidabian zhidu dao yinru biansujiaoyi: Lun beiguo biansu jiaoyizhidu de jiejianyiyi (From Guilty Pleas to Plea Bargaining: On Values of the US Plea Bargaining System). *Zhengzhi Yu Falv (politics and Law), 6*, 49–56.

China Law Year Book. (2022). *China Law Year Book (2010–2022)*. China Law Year Book Publishing.

Dyer, G. M., & Judge, B. (1989). Criminal Defendants' Waiver of the Right to Appeal—An Unacceptable Condition of a Negotiated Sentence or Plea Bargain. *Notre Dame L. Rev., 65*, 649.

Guangzhou Daily. (2021, March 22). Renzuirenfahou fanhui? Zhongpan! (Regretting Plea Leniency? Punished with a Sentence!). *Guangzhou Daily*. http://m.xinhuanet.com/gd/2021-03/22/c_1127238633.htm (Accessed 26 April 2023).

Han, X. (2021). Questions on the Effective Defence in Leniency for Guilty Pleas (Renzuirenfacongkuan anjianzhong youxiao falv bangzhu wenti yanjiu) 3 *Faxue zazhi* (Legal Magazine), 1–13.

He, X. (2023). Plea Leniency and Prosecution Centredness in China's Criminal Process. *The China Quarterly, 1–18*,. https://doi.org/10.1017/S03057410 2300022X

He, X., & Peng, X. (2020, September 14). Qiantan zai falv cengmian guiding jianchajiguan renzuirenfa jujieshu chehuiquan (A Discussion on the Right to Withdraw Cognisance by the Prosecution and its Legal Regulations) *Allbrightlaw*. https://www.allbrightlaw.com/CN/10475/cefb4049cb7ca2ae. aspx

Hu, Y. (2020). Wanshan renzuirenfacongkuan zhidu gaige de jige wenti (Several Questions on Perfecting Plea Leniency) *Zhongguo falv luntan (China Law Forum), 3*, 75–86.

Ivsan, I. (2017). To Plea or Not to Plea: How Plea Bargains Criminalize the Right to Trial and Undermine Our Adversarial System of Justice. *North Carolina Central Law Review, 39*(2), 135–165.

Ji, X. (2007). Yuwai biansu jiaoyi de fazhan jiqi qishi (The Development and Inspiration of Plea Bargaining). *Dangdai Faxue (modern Law), 21*(3), 23–30.

Lan, Y., & Zhao, H. (2020). Renzuirenfa anjian beigaoren shangsu zhidu goujian (The Construction of the Appeal System for Plea Leniency). *Journal of Central South University, 26*(6), 52–61.

Law Daily. (2019, October 25). "Lianggao liangbu" jiu zhunque shiyong renzuirenfacongkuanzhidu da jizhewen (The SPC, SPP, the Ministry of Justice and Ministry of Public Security press conference on Plea Leniency).

Li, E. (2022a). Chinese Courts' New Plea Leniency System: Scrutinizing the Efficacy of Mandatory Defense Counsel. *The China Journal, 88*(1), 78–99.

Li, E. (2022b). Haste Makes Waste: Why China's New Plea Leniency System is Doomed to Fail. *Asian Journal of Comparative Law, 17*(1), 76–105.

Liang, S. (2022). Renzuirenfacongkuanzhidu beizhuisuren fanhui yanjiu (Research on the Retraction of the Defendant) *Open Journal of Legal Science, 10*, 68.

Liu, S., & Halliday, T. C. (2016). *Criminal Defence in China: The Politics of Lawyers at Work*. Cambridge University Press.

Long, Z. (2020). Case Comment on Yu Jinping Case. *Zhongguo Falvpinglun (china Law Review), 3*, 87–96.

McConville, M., & Marsh, L. (2014). *Criminal Judges: Legitimacy, Courts and State-induced Guilty Pleas in Britain*. Edward Elgar Publishing.

McConville, M., et al. (2011). *Criminal Justice in China: An Empirical Inquiry*. Edward Elgar Publishing.

Min, C. (2017). Effective Defence in Leniency for Guilty Pleas. *Dangdai Faxue (Modern Law), 4*, 27–37.

Min, Z. (2021). Renzuirenfahou fanwei de baozhang yu guizhi (Safeguard and Regulation on the Retraction in Plea Leniency). *Zhongguo Xingshifa Zazhi (Chinese Criminal Law Magazine), 4*, 143–159.

Mou, Y. (2020). *The Construction of Guilt in China*. Hart Publishing.

Mou, Y. (2022). Accountable for a lifetime: Reforms in prosecutorial accountability in China. *China Law and Society Review, 6*(1), 36–78.

National People's Congress. (2020, October 16). SPP's Report on Plea Leniency Indicates Drastic Improvement in Efficiency of Criminal Justice. *The People's Daily*. http://www.npc.gov.cn/npc/c30834/202010/5ca8ef6d7a8d4013845d3200913b88fd.shtml

Reimelt, A. W. (2010). An Unjust Bargain: Plea Bargains and Waiver of the Right to Appeal. *Boston College Law Review, 51*, 871–904.

SPC. (2017). Zuigao renming fayuan yinfa "sanxiang guicheng" shenru tuijin xingshi tingshen shizhihua gaige (The SPC on Deepening the Trial Substantive Reform and Three Procedures) *The Supreme People's Procuratorate of the People's Republic of China*. https://www.court.gov.cn/zixun-xiangqing-75622.html (Accessed 14 March 2023).

SPC. (2018, March 15). Tingshen shizhihua fangfan yuancuoan: renmin fayuan tuijin yi shenpan weizhongxin de xingshi susong zhidu gaige zongshu (Substantiating Court Trials and Preventing Miscarriages of Justice). *The People's Court Gazette*. https://www.court.gov.cn/zixun-xiangqing-85282.html

SPC. (2019, February 27). *The Notice on Issuing and Circulating the Speech Delivered by the Vice President Li Shaoping on Promoting and Implementing the Work of Plea Leniency, The Supreme People's Procuratorate of the People's Republic of China*. Doc. Fa Ban 2019, no 49.

SPP. (2022). Zuigaojian mingque: zhezhong anjian yao kangsu! Kangshi weile bukang (A Clarification from the SPP: Those Cases must be Protested for the Sake of not to Protesting them in the Future). 14 January. *The Supreme People's Procuratorate of the People's Republic of China*. https://www.spp.gov.cn/zdgz/202201/t20220114_541676.shtml

SPP. (2023a). Renzuirenfacongkuan chulihou you xiang shangsu jianxing? Dong wainaojing keng le ziji (Appeal for a Mitigated Sentence after Receiving Plea Leniency? Outsmart the System to Harm Oneself 认罪认罚从宽处理后又想上诉减刑?动"歪脑筋"坑了自己!) *The Supreme People's Procuratorate of the People's Republic of China*. April 26. http://k.sina.com.cn/article_5053469079_12d35d19701900h4tj.html?from=pet.

SPP. (2023b). Zuigao renmin jianchayuan gongzuo baogao (The Supreme People's Procuratorate Work Report). *The Supreme People's Procuratorate of the People's Republic of China*. https://www.spp.gov.cn/spp/gzbg/202303/t20230317_608767.shtml (Accessed 14 March 2023).

Stuntz, W. J. (2004). Plea bargaining and criminal law's disappearing shadow, *Harvard Law Review*, *117*, 2548–2569.

Sun, C., & Tian, W. (2021). Empirical Research on Leniency for Guilty Pleas: A Sample of Two Levels of Courts in a City. *Xinanzhengfa Daxuexuebao (Southwest University of Political Science and Law Journal)*, *5*, 3–16.

Sun, H. (2021). The Pitfalls of High Approval Rates of Sentence Recommendations. *Peking University Law Journal*, *6*, 1503–1522.

Teeter, D. (2005, April). Contracts Analysis of Waivers of the Right to Appeal in Criminal Plea Bargains. *University of Kansas Law Review*, *53*(3), 727–766.

Wang, C. (2021). Renzuirenfa anjian beigaoren fanhui de chengxu yingdui (Procedural Reaction to the Defendant's Retraction of Guilty Pleas in Plea Leniency) Shenjing *falv pinglun*, 10(1), 109–129.

Wang, J. (2002). Biansu jiaoyi de lilun jichu (The Theoretical Foundation of Plea Bargaining). *Zhengfa Luntan (Politics and Law Forum), 6*, 14–18.

Wei, X. (2021). Renzuirenfacongkuan zhiduzhong de subian guanxi (The Prosecution-defence Relationship under Plea Leniency) *Zhongguo xingshifa zazhi (China Criminal Law Magazine), 6*, 52–66.

Xie, X. (2023). Renzuirenfacongkuan anjianzhong yi kangsu jingdui liangxing shangsu zhi zhiyi (A Question on the Counter-appeal Protest Against the Sentencing Decision in Plea Leniency Cases) *Huanqiu falv pinglun (Global Law Review), 2*, 193–209.

Yin, B., & Mou, Y. (2022). Centralized Law Enforcement in Contemporary China: The Campaign to "Sweep Away Black Societies and Eradicate Evil Forces". *The China Quarterly*, 1–15.

Yu, D. (2015). Guanyu jianchajiguan jixiao kaohezhidu de diaocha baogao: yi H sheng L xian renming jianchayuan gongsu jixiao kaohe zhidu wei yangben (Survey Report on the Appraisal System of the Procuratorate: A Sample of the People's Procuratorate in L County H Province). *Zhongguo Xingshifa Zazhi (china Criminal Law Magazine), 2*, 114–132.

Yuan, B., & Yuan, L. (2021). Renzuirenfazhiduzhong de shangsu wenti jiqi yingdui (The Appeal Issues and its Solution in Plea Leniency) *Fazhi yu shehui (Law and Society), 7*, 88–89.

Zachary, M. (2003). Interpretation of Problematic Federal Criminal Appeal Waivers. *Vermont Law Review, 28*(1), 149–172.

Zeng, H. (2021). The Rule of Dominance in the Sentencing Power of Leniency for Guilty Pleas *Xinyangnongling xuyuanxuebao (Journal of Xinyang Agriculture and Forestry University), 3*, 5–9.

Zhou, J. (2021, August 21). Lushi jieru jieru renzuirenfa anjian zhi lujin yanjiu (Research on How the Defence Lawyers Should Intervene Plea Leniency Cases), *Guikexueyuan*. https://www.fahejia.com/view?id=572f47fcd7d84999848b3c9df2345213&userid=68e3fc47451d482b9bb354d4f0cac5be&type=2

Is Plea Leniency Really a Bargain? An Empirical Study of Six Cities in China

Yuhao Wu

Introduction

In the criminal justice system, legal actors' decision-making is supposed to be guided by several focal concerns such as the severity of the crime, the blameworthiness of the defendant, and other practical considerations (Kutateladze & Lawson, 2018; Steffensmeier, 1980; Steffensmeier et al., 1998). Plea bargaining is usually defined as a process in which a defendant agrees to plead guilty in exchange for some concession from the prosecutor. A wealth of literature, mostly using data from American courts, has confirmed that many factors play a role in the decision-making around which cases are disposed by guilty plea versus proceeding to trial. These factors include legal factors such as the severity of the crime and prior criminal record as well as extralegal factors such as the gender and race of the defendant (Boylan, 2012; Dervan & Edkins, 2013; Meyer & Gray, 1997).

One common reason for most defendants to plead guilty is to avoid the 'trial penalty'. They expect that pleas could lead to a more favourable outcome in case dispositions—as getting a 'bargain' (Bushway & Redlich,

Y. Wu (✉)
Law School, Peking University, Beijing, China
e-mail: wyhpku@yeah.net

E. Li et al. (eds.), *Criminal Case Dispositions through Pleas in Greater China*, https://doi.org/10.1007/978-981-97-1856-6_5

2012; Bushway et al., 2014). Most jurisdictions also acknowledge that defendants entering a guilty plea could receive a reduction in their sentence compared to similarly placed defendants entering a trial (Langer, 2004; Rauxloh, 2011; Soubise, 2018). The law in practice, however, could be different from the law on the books. Several empirical studies indicate that pleading guilty is not always the better choice. In other words, whether defendants who pleaded guilty received true benefits remains contradictory (Albonetti, 1998; Brereton & Casper, 1981–1982; Bushway & Redlich, 2012; Uhlman & Walker, 1979).

In contrast, the opportunity for defendants to plead guilty and thereby avoid a full trial was alien to the Chinese criminal justice system for decades. The inquisitorial culture and socialist law tradition derived from the Chinese criminal justice system both conceive that the truth in a case cannot be bargained with or compromised. Nevertheless, due to the increasing caseload, recent reforms in China have introduced a new system to expedite the dispositional process of 'simple' cases. On September 3, 2016, the Supreme People's Court (SPC) and the Supreme People's Procuratorate (SPP) started a program called *renzui renfa congkuan* (*认罪认罚从宽 Imposing Lenient Punishments on Those Pleading Guilty and Accepting Punishments*) in several pilot cities, which is cited by some scholars as the Chinese version of plea bargaining (Gu, 2016; Jia, 2018). This 'plea leniency' program allows prosecutors to propose a sentence recommendation for a defendant who pleads guilty. Negotiations over pleas between defence and prosecution are also allowed thereafter. Finally, certain regulations explicitly state that leniency could be offered to defendants who plead guilty, agree with the prosecutor on the sentencing recommendation, and sign a plea agreement (SPC, 2016a, 2016b).

Plea leniency was described as a legal transplant from the plea bargaining system in Anglo-American courts (Chen, 2016; Gu, 2016). Consequently, some Chinese scholars have expressed similar concerns to those discussed in the Anglo-American practice of plea bargaining, that is, whether the sentence reduction truly happens in practice. Specifically, considering that China has a reputation for its unbalanced justice system in favour of the police and prosecutors, it is possible that the guilty plea is manipulated by the police and prosecutors and that defendants do not have the bargaining power to obtain a lighter sentencing outcome (Chen, 2016; Li, 2022a; Wang, 2017; Xiong, 2016). Also, because poor accused persons who are not familiar with the criminal justice system tend to accept the prosecutor's offer without negotiation, this raises further questions about whether a guilty plea could lead to more favourable results for defendants (Jia, 2018; Zuo, 2017). While these theoretical discussions offer an interesting insight into the implementation of the Chinese plea leniency, they do not provide empirical evidence on what actually happens in practice (He, 2023; Li, 2022b).

This study fills this gap by providing an empirical study of the mode of decision-making and its effect on case outcomes in plea leniency. Specifically, this study aims to answer two questions: what factors play a role in the decision to make a guilty plea versus proceeding to trial and whether the decision to plead guilty leads to more favourable results. I used data on DUI cases tried by courts located in six cities where the *renzui renfa congkuan* program was carried out. The influences of legal and extralegal factors in determining which cases are disposed of by plea versus trial were examined. The results show that the defendants who were more likely to plead guilty were those without a prior criminal record, a lower level of Blood Alcohol Concentrations (BACs), or those who had confessed. The findings suggest that defendants who failed to compensate the victims were also more likely to enter a guilty plea. Furthermore, using a propensity score weighting technique to control for potential confounding variables, this study answers the question of whether the defendants who pleaded guilty received leniency compared to the similarly situated defendants who were disposed of through full trial. Generally, my results support the conclusion that a guilty plea could lead to more favourable case outcomes. Defendants who pleaded guilty were more likely to be released before the trial and be granted probation. In addition, although defendants who pleaded guilty, on average, received a longer declared sentence length, their actual time served in jail was significantly shorter than defendants who did not plead guilty because a higher percentage of these defendants had their sentences suspended. Finally, whether a defendant pleaded guilty was not a significant predictor of the quantum of the fine imposed on defendants.

The remainder of this chapter has five parts: Part 2 introduces the background information of what plea leniency is like. Part 3 discusses the theoretical framework and prior literature. Part 4 presents the data. Part 5 describes the methodology. Part 6 presents empirical results. Part 7 reviews the findings and the limitations of this research.

Development of Plea Leniency in China

Two features of the Chinese criminal justice system explain why the formal plea bargaining system did not exist in China for decades. First, Chinese criminal procedure is inquisitorial in nature, which assumes that the criminal process is a neutral investigation conducted by the state to find factual truth. In this model, prosecutors are supposed to represent the wider public interest rather than pursuing the narrow interests of the prosecution's side (Rauxloh, 2014; Soubise, 2018). They play a role as state officials in supervising the criminal investigation. The idea that case outcomes can be negotiated between the prosecutor and the defendant is alien to the inquisitorial system. In practice, prosecutors document all the results of a criminal investigation in the dossiers. The judge conducts fact-finding through verifying the dossiers that have been prepared before trial (Chen, 2006; Goldstein & Marcus, 1977). Hence, while the fact that the defendant admits guilt is often recorded in the dossiers by the prosecutor and may be crucial to the judge's decision, the case must still go to trial before the judge can make a final determination (Soubise, 2018).

Second, as a socialist country, China's legal culture is also deeply influenced by the former Soviet Union's legal tradition and has a reputation for its unbalanced justice system in favour of the police and prosecutors. In this model, prosecutors play a role as a 'provider of justice', who cooperate with the police and the court to crack down on crime.[1] The judge does not require the prosecutor to present much evidence in the dossier and convictions heavily rely on defendants' confessions. Guided by the criminal justice policy of *leniency to those who confess, severity to those who resist* (*tanbai congkuan, kangju congyan* 坦白从宽，抗拒从严), defendants are encouraged to confess at a very early stage in the criminal process. As a result, most defendants who have confessed have no legal rights to trade in return for a reduced sentence with the prosecutor (Biddulph et al., 2017; Li, 2015; Lu & Kelly, 2008; Yan, 2013).

For a long time, this model of criminal proceedings has been criticized by many scholars for disregarding the defendant's rights and being

[1] Packer (1964, p. 11) vividly described this kind of criminal process as the Crime Control Model: "The image (of this model) that comes to mind is an assembly line or a conveyor belt down which moves an endless stream of cases, never stopping, carrying the cases to workers who stand at fixed stations and who perform on each case as it comes by the same small but essential operation that brings it one step closer to being a finished product, or, to exchange the metaphor for the reality, a closed file."

more likely to lead to miscarriages of justice (Biddulph et al., 2017; Chen, 2006, 2016). In practice, several remarkable wrongful convictions such as She Xianglin,[2] Zhang Gaoping,[3] and Huugjilt[4] have been exposed, suggesting the necessity of fundamental reforms in the criminal justice system.

On October 29, 2014, the Fourth Plenary Session of the 18th Central Committee of the Communist Party of China (CPC) released the Decision of the CPC Central Committee on Major Issues Pertaining to Comprehensively Promoting the Rule of Law. This decision was interpreted as a signal that the central government planned to start several reforms to the legal system. On the one hand, to increase the fairness of the criminal justice system, the decision proposed that placing the trial at the centre (*yi shenpan wei zhongxi* 以审判为中心) should be one of the future organizing principles of the justice system (CPC, 2014). This reform emphasized that in complicated cases, the judge should invest enough time in a court hearing to conduct the fact-finding process rather than heavily relying on dossiers to determine the facts of a case (Biddulph et al., 2017; Shen, 2015; Zhang, 2015).

On the other hand, however, the criminal justice system in China has also encountered pressure from increasing caseloads. This issue has been especially prominent in minor cases. First, China abolished its re-education through labour system on December 23, 2013. This system utilized administrative detention to punish people who committed minor crimes. After this system was abolished, a portion of these people were prosecuted within the criminal justice system, leading to a significant increase of cases handled by courts (Biddulph et al., 2017). Second, recent legal reforms also accelerated the professionalism of the judiciary in China. One of these measures was the internal reallocation of personnel roles within the courts (*yuan'ezhigaige* 员额制改革). This program set

[2] She Xianglin was convicted of murder in 1998 after he was tortured by the police and confessed. After he had spent seven years in prison, his wife reemerged and his conviction was overturned.

[3] Zhang Gaoping and his nephew Zhang Hui were convicted of rape and murder in 2003 due to forced confession. In 2013, another suspect's DNA was found to match their case. Their conviction was subsequently overturned.

[4] Huugjilt was an Inner Mongolian who was executed on June 10, 1996, for the rape and murder of a woman. On December 5, 2006, ten years after the execution, another suspect Zhao Zhihong admitted he had committed the crime. Huugjilt was posthumously exonerated and Zhao Zhihong was sentenced to death in 2015.

a mandatory quota of legal staff to be selected as judges to adjudicate cases while assigning the administrative work to other personnel (Li, 2016). As some scholars suggested, after this program was carried out, the number of legal staff with the title of judge decreased significantly, and thus the number of cases handled by each judge increased drastically (Feng, 2015). Finally, the trial-centeredness reform also required that the criminal justice system has sufficient resources to handle complicated and serious cases, consequently limiting resources available to deal with minor crimes. Therefore, the CPC's decision also stated that China aimed to improve the justice system to help it handle simple or straightforward cases in a more efficient manner. One solution was to establish the *renzui renfa congkuan* (plea leniency) system within criminal justice (CPC, 2014).

Two years later, the plea leniency system was implemented. On September 3, 2016, the Standing Committee of the National People's Congress formally passed a decision to authorize the Supreme People's Court and the Supreme People's Procuratorate to carry out the *renzui renfa congkuan* program. This program was first carried out in 18 cities as a pilot program for two years and then expanded nationwide.

According to official regulations, the core idea of the *renzui renfa congkuan* program is to impose leniency on defendants who plead guilty, follow the prosecutor's sentencing recommendation, and sign a plea agreement (SPC, 2016a, 2016b). Several characteristics of this program indicate its similarities to the conventional model of plea bargaining in Anglo-American Courts. First, this program allows defendants and prosecutors to reach a formal agreement on charges and sentences, which is then delivered to the judge for validation. Second, this program acknowledges that the defendant and the prosecutor can negotiate as two parties over pleas and sentences (SPC, 2018).[5] Last but not least, this program allows defendants to plead guilty in exchange for some concession from the prosecutor by stating that a lenient disposition could be imposed on defendants who reach an agreement with the prosecutor (SPC, 2016a, 2016b).

Nevertheless, some scholars underline two important differences between plea leniency and plea bargaining in Anglo-American courts.

[5] Previous qualitative studies indicate that, in practice, prosecutors decide whether to initiate the plea leniency process right after cases are sent to them. They would meet with the defendant when they think plea leniency is applicable to the case (Gu & Xiao, 2017).

First, the scope of plea leniency is narrower than that in Anglo-American courts. While sentence bargaining is at the centre of the Chinese plea leniency system, charge bargaining is not permitted. This means defendants cannot bargain with the prosecutor for lesser charges or to have some charges dropped (Gu, 2016; Zuo, 2017). Second, because the Chinese criminal justice system is inquisitorial in nature and based on the notion that the factual truth rather than the legal truth should be found in the courtroom, some scholars argue that the standard of proof cannot be lowered even in cases where defendants plead guilty (Chen, 2017; Sun, 2018).

After implementing this program in 18 pilot cities for two years, plea leniency was expanded nationwide. On October 26, 2018, the Standing Committee of the National People's Congress in China revised the criminal procedure law (CPL). One notable feature of the 2018 CPL is that it added several articles on the criminal proceedings of *renzui renfa congkuan*. Specifically, the first amendment of the 2018 CPL stated that 'criminal suspects or defendants who voluntarily and truthfully plead guilty, admit the facts of the crime as charged, and are willing to accept punishment could receive a lenient disposition' (Article 15). In addition, the 2018 CPL added some detailed articles on how this new criminal process should operate, such as the obligation of police to inform suspects of their right to a guilty plea (Article 120), the obligation of the prosecutor to record and transfer the plea agreement (Article 162), and the obligation of the judge to review the voluntariness of the guilty plea (Article 190). Moreover, the 2018 CPL also addressed the role of attorneys in plea leniency by stating that a retained lawyer or an on-duty lawyer (*zhiban lvshi* 值班律师) should be present when defendants sign a plea agreement with the prosecutor (Article 173).[6]

[6] However, these on-duty lawyers do not act as defence attorneys and they will not appear in court on behalf of the defendant. For example, in my sample, only around 12% of defendants had a lawyer to represent them. For the remaining defendants, according to the 2018 CPL, an on-duty lawyer would give them some legal advice before the trial, but these defendants would still be labelled as unrepresented during the trial.

Theoretical Framework and Prior Literature

Given that plea leniency is a newly established system in China, there has not yet been a quantitative study on plea leniency in China. By contrast, plea bargaining has been widely used in criminal cases in the U.S. since the late nineteenth century (Alschuler, 1979; Vogel, 1999). Now, most criminal cases in the U.S. are resolved through guilty pleas rather than trials.[7] Consequently, there has been considerable literature devoted to the empirical legal study of the practice of plea bargaining in U.S academia. There are two research questions concerning the empirical study of decision-making in plea bargaining systems. First, what factors influence the decision between a guilty plea versus a trial. Second, whether the decision of pleading guilty results in favourable case outcomes.

Factors Affecting a Guilty Plea Decision

The decision of a guilty plea is normally believed to be a result of the discretion exercised by both the prosecutor and the defendant. Prior research has acknowledged that both legal and extralegal factors influence the decision-making of plea bargaining.

Among the legal factors, crime severity has been considered to play a critical role. Some qualitative studies in U.S. courtrooms indicate that prosecutors differentiate between serious and nonserious cases. Specifically, prosecutors tend to take more serious cases to trial because they believe these cases deserve more resources and time than nonserious cases (Burke, 2007; Ulmer, 1997). This hypothesis was also supported by several quantitative studies. Meyer and Gary (1997) found that in DUI cases, defendants facing longer jail sentences were more likely to plead not guilty. Similarly, using the effect of judge assignment, Boylan (2012) found that a 10-month increase in prison sentences raises trial rates by 1 percentage point.

Whether a defendant had a prior criminal record is another potential legal factor that could influence the plea bargaining decision. However, evidence provided by prior empirical work is mixed. Some found that

[7] In the federal system, out of 78,155 convictions from October 1, 2013, to September 30, 2014, 76,163 were obtained through guilty plea. This proportion has reached 97.5%. In the state system, 94% of felony offenders sentenced in 2006 pleaded guilty (Bureau of Justice Statistics, 2009, 2017).

defendants with prior arrests or convictions pleaded guilty more often than those without prior criminal records (Kutateladze & Lawson, 2018; Myers, 1982), while other studies indicated that prior convictions do not affect plea bargaining (Meyer & Gray, 1997), or affect it in the opposite direction (Myers & Hagan, 1979).

Last but not the least, previous studies have also suggested that some extralegal characteristics of defendants such as race, gender, and age could also influence the decision to go to trial. For example, there is evidence showing that males and older defendants are more likely to proceed to trial (Myers & Hagan, 1979). Previous studies indicated that Caucasians were more likely than other ethnic groups to plead not guilty (Meyer & Gray, 1997). However, several other studies have found that race has no influence (Ball, 2006; Frenzel & Ball, 2007; Kutateladze & Lawson, 2018).

This study anticipates that legal and extralegal factors might influence the plea decision in the Chinese context. Instead of using the prison sentence, this paper uses several characteristics of DUI crimes such as the BACs and the harm caused by DUI as a proxy for offence severity. In addition, other legal factors indicating blameworthiness such as victim compensation and confession are also included in my model.[8] Finally, whether extralegal factors such as gender and ethnicity have an impact on the discretion of plea leniency was also tested in this study.

Plea Leniency and Case Outcomes

There are several theoretical frameworks that explain why sentence disparities exist between cases disposed by guilty plea and cases convicted at a trial. First, a guilty plea indicates that defendants acknowledge guilt and manifest a willingness to assume responsibility for their actions. Therefore, the sentence imposed on these defendants should be more lenient because they have expressed remorse and thus are less blameworthy (Bowers, 2008; Church, 1979).

Second, regarding practical issues, prosecutors need to maintain the expeditious movement of case dispositions to overcome increasing

[8] In China, most confessions occur during the investigation stage. Police record whether the suspect confessed and deliver dossiers to prosecutors. Therefore, confession is believed to affect a set of prosecutorial discretions including plea leniency (Chen, 2006; Goldstein & Marcus, 1977).

caseload pressures. Plea bargaining makes prosecutors more administratively efficient and gives them a better chance of securing convictions for those cases that do still go to trial. Consequently, the criminal justice system should reward defendants who plead guilty with better case outcomes (Bowers, 2008; Easterbrook, 1983; Fisher, 2000; Guidorizzi, 1998).

Finally, some criminologists posit that the plea offer made by prosecutors is a function of perceived probable outcomes of a trial. This 'shadow of the trial' theory indicates that defendants pleading guilty receive a sentence discount because a defendant may not be convicted at trial. Specifically, according to this theory, a plea sentence reached by prosecutors and defence attorneys equals the possible sentence at trial, discounted by its conviction probability (Bushway & Redlich, 2012; Bushway et al., 2014; Yan & Bushway, 2018).

In summary, all these theories suggest that the better case outcomes associated with a guilty plea have legitimate foundations. Previous quantitative studies in the U.S. also show that defendants who pleaded guilty, on average, received better case outcomes than similarly situated defendants who were convicted at trial (Brereton & Casper, 1981–1982; Bushway et al., 2014; Meyer & Gray, 1997; Yan, 2020).

However, China has a criminal justice system that is significantly different from that of the U.S. For example, in China, the criminal justice system has a conviction rate that exceeds 99.9% (China Law Society, 2018). Consequently, the 'shadow of the trial' theory can hardly be applied in the Chinese context. Also, many scholars are concerned about China's reputation for bias in its justice system in favour of the police and prosecutors. Therefore, it is possible that the guilty plea is coerced by the police and prosecutors and that defendants do not have the bargaining power to obtain a lighter sentencing outcome (Chen, 2016; Xiong, 2016; Wang, 2017). Therefore, empirical studies conducted in the American criminal justice system cannot offer straight *ex ante* predictions for the decision-making in plea leniency system.

The current study is the first to quantitatively assess the effect of a guilty plea on sentence outcomes in the Chinese context. Specifically, a propensity score weighting technique is used to determine the treatment effect of plea leniency. This methodology allows the comparison between the defendants who pleaded guilty and the defendants who did not plead guilty but had the same joint distribution of observed legal and extralegal features. Additionally, apart from the sentencing outcome, this paper examines other treatment effects such as pretrial detention and fines imposed on the defendants to answer whether the decision of a guilty plea truly benefits the defendant.

Data

This study uses data on 6826 DUI cases processed by courts located in six cities—Beijing, Shanghai, Hangzhou, Fuzhou, Xiamen, and Qingdao. All six cities are located along the east coast, which is the most developed area in China. They are among the 18 pilot cities in which plea leniency was initially implemented in 2016. Compared to other cities, these did a better job of publishing court judgements online.[9]

My sample is constructed in two steps: First, I downloaded all the DUI case files adjudicated in these six cities from a website established by the Supreme People's Court in China: China Court Judgments (*zhongguo caipan wenshuwang* 中国裁判文书网).[10] Starting from July 2013, the SPC requested that local courts upload all documents that reflect the disposition of a case on this website.[11] Therefore, I assumed that case files downloaded from this website should cover most DUI cases adjudicated in my sample cities. Second, from each case file, I coded a series of legal and extralegal variables including prior criminal record, crime severity, gender, and ethnicity.[12] Additionally, case outcome variables including the pretrial detention decision and sentencing outcomes were

[9] For example, I found that in some other pilot cities such as Xi'an, courts removed some important information such as whether there was pretrial detention or a criminal attorney present before uploading these judgements online.

[10] For other recent work using this database, see Liebman (2015) and Wei and Xiong (2019).

[11] The latest version of the regulation states that local courts should upload any judgements online within seven days from the date the case is disposed (Article 7) unless this case falls into an excluded category including cases involving state secrets, juvenile criminal cases, disputes concluded through mediation, divorce, and adoption cases (Article 4). Moreover, the regulation requires local courts to disclose the Case ID, the name of the court, the filing date, and the explanation whenever they decide not to release a specific case (Article 6) (SPC, 2016a, 2016b). This rule further institutionalized the publicization of the court decisions.

[12] Ethnic minorities in China are the non-Han Chinese population. China officially recognizes 55 ethnic minority groups within China in addition to the Han majority. As of 2010, the combined population of officially recognized minority groups comprised 8.49% of the population of mainland China.

also included. Most importantly, each judgement also recorded information about whether the offender pleaded guilty and reached a deal with the prosecutor. Because the plea leniency pilot program was implemented on November 11, 2016, I began the observation period exactly on that day. The last judgement in my dataset was tried on July 22, 2018.

Drunk driving behaviour has been criminalized in China since 2011 when the eighth amendment of the criminal law was enacted. According to the current Chinese law, drivers would be sentenced to jail time from 1 to 6 months if the alcohol level in their blood surpasses 80 milligrams per 100 millilitres. This study focuses on DUI cases for two primary reasons. First, as noted previously, China established the plea leniency system to expedite the disposition of minor cases. DUI is one of the most common misdemeanours across the world. According to a Chinese annual report, the number of DUI cases disposed of through plea leniency is the largest among all types of crime (Shangquan Law Office, 2018). Therefore, how the courts dispose of DUIs would be a good indicator of the decision-making contrast in plea leniency versus trial.[13] Second, from the perspective of empirical design, compared to other criminal cases, the judgement of the DUI cases is relatively simple to code. Few DUI cases involve co-offenders. Moreover, in every DUI case, the judgement lists the blood test result of the defendant, which is the most critical indicator of the crime severity. The existence of this evidence enables us to control the decisive factors that influence the sentencing outcomes in our empirical analysis, helping to identify the real effect of the guilty plea decision itself.

Table 1 provides summary statistics of my data. As shown in the table, among 6826 DUI cases, there are 1388 DUI cases in which the defendant pleaded guilty. According to the current version of criminal procedure law in China, there are three types of criminal procedure in the Chinese criminal justice system (from the most complete to the most compacted): the ordinary procedure, the summary procedure, and the speedy trial.[14] Compared to other cases, plea leniency cases are more

[13] Admittedly, according to the 2018 CPL, plea leniency could be applied to felony crimes as well. However, in practice, plea leniency is much less used in felony cases than in minor cases such as DUI.

[14] In the ordinary procedure, the defendant is supposed to receive a full trial. In the summary procedure, cases are allowed to be tried by a single judge, thus eliminating several criminal processes such as interrogating the defendant, questioning the witnesses

likely to be disposed of through speedy trial and less likely to be disposed of through the ordinary and summary procedure.[15] In addition, Table 1 shows that there exist several differences in legal factors between the cases in which defendants pleaded guilty and in which defendants did not. On average, defendants who pleaded guilty had a lower level of blood alcohol concentrations (BACs) and their DUI behaviours were less likely to cause accidents, which indicates their crimes were overall less serious. Finally, regarding sentencing outcomes, it is surprising to find that the mean sentence declared by the judge for defendants who pleaded guilty was longer than for other defendants. However, this does not necessarily indicate that their sentence was harsher. The table also shows that a higher percentage of plea leniency defendants (41.5%) were granted probation.

Methodology

This study has two goals: First, it assesses what factors affect the decision of whether to plead guilty or go to trial. Second, it tests whether the decision of a guilty plea results in better case outcomes for defendants.

To examine the factors affecting a guilty plea decision, I used logistic regression and the odds ratio to estimate a series of legal and extralegal factors on the likelihood that plea leniency occurs to a specific type of case. The model is presented in the following form:

$$\log\frac{P_i(plead\ guilty)}{1-P_i(plead\ guilty)} = \beta_0 + \beta_1 criminal\ procedure_i + \beta_2 prior\ record_i + \beta_3 BACs_i + \beta_4 accident_i + \beta_5 confession_i + \beta_6 victim\ compensation_i$$

and expert witnesses, and cross-examination. In addition, the time required for trial is reduced from three months to twenty days. In the speedy trial, defendants plead guilty, agree with the prosecutor on the sentencing recommendation, and sign a plea agreement before the trial. Cases disposed of through the speedy trial can be expedited by omitting both court investigation [*fating diaocha*] and court debate [*fating bianlun*].

15 Summary procedure and speedy trial apply to cases in which the facts are clear, the evidence is concrete and sufficient, and the defendants have no objection to the facts of the crime. Therefore, the case procedure type variable is used to control for how complex a case is. However, it is admitted although plea leniency could apply in all types of criminal procedures, in certain circumstances, whether a defendant pleads guilty could influence the criminal procedure as well, which raises a question on the causal relationship between case procedure and plea leniency. I will return to this point in the discussion part.

Table 1 Summary statistics of DUI cases in six cities

Case disposition	*Full sample (N = 6826) (I)*	*Plead guilty (N = 1388) (II)*	*Plead not guilty (N = 5438) (III)*	*T-STAT p-value (II)–(III)*
Case Procedures				
Ordinary Procedure	3.28%	2.52%	3.48%	0.05
Summary Procedure	36.13%	18.37%	36.52%	<0.01
Speedy Trial	60.69%	79.68%	55.72%	<0.01
Legal Factors				
Having Prior Record	9.29%	8.86%	9.40%	0.54
BACs (mg/ 100 ml)	154.13	147.84	155.69	<0.01
Accident Involved	38.64%	29.03%	41.09%	<0.01
Confession	92.98%	96.97%	91.94%	<0.01
Victim Compensation	16.64%	11.82%	17.86%	<0.01
Having an Attorney	12.48%	10.66%	12.93%	0.02
Extralegal Factors				
Male	97.26%	97.05%	97.32%	0.59
Minority	3.69%	3.60%	3.71%	0.84
Pretrial Detention	68.25%	60.81%	70.15%	<0.01
Sentencing Outcome				
Declared Sentence (months)	2.19	2.32	2.15	<0.01
Probation Decision	31.20%	41.50%	28.50%	<0.01
Fine (yuan)	3464	3216	3527	<0.01
Cities				
Beijing	32.98%	35.23%	32.40%	0.05
Shanghai	23.18%	14.12%	25.49%	<0.01
Hangzhou	9.79%	13.54%	8.83%	<0.01
Fuzhou	8.88%	2.45%	10.52%	<0.01
Xiamen	19.65%	27.67%	17.60%	<0.01
Qingdao	5.54%	6.99%	5.17%	0.01

Note Column I displays the descriptive statistics of variables regarding the characteristics of the full sample. Column II and Column III show average characteristics of defendants pleading guilty and pleading not guilty, respectively. The last column reports the associated *p*-value for a test of the null hypothesis of equal means across these two groups of defendants for each variable

$$+ \beta_7 legal\ representation_i$$
$$+ \beta_8 gender_i$$
$$+ \beta_9 ethnicity_i + court_{c(i)} + \epsilon_{it} \quad (1)$$

plead guilty is a variable to indicate whether the defendant, in this case, pleaded guilty. And exp (β_1) to exp (β_9) indicates the effects of a series of legal and extralegal factors on the odds of the cases being plea bargained (versus not being plea bargained).

Table 1 shows that defendants who pleaded guilty tended to have a lower level of BACs and were less likely to cause an accident. If defendants who committed less severe crimes were more likely to plead guilty, the leniency of case outcomes cannot necessarily be attributed to the decision of pleading guilty.

Therefore, in order to examine the relationship between a guilty plea and better case outcomes, statistical adjustments need to be used to control alternative explanations. One conventional way to address this methodological issue is to include these confounding variables in a simple linear regression. However, this method was criticized as being highly sensitive to the form of the model and the inclusion of important interaction terms (Imbens, 2004; Ridgeway, 2006).[16] Instead, this study uses a double regression estimation to identify the effect of guilty pleas on case outcomes. This method combines a form of outcome regression with a model for the exposure (i.e. the propensity score) to estimate the causal effect of an exposure on an outcome (Funk et al., 2011). It has been widely used in natural and social science (Jiang et al., 2017; Uysal, 2015) and was applied in criminology research to assess the effect of race bias in post-traffic stops (Ridgeway, 2006). In my study, applying this methodology includes two steps: First, I used a propensity score weighting technique to construct a 'comparison group' (e.g. defendants who did not plead guilty) whose distribution of potential confounding variables equals the 'target group' (e.g. defendants who pleaded guilty). Generalized boosted models (GBM), a multivariate nonparametric regression technique, was used to estimate the propensity score. Specifically, I included all the legal and extralegal factors listed in Table 1 to calculate

[16] For example, in my research context, the effects of some legal factors such as Blood Alcohol Concentrations on case outcomes may not be linear. Also, some control variables may correlate with each other, thus making certain interactive effects possible. Therefore, simply applying multicollinearity models on the raw sample could be problematic.

the propensity score.[17] Because the GBM modelling algorithm allows for flexible, non-linear relationships between all these control variables, this method would overcome the pitfalls of using a multicollinearity model, which requires variable selection and thus is highly sensitive to the form of the model.[18]

Second, after the new sample was constructed, several regression models were applied to identify the effect of a guilty plea on case outcomes. In the regression models, the same set of legal and extralegal variables was included. Notably, however, the propensity score weighting technique in the first step already allowed the two groups of defendants (plea versus trial) to have the same distribution of these confounding variables. Therefore, including these legal and extralegal variables would no longer change the estimation of the effect of a guilty plea on case outcomes. All estimates of these variables reveal their direct effect on case outcomes.

Table 2 shows the first step of doubly robust estimation. Different from the conventional propensity score matching method, propensity score *weighting* does not abandon any observation. This method weights each observation according to a propensity score. The effective sample size (ESS) gives an estimate of the number of comparison participants that are comparable to the target group after weighting. In my sample, after propensity score weighting, there are effectively 2587 non-plea leniency cases that have features similar to the plea leniency cases.

In Table 2, the fourth column displays the raw percentages. It indicates that the plea leniency cases and non-plea leniency cases indeed have different features. However, after using the propensity score weighting technique, the third column shows that the weighted percentages for the comparison group are uniformly close to the percentages for the target group. Whether the defendant pleaded guilty, therefore, is the only factor differing between the groups by design.

[17] These variables include the BACs of the defendant, whether an accident was involved, whether the defendant has a prior criminal record, whether the defendant confessed, and whether the defendant compensated the victim. Also, I included extralegal factors reflecting personal characteristics, including gender and ethnicity.

[18] A more detailed technical explanation of GBM propensity score calculation, *see* Ridgeway (2006). Assessing the Effect of Race Bias in Post-traffic Stop Outcomes Using Propensity Scores. *Journal of Quantitative Criminology*, 22(1), 1–29.

Table 2 Assessment of the comparison samples of defendants who did not plead guilty for a target sample of defendants who pleaded guilty from the propensity weighting

	Plead guilty *N = 1388*	*Not plead guilty* *(Weighted)* *ESS = 2587.1*	*Not plead guilty* *(Unweighted)* *N = 5438*
Legal Factors			
Having Prior Record	8.86%	9.05%	9.40%
BACs (mg/100 ml)	147.84	148.40	155.75
Accident Involved	29.03%	29.89%	41.10%
Confession	96.97%	96.59%	91.96%
Victim Compensation	11.82%	12.49%	17.87%
Having Criminal Attorney	10.66%	11.20%	12.93%
Procedures			
Speedy Trial	79.68%	78.66%	55.72%
Summary Procedure	18.37%	18.60%	36.52%
Extralegal Factors			
Minority	3.60%	3.40%	3.71%
Male	97.05%	97.47%	97.32%
Cities			
Beijing	35.23%	36.89%	32.40%
Shanghai	2.45%	2.92%	10.52%
Hangzhou	13.54%	11.92%	8.83%
Fuzhou	6.99%	6.61%	5.17%
Xiamen	14.12%	14.85%	25.49%
Qingdao	27.67%	26.81%	17.60%

Assuming whether there was a guilty plea is now the only factor differing between the groups of defendants and no other factors influence the relationship between the decision to plead guilty and case outcomes, I used the following models to assess the effect of a guilty plea on case dispositions. To examine the effect of the decision of a guilty plea on pretrial decisions and probation decisions, I used logistic regression and the odds ratio to estimate the likelihood that one outcome will occur. For example, the model of effects on pretrial decisions is:

$$\log\frac{P_{it}(released\ before\ trial)}{1-P_{it}(released\ before\ trial)} = \beta_0 + \beta_1 plead\ guilty + \beta_2 criminal\ procedure_i + \beta_3 prior\ record_i$$

$$+ \beta_4 BACs_i + \beta_5 accident_i$$
$$+ \beta_6 confession_i$$
$$+ \beta_7 victim\ compensation_i$$
$$+ \beta_8 legal\ representation_i$$
$$+ \beta_9 gender_i$$
$$+ \beta_{10} ethnicity_i + court_{c(i)} + \epsilon_{it}. \quad (2)$$

released before trial is a dummy variable to indicate whether the defendant, in this case, is released before trial. The variable *guilty plea* is the coefficient of interest. It is a dummy variable which becomes 1 if this defendant pleaded guilty. Consequently, exp (β_1) indicates the effect of plea leniency on the odds of the defendant being released (versus not being released). Also, a number of legal and extralegal variables were included in the model. β_2 to β_{10} reveals the direct effect of these factors on case outcomes. As noted previously, due to the design of doubly robust estimation, including these variables does not affect the estimation of β_1.

Regarding the effect of a guilty plea on sentence length and fine amount, similar OLS models are used:

$$\begin{aligned} sentence\ length = {} & \beta_0 + \beta_1 plead\ guilty + \beta_2 criminal\ procedure_i \\ & + \beta_3 prior\ record_i + \beta_4 BACs_i + \beta_5 accident_i \\ & + \beta_6 confession_i + \beta_7 victim\ compensation_i \\ & + \beta_8 legal\ representation_i + \beta_9 gender_i \\ & + \beta_{10} ethnicity_i + court_{c(i)} + \epsilon_{it}. \end{aligned} \quad (3)$$

sentence length is a continuous variable to indicate the length of the sentence imposed on the defendant. Similarly, β_1 is the coefficient of interest, suggesting the average difference of the sentence length of defendants who plead guilty and defendants who did not after controlling for a series of variables.

However, although this study uses the adaptive and flexible method of doubly robust estimation to control for confounding variables, there is still potential concern that the estimates of a guilty plea's effect on case outcomes may be biased because defendants who pleaded guilty could have some unobserved characteristics from defendants who went to trial.

This is a universal limitation in cross-sectional analysis (Baumer, 2013; Yan, 2020). I will return to this point in the discussion section.

Results

Factors Affecting a Guilty Plea Decision

To answer the first question of which variables affected the decision of a guilty plea, I applied logistic regression analysis using the full sample. Table 3 shows the regression results. As shown in the table, the prior criminal record does affect the odds of defendants being disposed of through plea leniency. For a defendant who had a prior criminal record, the odds of pleading guilty (versus not pleading guilty) decrease by a factor of 0.78. In addition, certain variables regarding offence severity influence whether defendants plead guilty. For example, for a defendant whose DUI offence caused an accident, the odds of plea leniency decrease by a factor of 0.76. However, another determinant of crime severity, such as blood alcohol concentration, is not associated with the decision of pleading guilty. In conclusion, I found that defendants who had a criminal record and caused harm were less likely to plead guilty and reach an agreement with the prosecutor.

Also, confession does increase the likelihood that the defendant pleaded guilty. The odds of pleading guilty for confessed defendants are 3 times that of defendants who did not plead guilty. Victim compensation decreases the likelihood of plea leniency. After controlling for the *accident* variable, for a defendant who compensated the victim, the odds of plea leniency decrease by a factor of 0.76. This echoes the concerns of some scholars that victim compensation is not so readily incorporated into plea negotiations (Chen, 2016; Xiong, 2016).

Finally, extralegal factors such as gender and ethnicity do not significantly affect the decision to plead guilty. Perhaps it is because of the negligible role that the small number of defendants with certain characteristics could play in a multivariate model. Indeed, less than 3% per cent of defendants in our data were either female or minorities.

Plea Leniency and Pretrial Detention

After assessing the effects of legal and extralegal factors on the decision of a guilty plea, I examined whether a guilty plea resulted in better

Table 3 Legal and extralegal factors affecting plea leniency ($N = 6826$)

	Plea bargain		
	Odds ratio	*2.5%*	*97.5%*
Legal Factors			
Having Prior Criminal Record	0.78***	0.60	0.92
BACs higher than 80 (mg/100 ml)	1.00	1.00	1.00
Accident Involved	0.76***	0.61	0.95
Confession	3.00***	1.98	4.64
Victim Compensation	0.76**	0.59	0.99
Having Attorney	0.91	0.69	1.19
Summary Procedure	2.68***	1.86	3.92
Speedy Trial	9.48***	6.52	13.98
Extralegal Factors			
Female	1.24	0.84	1.80
Minority	0.94	0.61	1.44
Court Fixed	Yes		

*$p < 0.1$, ** $p < 0.05$, *** $p < 0.01$

case outcomes using the sample created by propensity score weighting. As noted in the methodology, the propensity score weighting technique effectively created 2587.1 non-plea leniency cases that have features similar to the plea leniency cases. My target group has 1388 defendants who did not plead guilty. Therefore, the effective sample size (ESS) for my analysis becomes 3975.1.

First, I examined whether the guilty plea is associated with a lower likelihood of pretrial detention. The excessive use of pretrial detention was addressed and criticized by many scholars (Lin & Shen, 2016; Yi, 2016). In practice, more than 85% of defendants were detained before trial and this percentage was even higher in felony crimes such as robbery (Xiong & Wei, 2017). Even for misdemeanour cases like DUI in my sample, only 31% of defendants were released before the trial.

Pretrial detention in China is not subject to judicial review and prosecutors serve as decision-making agents to evaluate the necessity of the continued detention of the defendant (Li, 2022a; Lin & Shen, 2016; Yi, 2016). In the meantime, qualitative studies indicate that, in practice, prosecutors decide whether to initiate the plea leniency process right after cases are delivered to them and pretrial detention is one area of negotiation in plea leniency (Gu & Xiao, 2017; You, 2016).

Therefore, if prosecutors offer concessions in pretrial detention decisions due to a plea, the decision of a guilty plea is expected to increase the likelihood of a defendant being released before the trial. The first three columns in Table 4 display the results of the logistic regression model of the effect of plea leniency on pretrial decisions using a doubly robust estimation. Column 2 shows the odds of being released before trial for plea cases is 6.35 times that of trial cases. This suggests that plea leniency results in a more lenient disposition in pretrial detention.

For other legal factors, I found that those who confessed had odds of pretrial release 2.44 times as high as those who did not confess. Surprisingly, defendants in cases involving an accident are more likely to be released before a trial. Case disposition could also influence pretrial detention. Specifically, defendants disposed of through the speedy trial procedure are less likely to be granted a pretrial release. Finally, neither gender nor ethnicity has an effect on pretrial detention.

Table 4 Weighted logistic regression models of the effect of plea leniency on case outcomes using the Doubly Robust Estimation (ESS = 3975.1)

	Released prior to trial			*Probation granted*		
	Odds ratio	*2.50%*	*97.50%*	*Odds ratio*	*2.50%*	*97.50%*
Plea Bargain	6.35***	4.45	9.05	2.43***	2.01	2.94
Having Prior Criminal Record	1.39	0.81	2.37	0.28***	0.18	0.44
BACs higher than 80 (mg/100 ml)	1.00	1.00	1.00	0.99***	0.99	0.99
Accident Involved	1.71**	1.07	2.73	0.27***	0.18	0.39
Confession	2.44***	1.28	4.67	0.56*	0.31	1.02
Victim Compensation	1.42	0.76	2.62	0.91	0.56	1.51
Having Attorney	1.05	0.51	2.15	0.91	0.59	1.41
Speedy Trial	1.11***	1.05	1.24	1.08	0.61	1.93
Summary Procedure	1.65	0.78	3.53	0.83	0.47	1.45
Minority	0.77	0.39	1.53	0.53**	0.29	0.98
Female	1.18	0.63	2.21	1.2	0.61	2.37
Court Fixed			Yes			

Note ESS refers to the Effective Sample Size * $p < 0.1$, ** $p < 0.05$, *** $p < 0.01$

Plea Leniency and Probation Decision

A common indicator that a defendant in a misdemeanour case received a lenient sentencing outcome is that they were not incarcerated after the trial. According to Chinese criminal law, defendants who are sentenced to fewer than three years' imprisonment are eligible for probation (*huanxing* 缓刑). These defendants do not serve their declared sentence in jail *from the very beginning* unless they commit new crimes or seriously violate rules of probation during the probationary period, which rarely happens in practice.

In misdemeanour cases, the probation recommendation is a key area of plea agreement. A large portion of defendants plead guilty in exchange for the concession that a probation recommendation would be written in the plea deal (Gu & Xiao, 2017; You, 2016). Given that more than 92% of sentencing recommendations offered by prosecutors are accepted by judges in the Chinese plea leniency context (SPC, 2017), this plea agreement, if reached, is very likely to be beneficial.

To examine whether the decision of plea leniency had an effect on probation decisions, the last three columns in Table 4 show the logistic regression results. As shown in the table, the fifth column shows that the odds of being granted probation for plea cases are 2.43 times that of trial cases. This supports the argument that plea leniency results in lenient sentencing outcomes.

In addition, many other legal and extralegal factors are also significant predictors of the probation decision. For example, I found that having a prior criminal record and a previous accident could decrease the odds of probation by a factor of 0.28 and 0.27, respectively. Interestingly, being a minority decreases the odds of receiving probation by a factor of 0.53.

Plea Leniency and Sentence Length

According to Chinese criminal law, DUI offences are subject to punishment of fewer than six months in jail. In my sample, every defendant received a declared jail sentence between one and six months. If a guilty plea resulted in leniency in the sentencing outcome, the average declared sentence length is expected to be shorter for defendants who pleaded guilty than for defendants who did not after controlling for all confounding variables.

The first three columns in Table 5 display the results of the OLS regression of the effect of plea leniency on declared sentence length. Contrary to our expectations, I found that, on average, defendants who pleaded guilty received 0.27 months longer declared sentence length than defendants who did not.

Tables 4 and 5 interestingly suggest contradictory conclusions on whether the guilty plea results in leniency. While Table 4 shows that defendants who pleaded guilty are more likely to be granted probation, Table 5 suggests that they received longer declared sentence lengths. To resolve this contradiction and examine whether plea leniency results in greater leniency, I created a new variable: actual time served in jail. For defendants who did not receive probation, their actual time served in jail equals the sentence declared by the judge. However, as noted before, defendants who were granted probation do not need to serve their declared sentence in jail. Therefore, their actual time served in jail equals zero.[19] The middle three columns in Table 5 show the OLS regression results of a plea on this dependent variable: for defendants who pleaded guilty, the average actual time served in jail decreases by 0.22 months.

In addition, I also find a number of legal variables have a significant effect on sentence length. For example, having a prior criminal record increases the actual time served in jail, on average, by 0.54 months. One unit increase of BACs could result in an increase of actual time served in jail by 0.01 months. A prior accident increases actual time served in jail, on average, by 0.42 months. Finally, I also find that male defendants have 0.27 months longer actual time served in jail than female defendants.

Plea Leniency and Fine Amount

Finally, I examined whether the guilty plea had an effect on the quantum of the fine imposed on defendants. The last three columns in Table 5 show the OLS regression results of the effect of plea leniency on the amount of the fine. They suggest that whether the defendants pleaded

[19] Theoretically, probation could be revoked if defendants commit a new crime or seriously violate the rules of probation. In this case, defendants need to serve their declared sentence in jail. However, in practice, this rarely happens. Empirical studies suggest that the overall revocation rate in China is below 1% (Zhao, 2018). Therefore, given that data on the actual time served by defendants is not available, labelling their actual time served in jail as zero, though not completely precise, would not cause much bias.

Table 5 Weighted OLS regression models of the effect of plea leniency on case outcomes using the Doubly Robust Estimation (ESS = 3975.1)

	Declared sentence length (Month)			*Actual time served in jail (Month)*			*Fine amount (Yuan)*		
	Estimate	*Std. error*	p-*value*	*Estimate*	*Std. error*	p-*value*	*Estimate*	*Std. error*	p-*value*
Plea Bargain	0.27 ***	0.03	<0.001	–0.22 ***	0.03	<0.001	5.1	60.41	0.93
Having Prior Criminal Record	0.14 *	0.09	0.09	0.54 ***	0.09	<0.001	196.37	129.44	0.13
BACs higher than 80 (mg/100 ml)	0.01 ***	0.001	0.00	0.01 ***	0.00	<0.001	15.81***	1.43	0.00
Accident Involved	–0.05	0.06	0.48	0.42 ***	0.07	<0.001	133.81	116.12	0.25
Confession	0.26 ***	0.08	0.001	0.37 ***	0.08	<0.001	397.71**	158.68	0.01
Victim Compensation	0.1	0.09	0.24	0.06	0.08	0.45	195.86	166.08	0.24
Having Defense Attorney	–0.11 **	0.07	0.10	–0.07	0.07	0.28	694.73***	127.72	0.00
Speedy Trial	–0.21	0.22	0.33	–0.17	0.2	0.39	–433.8	475.25	0.36
Summary Procedure	–0.15	0.22	0.50	–0.02	0.2	0.93	–819.96*	472.91	0.08
Minority	–0.21 **	0.09	0.01	0.04	0.07	0.52	–78.79	119.11	0.51
Female	–0.05	0.12	0.68	–0.27 ***	0.09	<0.001	–71.53	234.26	0.76
Court Fixed				Yes					

Note ESS refers to the Effective Sample Size * $p < 0.1$, ** $p < 0.05$, *** $p < 0.01$

guilty is not a significant predictor of the amount of the fine. In contrast, other variables indicating the severity of the crime could significantly influence the amount of the fine. Specifically, one unit increase of the BACs of the defendant could increase the fine amount by 15 yuan.

Discussion

One practical issue, which is true all over the world, is that the criminal justice system needs to maintain its efficiency without significantly compromising the rights of defendants. Plea-based case disposition is believed to be a potential solution because it can help lighten the caseload for prosecutors, save defendants from the discomfort of trial proceedings, and provide an extra opportunity for more favourable case outcomes (Bowers, 2008; Easterbrook, 1983; Fisher, 2000; Guidorizzi, 1998).

The plea leniency system is relatively new in China. However, driven by similar motivations, such as expediting the dispositional process of 'simple' cases and providing defendants with an extra opportunity to receive lenient sentencing, in September 2016, China started to carry out its own version of 'plea bargaining' program in several pilot cites. The present study is the first study to examine what factors influence a guilty plea decision and its relationship with case outcomes in the Chinese criminal justice system.

Using DUI cases in six cities as my research context, my study finds that several legal factors such as prior criminal record and crime severity have a significant effect on whether cases were disposed of through guilty pleas versus trial. Specifically, more serious crimes such as DUIs causing an accident and more dangerous offenders such as those with a criminal record are less likely to be disposed of through guilty pleas. This finding is consistent with prior studies done in American courts (Kutateladze & Lawson, 2018; Meyer & Gray, 1997). There exist several possible explanations for this. First, due to the actual harm of certain DUI cases or elevated blameworthiness of certain defendants, prosecutors expect that these defendants are more likely to receive a harsher sentence if they go to trial. Therefore, they tend to make more punitive offers in these cases, which in turn discourage defendants from accepting them. Second, because the policy goal of this program is to expedite the handling of 'simple' cases, prosecutors are therefore able to allocate more resources to complicated cases. It is highly possible that prosecutors may use this program as a case management system. Prosecutors could have a screening process and prefer to reach an agreement with defendants who are less blameworthy. This mechanism, if it existed, could also explain why prior criminal records and crime severity significantly affect the decision of whether a case was disposed of through plea leniency.

Notably, my study shows that cases without victim compensation are more likely to be disposed of through a guilty plea (versus going to trial). This is either because defendants who are not able to compensate for victims tend to plead guilty in exchange for some sentence reductions or because defendants who pleaded guilty feel it is unnecessary to compensate defendants. If the latter causal relationship exists, this supports the argument that an agreement between the prosecutor and the defendant does marginalize the role of victims in the criminal process (Chen, 2017). In the U.S. criminal justice system, there are several activities that define the emergence of the modern crime victims' rights movement (CVRM). The establishment of state victim compensation programs is a vital part of this (Young & Stein, 2004). Some scholars have also discussed approaches to protect the role of victims in plea leniency cases (Manikis, 2012; O'Hear, 2007). My study suggests that the protection of victim rights should be a concern for policymakers in the future both in and outside of China.

Regarding the question of whether the decision of pleading guilty led to more favourable case outcomes, although there have been theoretical debates over whether the leniency resulting from a guilty plea is legitimate (Xiong, 2016; Zhu, 2016; Zuo, 2017), my study reveals that in practice, defendants who pleaded guilty did receive better dispositions throughout the whole criminal process. Shockingly, my results show that defendants who pleaded had odds of pretrial release 6.4 times higher than those who went to trial. As for the sentencing outcomes, my study shows that the odds of being granted probation for defendants who pleaded guilty are 2.43 times that of defendants who did not plead guilty. Although defendants who pleaded guilty, on average, received a longer declared sentence, the actual time they served in jail was significantly shorter. The disparity between these two groups of defendants can occur through two mechanisms. One explanation is that the plea leniency system offered an extra opportunity for defendants to receive leniency as promised. Therefore, defendants who pleaded guilty were granted extra 'plea discounts'. Another explanation, however, is that considering the Chinese criminal justice policy of leniency to those who confess and severity to those who resist, the criminal justice system in China could have utilized this system to facilitate case dispositions by threatening to impose the 'trial penalty' on defendants who refused to plead guilty. If this is true, the development of a plea leniency system in China can hardly be said to bring benefits to defendants.

In a broad sense, this chapter reveals that, in a country where almost everyone would be convicted at trial, a plea could still result in relatively better case outcomes. Consequently, the 'shadow of the trial' theory proposed by American scholars, at least, is not the only reason for sentencing disparities between plea and trial cases. To the contrary, my study shows that prosecutors could make concessions in plea cases even if they deem the defendant would certainly be convicted at trial. Therefore, findings in this study support other frameworks to understanding the sentencing disparity between plea-based dispositional process and trial such as prosecutors using plea leniency to expedite case dispositions as well as to reward remorseful defendant (Bowers, 2008; Easterbrook, 1983; Fisher, 2000; Guidorizzi, 1998).

This study is subject to several limitations. First, although it is true that courts are required to upload all decisions except for certain types of cases which are exempted, existing literature shows that local courts may fail to publish a portion of the cases due to various reasons, and the missing data varies widely by court and case type (Liebman et al., 2020; Roberts et al., 2010). If the missing data issue is associated with certain case variables, it could generate biased estimates.

Second, this study is restricted to one type of criminal case—DUI. Although DUI is a typical type of simple case disposed of through plea leniency, it has some characteristics that may prevent the accused party in DUI cases from significantly changing their case outcomes. For example, DUI cases have a relatively narrow sentencing range, which is from 1 to 6 months. Additionally, the result of a defendant's blood test provides prosecutors in DUI cases with strong evidence, and thus, few defendants have the chance to refuse to plead guilty. It is possible that the results extracted from another type of crime might be different. To comprehensively evaluate the plea leniency system in China, more research should be done on additional types of crimes.

Third, although I tried to control for a number of legal and extralegal variables to examine the effect of a guilty plea on case outcomes, there are still some potential confounding variables that are not included in my study. For example, I do not have information about the socioeconomic status of each defendant. Some scholars argue that most underprivileged defendants are not familiar with the criminal justice system. Therefore, whether they fully understand the potential consequences of a guilty plea is highly questionable (Chen, 2016; Zuo, 2017). Future studies could assess whether these characteristics of defendants influence the decision to plead guilty and its relationship with certain case outcomes. Also, some control variables in my model could have some reverse causality issues. For example, I use the type of criminal procedure to control for how complex the case is. However, in some circumstances, the fact that a defendant pleads guilty would affect the criminal procedure type as well. Therefore, one should be cautious to interpret estimates of certain variables in my model as having a causal effect.

Fourth, this study proposes several potential explanations for the empirical findings. However, due to the limitations of quantitative studies, most of them cannot be tested through data analysis. The interpretation of results could be more convincing if future studies combine quantitative research with qualitative research. Interviews with judges, attorneys, and prosecutors may provide new insights in understanding possible explanations of the results of this study (Li, 2022b).

Finally, my analysis focuses on six cities located in China's developed areas, which suggests the need for broader analyses focusing on other places. In future studies, researchers could study the plea leniency system in mid-western Chinese cities. Because these cities are located in less developed areas and have fewer legal resources, the plea leniency system may have been carried out in a different way.

References

Albonetti, C. A. (1998). Direct and Indirect Effects of Case Complexity, Guilty Pleas, and Offender Characteristics on Sentencing for Offenders Convicted of a White-collar Offense Prior to Sentencing Guidelines. *Journal of Quantitative Criminology, 14*(4), 353–378.

Alschuler, A. W. (1979). Plea Bargaining and its History. *Columbia Law Review, 79*(1), 1–43.

Ball, J. D. (2006). Is it a Prosecutor's World? Determinants of Count Bargaining. *Journal of Contemporary Criminal Justice, 22*, 241–260.

Baumer, E. P. (2013). Reassessing and Redirecting Research on Race and Sentencing. *Justice Quarterly, 30*(2), 231–261.

Biddulph, S., Nesossi, E., & Trevaskes, S. (2017). Criminal Justice Reform in the Xi Jinping Era. *China Law and Society Review, 2*, 63–128.

Bowers, J. (2008). Punishing the Innocent. *University of Pennsylvania Law Review, 156*(5), 1117–1179.

Boylan, R. T. (2012). The Effect of Punishment Severity on Plea Bargaining. *The Journal of Law & Economics, 55*(3), 565–591.

Brereton, D., & Casper, J. D. (1981–1982). Does it Pay to Plead Guilty? Differential Sentencing and the Functioning of Criminal Courts. *Law & Society Review, 16*(1), 45–70.

Bureau of Justice Statistics. (2009). *Felony Sentences in State Courts, 2006—Statistical Tables*. U.S. Department of Justice.

Bureau of Justice Statistics. (2017). *Federal Justice Statistics, 2014—Statistical Tables*. U.S. Department of Justice.

Burke, A. S. (2007). Prosecutorial Passion, Cognitive Bias, and Plea Bargaining. *Marquette Law Review, 91*(1), 183–212.

Bushway, S. D., & Redlich, A. D. (2012). Is Plea Bargaining in the "Shadow of the Trial" a Mirage? *Journal of Quantitative Criminology, 28*(3), 437–454.

Bushway, S. D., Redlich, A. D., & Norris, R. J. (2014). An Explicit Test of Plea Bargaining in the "Shadow of the Trial." *Criminology, 52*(4), 723–754.

Chen, R. (2006). Dossier Centralism: A re-Examination of China's Criminal Trial Methods [Anjuan Bilu Zhongxinzhuyi—dui Zhongguo Xingshi Shenpan Fangshi de Chongxin Kaocha]. *Chinese Journal of Law [faxue Yanjiu], 4*, 63–79.

Chen, R. (2016). Theoretical Reflection on Plea Bargaining Reform—Based on the Experience of Operation Ofspeedy Trial ["Renzui Renfa Congkuan" Gaige de Lilun Fansi—Jiyu Xingshi Sucai Chengxu Yunxing Jingyan de Kaocha]. *Contemporary Law Review [dangdai Faxue], 32*(2), 3–13.

Chen, R. (2017). Several Controversial Issues on the Imposing Leniency on Defendants who Plead Guilty and Admit Punishment [Renzui renfa Congkuan Zhidu de Ruogan Zhengyi Wenti]. *Chinese Legal Science [zhongguo Faxue], 1*, 36–52.

China Law Society. (2018). *Law Yearbook of China*. The Press of Law Yearbook of China.

Church, T. W. (1979). In Defense of "Bargain Justice." *Law & Society Review, 13*(2), 509–525.

CPC. (2014, October 29). *Decision of the CPC Central Committee on Major Issues Pertaining to Comprehensively Promoting the Rule of Law. [zhonggong Zhongyang guanyu quanmian tuijin yifa zhiguo ruogan zhongda wenti de jueding]*. http://cpc.people.com.cn/n/2014/1029/c64387-25927606.html

Dervan, L. E., & Edkins, V. A. (2013). The Innocent Defendant's Dilemma: An Innovative Empirical Study of Plea Bargaining's Innocence Problem. *The Journal of Criminal Law and Criminology, 103*(1), 1–48.

Easterbrook, F. H. (1983). Criminal Procedure as a Market System. *Journal of Legal Studies, 12*(2), 289–332.

Feng, L. (2015). Policy Goals and Strategies Of Reallocation of Personnel Roles Within the Courts [faguan yuanezhi de gaige mubiao yu celve]. *Contemporary Law Review [dangdai Faxue]*, *5*, 140–148.

Fisher, G. (2000). Plea Bargaining's Triumph. *The Yale Law Journal, 109*(5), 857–1086.

Frenzel, E. D., & Ball, J. D. (2007). Effects of Individual Characteristics on Plea Negotiations under Sentencing Guidelines. *Journal of Ethnicity in Criminal Justice, 5*, 59–82.

Funk, M. J., Westreich, D., Wiesen, C., Stürmer, T., Brookhart, M. A., & Davidian, M. (2011). Doubly Robust Estimation of Causal Effects. *American Journal of Epidemiology, 173*(7), 761–767.

Goldstein, A., & Marcus, M. (1977). The Myth of Judicial Supervision in Three Inquisitorial Systems: France, Italy, and Germany. *Yale Law Journal, 87*(2), 240–283.

Gu, Y. (2016). Theoretical Issues on the Improvement of the Plea Bargaining in China [Guanyyu Wanshan Renzui Renfa Zhidu Zhong de Jige Lilun Wenti]. *Contemporary Law Review [dangdai Faxue], 6*, 129–137.

Gu, Y., & Xiao, P. (2017). Observations, Thinkings, and Suggestions on the Imposing Lenient Punishments on Those Pleading Guilty [wanshan renzui renfa zhidu de qinli guancha yu sikao jianyi]. *Research on Rule of Law [fazhi Yanjiu], 1*, 56–70.

Guidorizzi, D. D. (1998). Should We Really Ban Plea Bargaining: The Core Concerns of Plea Bargaining Critics. *Emory Law Journal, 47*(2), 753–784.

He, X. (2023). Plea Leniency and Prosecution Centredness in China's Criminal Process. *The China Quarterly, 254*, 448–465.

Imbens, G. W. (2004). Nonparametric Estimation of Average Treatment Effects under Exogeneity: A Review. *The Review of Economics and Statistics, 86*(1), 4–29.

Jia, Z. (2018). On Effective Assistance of Counsel in the Cases of those Confessing to their Crimes and Accepting Punishments: From the Perspective of Litigation Consensus Theory [Lun Renzui Renfa Anjian Zhong de Youxiao Bianhu: Yi Susong Heyi de Shijiao]. *Tribune of Political Science and Law [zhengfa Luntan], 2*, 171–184.

Jiang, R., Lu, W., Song, R., Hudgens, M. G., & Naprvavnik, S. (2017). Doubly Robust Estimation of Optimal Treatment Regimes for Survival Data—With Application to an HIV/AIDS Study. *Annals of Applied Statistics, 11*(3), 1763–1786.

Kutateladze, B. L., & Lawson, V. Z. (2018). Is a Plea Really a Bargain? An Analysis of Plea and Trial Dispositions in New York City. *Crime and Delinquency, 64*(7), 856–887.

Langer, M. (2004). From Legal Transplants to Legal Translations: The Globalization of Plea Bargaining and the Americanization Thesis in Criminal Procedure. *Harvard International Law Journal, 45*(1), 1–64.

Li, A. H. (2016). Centralisation of Power in the Pursuit of Law-based Governance: Legal Reform in China under the Xi Administration. *China Perspectives, 2*(106), 63–68.

Li, X. (2015). Confession Governance and Chinese Criminal Judicial Referee [Kougong Zhili yu Zhongguo Sifa Caipan]. *Social Science in China [zhongguo Shehui Kexue], 1*, 119–205.

Li, E. S. (2022a). Haste Makes Waste: Why China's New Plea Leniency System is Doomed to Fail. *Asian Journal of Comparative Law, 17*(1), 76–105.

Li, E. S. (2022b). Chinese Courts' New Plea Leniency System: Scrutinizing the Efficacy of Mandatory Defense Counsel. *The China Journal, 88*, 78–99.

Liebman, B. L. (2015). Leniency in Chinese Criminal Law: Everyday Justice in Henan. *Berkeley Journal of International Law, 33*(1), 153–222.

Liebman, B., Roberts, M., Stern, R., & Wang, A. (2020). Mass Digitization of Chinese Court Decisions: How to Use Text as Data in the Field of Chinese Law. *Journal of Law and Courts, 8*(2), 177–201.

Lin, X., & Shen, W. (2016). Reforms to China's Pretrial Detention System: The Role of the Procuratorate. *International Journal of Law, Crime and Justice, 44*, 183–211.

Lu, H., & Kelly, B. (2008). Courts and Sentencing Research on Contemporary China. *Crime, Law and Social Change, 50*(3), 229–243.

Manikis, M. (2012). Recognizing Victims' Role and Rights during Plea Bargaining: Fair Deal for Victims of Crime. *Criminal Law Quarterly, 58*(3 and 4), 411–441.

Meyer, J., & Gray, T. (1997). Drunk Drivers in the Courts: Legal and Extra-legal Factors Affecting Pleas and Sentences. *Journal of Criminal Justice, 25*(2), 155–163.

Myers, M. A. (1982). Common Law in Action: The Prosecution of Felonies and Misdemeanors. *Sociological Inquiry, 52*, 1–15.

Myers, M. A., & Hagan, J. (1979). Private and Public Trouble: Prosecutors and the Allocation of Court Resources. *Social Problems, 26*, 439–451.

O'Hear, M. M. (2007). Plea Bargaining and Victims: From Consultation to Guidelines. *Marquette Law Review, 91*(1), 323–348.

Packer, H. L. (1964). Two Models of the Criminal Process. *University of Pennsylvania Law Review, 113*(1), 1–68.

Rauxloh, R. E. (2011). Formalization of Plea Bargaining in Germany: Will the New Legislation be able to Square the Circle. *Fordham International Law Journal, 34*(2), 296–331.

Rauxloh, R. E. (2014). Plea Bargaining in Germany Doctoring the Symptoms Without Looking at the Root Causes. *Journal of Criminal Law, 78*(5), 392–406.

Ridgeway, G. (2006). Assessing the Effect of Race Bias in Post-traffic Stop Outcomes Using Propensity Scores. *Journal of Quantitative Criminology, 22*(1), 1–29.

Roberts, A. L., Gilman, S. E., Fitzmaurice, G., Decker, M. R., & Koenen, K. C. (2010). Witness of Intimate Partner Violence in Childhood and Perpetration of Intimate Partner Violence in Adulthood. *Epidemiology, 21*(6), 809–818.

Shangquan Law Office. (2018, August 11). *Big Data Report on Imposing Leniency on Defendants who Pleaded Guilty and Accepted Punishments.* Shangquan Law Office. Retrieved March 2, 2020, from http://www.sqxb.com/aboutNewsInfo.php?SysID=1123

Shen, D. (2015). On the Reform of the Criminal Justice System Centered on Trial [Lun yi Shenpan wei Zhongxin de Susong Tizhi Gaige]. *China Legal Science [zhongguo Faxue], 3*, 5–19.

Soubise, L. (2018). Guilty Pleas in an Inquisitorial Setting—An Empirical Study of France. *Journal of Law and Society, 45*(3), 398–426.

SPC. (2016a, August 29). *Guanyu renmin fayuan zai hulianwang gongbu caipan wenshu de guiding [Regulations on the Publicizing Court's Decisions Online].* Supreme People's Court of the People's Republic of China. http://www.court.gov.cn/zixun-xiangqing-25321.html

SPC. (2016b, November 16). *Notice on Issuing the Measures for the Pilot Program of Imposing Lenient Punishments on Those Confessing to Their Crimes and Accepting Punishments in Criminal Cases [guanyu <guanyu shouquan zai bufen diqu kaizhan xingshi anjian renzuirenfa congkuan>].* The Supreme People's Court in China. http://www.scxsls.com/a/20161207/117400.html

SPC. (2017). *Midterm Report on the Pilot Program of Imposing Lenient Punishments on those Pleading Guilty and Accepting Punishments [Guanyu zai bufen diqu kaizhan xingshi anjian renzui renfa congkuan shidian gongzuoqingkuang de zhongqi baogao].* The Supreme People's Court.

SPC. (2018). *Report on the "Imposing Lenient Punishments on those Pleading Guilty and Accepting Punishment" [renmin fayuan tuijin renzui renfa congkuan gaige shidian zongshu].* People's Court Daily. Retrieved October 18, 2019, from https://www.chinacourt.org/article/detail/2018/03/id/3231253.shtml

Steffensmeier, D. (1980). Assessing the Impact of the Women's Movement on Sexbased Differences in the Handling of Adult Cases. *Crime & Delinquency, 26*, 344–357.

Steffensmeier, D., Ulmer, J., & Kramer, J. (1998). The Interaction of Race, Gender, and Age in Criminal Sentencing: The Punishment of Being Young, Black, and Male. *Criminology, 36*, 763–797.

Sun, C. (2018). The Proof Standard for Conviction in Plea Bargaining Cases [Renzui Renfa Anjian de Zhengming Biaozhun]. *Chinese Journal of Law [faxue Yanjiu], 1*, 167–187.

Uhlman, T. M., & Walker, N. D. (1979). A Plea is No Bargain: The Impact of Case Disposition on Sentencing. *Social Science Quarterly, 60*(2), 218–234.

Ulmer, J. T. (1997). *Social Worlds of Sentencing: Court Communities under Sentencing Guidelines*. SUNY Press.

Uysal, S. D. (2015). Doubly Robust Estimation of Causal Effects with Multi-valued Treatments: An Application to the Returns to Schooling. *Journal of Applied Econometrics, 30*(5), 763–786.

Vogel, M. E. (1999). The Social Origins of Plea Bargaining: Conflict and the Law in the Process of State Formation, 1830–1860. *Law and Society Review, 33*(1), 161–246.

Wang, M. (2017). Key Issues on Imposing Lenient Punishments on Those Confessing to Their Crimes and Accepting Punishments [Renzui renfa Congkuan zhidu Yinan Wenti Yanjiu]. *Chines Legal Science, 1*, 17–34.

Wei, S., & Xiong, M. (2019). Judges' Gender and Sentencing in China: An Empirical Inquiry. *Feminist Criminology*, 1–34.

Xiong, M., & Wei, S. (2017). Unequal Treatment in Pretrial Detention in China. *British Journal of Criminology, 57*(6), 1398–1419.

Xiong, Q. (2016). Theoretical Review and Systematic Improvement of Plea Bargaining [Renzui Renfa Congkuan de Lilun Shenshi he Zhidu Wanshan]. *Law Science [faxue], 10*, 97–110.

Yan, S. (2013). Comments on the Confession Centralism [Kougong Zhongxinzhuyi Pingxi]. *Evidence Science [zhengju Kexue], 4*, 437–452.

Yan, S. (2020). What Exactly Is the Bargain? The Sensitivity of Plea Discount Estimates. *Justice Quarterly*. https://doi.org/10.1080/07418825.2019.1707856.

Yan, S., & Bushway, S. D. (2018). Plea Discounts or Trial Penalties? Making Sense of the Trial-Plea Sentence Disparities. *Justice Quarterly, 35*(7), 1226–1249.

Yi, Y. (2016). Arrest as Punishment: The Abuse of Arrest in the People's Republic of China. *International Journal of Law, Crime and Justice, 44*, 183–211.

You, T. (2016). Fulfillment of Sentencing Standardization of Imposing Lenient Punishments on those Pleading Guilty [renzui renfa congkuan zhidu zhong de liangxing guifanhua quanliucheng shixian]. *Journal of Law Application [falv Shiyong], 11*, 28–34.

Young, M., & Stein, J. (2004). *The History of the Crime Victims' Movement in the United States*. US Department of Justice, Office of Justice Programs, Office for Victims of Crime.

Zhang, J. (2015). The Essence of Trial Centralism Connotation and the Way of Realization [Shenpan wei Zhongxin Zhuyi de Shizhi Neihan he Shixian Lujin]. *Peking University Law Journal [zhongwai Faxue]*, *4*, 861–878.

Zhao, J. (2018). *Empirical Study on Probation: Observation from A City in J Province [huanxing zhidu de shizheng yanjiu—yi J sheng A shi de huanxing qingkuang wei li]*. CNKI.

Zhu, X. (2016). Several Questions on the Imposing Leniency on Admission of Guilty and Acceptance of Punishment [Renzui renfa congkuan zhidu zhong de jige wenti]. *Research on Rule of Law [fazhi Yanjiu]*, *5*, 35–44.

Zuo, W. (2017). Why Impose Leniency on Admission of Guilty and Acceptance of Punishment: Misunderstanding and Clarification [Renzui Renfa Heyi Congkua: Wuqu he Zhengjie]. *Chinese Journal of Aw [faxue Yanjiu]*, *3*, 160–175.

Behind the Scenes: Exploring the Legal and Cultural Factors of Taiwan's Plea Bargain System

Mong-Hwa Chin

Introduction

This chapter aims to explore why the plea bargain system in The Republic of China (hereinafter Taiwan) has not gained widespread acceptance, presenting this analysis from a legal and cultural perspective. The plea bargain system has been controversial for many years. Despite being revised in 1997 and 2004, the system has not been widely used in practice (Ministry of Justice, 2022). In theory, the plea bargain system poses potential benefits for all parties involved: defendants may receive a lighter punishment and a definite answer earlier in the legal process, avoiding the stress of lengthy procedures; victims avoid drawn out procedures and may receive financial compensation; and judicial resources can be saved by diverting judges and prosecutors to more complex cases.

This chapter is divided into three main sections. The first section briefly introduces the historical development of the plea bargain system in Taiwan and presents the practical aspects of the plea bargain system, including the number of cases and its current operational status. The

M.-H. Chin (✉)
National Yang Ming Chiao Tung University School of Law, Hsinchu, Taiwan
e-mail: mhchin@nycu.edu.tw

E. Li et al. (eds.), *Criminal Case Dispositions through Pleas in Greater China*, https://doi.org/10.1007/978-981-97-1856-6_6

second part illustrates the possible factors that may influence the adoption of plea bargaining, including: the legal restrictions that limit the scope of plea bargains, the traditional inquisitorial approach allowing judges to dominate the case narrative and the public's skepticism toward the judiciary as a whole, and finally, the preference for other expedited procedures, such as summary judgment and simplified trial procedures. The last section discusses how the Citizen Judge System poses new challenges to Taiwan's judicial resources and explores possible ways to reform the current plea bargain system.

The Legal Framework of Plea Bargaining in Taiwan

Plea bargaining was first introduced in 1997 and then expanded in 2004 under amendments to the Code of Criminal Procedure to respond to the growing backlog of cases and to increase judicial efficiency (Chin & Su, 2022; Wang, 2008). The 1997 model is embedded in the summary judgment rules. Summary judgment, as provided in Article 449 of the Code of Criminal Procedure, is a legal procedure that allows a court to decide a case without a full trial based on the evidence and arguments presented in the initial stages of the proceedings. Summary judgment is used when the prosecutor and court determine that no material issues of fact are in dispute and that the case can be resolved as a matter of law.

Article 451-1 of the Code of Criminal Procedure as introduced in 1997, stipulates a process called 'Specific Sentence Requested by a Prosecutor'. This model provides that a defendant who confesses during an investigation may express their willingness to accept punishment or probation to the prosecutor. If the prosecutor agrees, the statement is recorded and used as the basis to request punishment (such as a term of imprisonment or a fine) or probation from the court. Before requesting punishment or probation, the prosecutor may consult with the victim and consider all the circumstances surrounding the case. With the victim's consent, the defendant can be ordered to issue an apology and/or pay a reasonable amount of compensation to the victim. This procedure can be activated either during the investigation or the first instance trial. If the court agrees to the plea, the court rules in accordance with the terms of the plea agreement.

The 2004 model is an expanded version of the 1997 model which specifies a 'Bargaining Process'. According to the legislature's note, the purpose of the new amendment was to fulfill the ideal of 'speedy judgment for clear-cut cases, cautious discretion for doubtful cases' (明案速判, 疑案慎斷). This reform was in response to the practical needs of the judicial system. In 2002, the Code of Criminal Procedure was amended to grant both parties control over the presentation of evidence, which incorporated an element of the adversarial system into the inquisitorial procedure (Lewis, 2009). In 2003, cross-examination was incorporated into the criminal procedure in Taiwan. Together, these reforms created concern that case processing would slow down and so expedited procedures such as plea bargaining were introduced in response (Wang, 2008).

As part of these reforms, Article 455-2 allows prosecutors to negotiate with defendants in cases where the defendant is not facing the death penalty, life imprisonment, or prison sentences of three years or more, and where the case is at first instance or being dealt with through a summary judgment procedure. Before approving a plea bargain, the prosecutor may first seek the victim's opinion. Most scholars in Taiwan consider consulting with the victim a recommendation rather than a strict requirement to encourage the use of the plea bargain system (Tsai, 2004). The defendant must also agree to the terms of the plea agreement, which includes admitting guilt and one or more of the following items: accepting a specific sentence, apologizing to the victim, making restitution to the victim, or paying a certain amount of money to the public treasury. While the law does not explicitly guarantee a lower sentence for making restitution to the victim, in practice, an offer of restitution significantly increases the willingness of a prosecutor to negotiate a sentence.

If the defendant agrees to the plea agreement, the prosecutor can then petition the court to impose the agreed-upon sentence upon the defendant. The court may accept or reject the plea agreement based on whether it is in the interests of justice and whether it complies with the law. However, the court cannot change the terms of the plea agreement. If the court accepts the plea agreement, they will sentence the defendant accordingly.

Both models emphasize judicial oversight. Article 451-1 provides four elements which, if present, excludes the acceptance of the sentence requested by the prosecutor: first, if the crime does not meet the requirements for summary judgment; second, if the court finds that the facts of the crime established are obviously inconsistent with those on which the prosecutor based their accusation or discovers during the trial other criminal facts sufficient to determine that the prosecutor's request for punishment is obviously inappropriate; third, if the court determines after the trial that the defendant is innocent or exempted from prosecution, the case is not accepted, or a mistake in jurisdiction; and fourth, if the prosecutor's request is obviously inappropriate or unfair.

Article 455-4 outlines seven situations where the court cannot confirm a bargaining agreement, including cases where the defendant withdraws consent or the application to start the negotiation; the defendant's agreement to negotiate was not made freely; the negotiated agreement is obviously inappropriate or unfair; the crime committed is not subject to a request for negotiation judgment; the facts determined by the court clearly differ from those agreed upon in the negotiation; and the facts indicate that the defendant has other criminal acts with a heavier penalty. If none of these apply, the court shall make a judgment within the scope of the negotiated agreement without a trial.

The law allows additional and significant protections for the defendant in the 2004 model. Article 455-7 stipulates that if the court does not make a judgment based on the negotiation, the statement made by the defendant or their agent or defense counsel during the negotiation process shall not be used as evidence against the defendant or other accomplices in this case or other cases. Article 455-5 stipulates that in cases where negotiation is involved and there is no defense lawyer, the court shall appoint a public defense lawyer or attorney to assist the bargaining process if the defendant expresses willingness to accept a sentence of more than six months of imprisonment not subject to a suspension. Article 455-3 mandates that the court informs the defendant of the charges, statutory penalties, and the rights forfeited if the defendant accepts the plea agreement. These rights include, as described by Judicial Yuan orders, (1) the right to a public trial in accordance with the regular procedures of the court; (2) the right to examine witnesses and to confront witnesses; (3) the right to remain silent; and (4) the right to appeal, except in cases provided for by law.

Article 455-8 states that if the court accepts the result of a plea bargain, a simplified written verdict will be produced, which includes only the facts, evidence, applicable rules, and final conclusion. The court is not required to provide a detailed written verdict, as per Article 310, that includes the reasoning behind the verdict, such as an explanation of how the evidence, whether incriminating or exonerating, was interpreted by the court. According to Article 455-10, in principle, verdicts that result from plea bargains cannot be appealed unless there are plain errors. This feature arguably provides the strongest incentive for judges to use the new system (Wang, 2008).

Overall, Article 451-1 and Article 455-2 of the Code of Criminal Procedure establish the two models facilitating plea bargains in criminal cases in Taiwan, namely the program of 'Specific Sentence Requested by a Prosecutor' and the program of 'Bargaining Process'. Although each specify various requirements and restrictions, the ultimate decision on whether to accept a plea agreement rests with the court.

Plea Bargain in Practice

Despite the reforms outlined above, the number of plea bargains in Taiwan has been decreasing in recent years. According to Ministry of Justice records, 7197 people received a finalized verdict based on plea bargains at the first instance in 2011. This number increased to 9056 in 2012 but dropped sharply to only 5615 in 2015 and 2243 in 2021 (Ministry of Justice, 2022).

Furthermore, the occurrence of plea bargaining has a relatively insignificant presence within final outcomes. Between 2017 and 2021, the average number of people convicted of offenses and receiving finalized verdicts was 177,108 annually. During the same time frame, the average number of people receiving guilty verdicts based on plea bargains was 4513 annually (2.54% of all convictions).

Although the 'Specific Sentence' model under Article 451-1 is primarily intended to increase the likelihood of using summary judgment procedures, the lack of available statistics makes assessing its practical application difficult. However, with regard to the 'Bargaining Process' model under Article 455-2, negotiations under the Specific Sentence' model is not likely a significant contributing factor to using summary judgments.

Although the number and impact of plea bargains in Taiwan have decreased over the years, there is research indicating that they seem to benefit defendants in terms of the punishment received. For example, Sun (2008) analyzed proceedings for various crimes: 'offenses against public safety', 'forgery of instruments or seals', 'offenses against morality', 'gambling', 'offenses against freedom', 'theft', and offenses outlined in the Narcotics Hazard Prevention Act and the Controlling Guns, Ammunition, and Knives Act. With a few exceptions, the study found that plea bargains resulted in more lenient outcomes for defendants than regular procedures. In a questionnaire-based study of 49 practitioners (judges, prosecutors, and defense attorneys) in Kaohsiung, 29 (58%) believed that plea bargains result in more lenient outcomes for defendants (Tu, 2007). Although research on the topic is limited, some studies suggest that judges welcome plea bargains to save time and energy (Su, 2022; Wang, 2008). After the negotiation, judges can announce the final verdict immediately, as they are not required to explain their reasoning. Additionally, limiting the right to appeal also reduces the number of cases in workloads.

Article 455-2 prohibits judges from intervening during the initial stages of plea bargain negotiations, on the premise that any judicial intervention would pressure the defendant into negotiations. If the defendant refuses to negotiate or does not reach an agreement with the prosecutor, the judge's presence during the negotiation process could become a liability during a future trial (Lin, 2004). Therefore, judges can only passively participate in the process. They cannot initiate or participate in the negotiation process, nor can they modify the outcome (Liu, 2004). However, an empirical study noted that in practice, if a judge learns during the trial that the defendant has pled guilty and the case meets the statutory requirements for a plea bargain, they may inquire, either explicitly or implicitly, whether there is room for negotiation in the case (Su, 2022). If the prosecutor and defendant agree to negotiate, the judge will leave the bench to allow the negotiation to occur. In some instances, however, presiding judges remain seated in the courtroom to observe the negotiation process.

Prior to reaching an agreement with the defendant, the trial prosecutor must obtain approval from their counterparts in the investigative prosecutors' team (公訴組檢察官) and their superiors. As plea bargains are not a default practice, approval must be sought from their colleagues after the initial negotiation process in order to proceed (Su, 2022). This is because, in Taiwan, the prosecutors who appear in court are not the same prosecutors who decide to indict the defendant; the power to indict the defendant rests with the investigative prosecutors.

Limited Application of Plea Bargains

Although plea bargaining has the potential to produce favorable outcomes for defendants and reduce the caseload of the judiciary, it has not gained popularity and prominence in the Taiwanese justice system. This section explores the various reasons for this, which have been distilled into four main factors: the legal limitations, the judicial dominance on case narratives, the cultural resistance to plea bargains, and the tendency to use other summary procedures for handling cases.

Legal Limitations to the Application of Plea Bargain

The law imposes limitations on the possible results from the plea bargaining process. In the 1997 model, the options for punishment are limited to those from summary judgment as plea bargain negotiations are part of the summary judgment process. According to Article 449, possible forms of punishment include probation, fixed-term imprisonment that is convertible to a fine or community service, detention (1–60 days of imprisonment, which can be extended to 120 days), or a fine. As for the 2004 model, Article 455-4 limits the punishment imposed in such cases to probation, imprisonment for no more than two years, detention, or a fine. Evidently, the application of the plea bargain system has been reserved for minor cases.

The lack of prosecutorial discretion is another critical limitation of Taiwan's plea bargain system. Since the US plea bargain regime is arguably the most well-known, comparing the two approaches regarding prosecutorial discretion is of assistance to articulate this point. In the US, prosecutors have significant discretion regarding charges and plea bargains. They can decide whether to bring charges against a defendant, which charges to bring, and whether to negotiate a plea bargain. Prosecutors in the US may use plea bargains to manage their caseloads, to secure a conviction in a case that might be difficult to win at trial, or to achieve other policy objectives. However, prosecutors in Taiwan have more limited prosecutorial discretion than US prosecutors (Wen, 2018). Both Article 451-1 and Article 455-2 only grant the defendant the option to accept or reject the charge presented by the prosecutor. The law prohibits the defendant from proposing a plea for a lesser charge that was not initially offered by the prosecutor (Tsai, 2004). Moreover, the law does not allow the prosecutor to offer a lesser charge. As a result, the only opportunity for the defendant to negotiate is on sentencing after being charged on indictment.

A third important limitation to Taiwan's plea bargain system is that Article 455-2 only applies to the trial phase of the procedure. Therefore, with the exception of Article 451-1, plea bargains in Taiwan can only occur after the indictment and after the prosecutor decides the charges. This is another fundamental point of difference from the plea bargain system in the US. As mentioned above, because prosecutors in the US have broad prosecutorial discretion, there are no time limits on initiating negotiations.

Unsurprisingly, most plea bargain negotiations in the US occur during the investigation phase to save time and resources for both the defense and the prosecution (Henning et al., 2016). During this stage, before an indictment, the defendant has not yet been formally charged with a crime and the prosecution may still be gathering evidence to build their case. There is therefore more flexibility to negotiate a plea deal favorable to both parties. In addition, prosecutors are incentivized to conclude the matter at this stage as it removes the need for a trial and the associated costs and uncertainties of a trial outcome.

In contrast, prosecutorial discretion is highly constrained in Taiwan. Prosecutors lack the authority to pursue a lesser charge, which would expedite the process and conserve resources. Indeed, the Taiwanese legislature intentionally altered the language of relevant legislation to limit plea bargains to the trial phase (Wu, 2003), that is, after an indictment has been presented on the evidence as it supports the charge(s). The underlying idea is that prosecutors must proceed with an indictment if the evidence supports it, leaving the negotiation of the sentence as the only viable point for discussion. Scholars and practitioners have criticized this limitation for creating insufficient incentives for prosecutors to use the new plea bargain system (Tsai, 2004).

These legal restrictions significantly narrow the application of the plea bargain system in Taiwan, demonstrating a fundamental lack of trust by the legislators in the plea bargain system. This lack of trust originates not only from the legal professional community but also from the general public, as will be further discussed below.

Judicial Dominance on Case Narratives

Prior to 2003, Taiwan's criminal justice system was primarily inquisitorial in nature. It emphasized the discovery of objective truth and placed a significant amount of responsibility on the judge to seek that truth (Lewis, 2009). In this system, prosecutors and judges worked collaboratively, with prosecutors gathering evidence and presenting it to the court and judges continuing to investigate the case to determine the objective facts. Prosecutors compile the evidence they gather into a dossier of the case, which they submit to the judge along with the indictment.

The judge then takes over the investigation, actively questioning witnesses and investigating the facts of the case. The trial itself is considered insignificant, as judges are expected to review the dossier before trial, and trial dates are not usually held on consecutive days. A single hearing may take several court sessions and over a year to complete. During this period, judges can continue to gather evidence and conduct investigations outside the courtroom by exchanging documents. This model enables judges to spend minimal time at trials and resolve most issues outside the courtroom.

As judges are expected to take the lead in investigating the case, the role of prosecutors during the trial phase is minimized. Prosecutors do not have an essential role during the trial (Lewis, 2009; Tsai, 1998). Indeed, prosecutors are required to say nothing more than a few words to the judge, such as 'Please refer to the indictment' or 'Please make rulings according to Law'. Moreover, prosecutors and defense attorneys are only allowed to question witnesses after a judge has completed their inquiries.

In an inquisitorial system, the narrative is singular to reflect one version of the truth. Limiting the roles of prosecutors and defense attorneys during trial in this way aligns with the goals of the inquisitorial system, as the court can easily control the narrative and ensure only one version of the truth prevails. Against this context, one can expect that the presiding judge can be active to exercise their investigative powers to fill any gaps in the narrative.

Another mechanism in Taiwan's criminal justice system aimed to achieve the objective truth is the 'single case doctrine' established through court rulings. Article 267 of the Code of Criminal Procedure states that if a prosecutor presents an indictment regarding the partial facts of a crime, the legal effect of the indictment extends to all facts related to the crime. This stipulation allows judges to expand the charges brought by the prosecutor and include them in the trial, forming a 'single case'. Although there are limitations to this expansion based on substantive criminal law, and legal precedents have developed a sophisticated set of rules to determine these limitations, the single case doctrine effectively allows judges to assume the prosecutor's role and decide the breadth of an indictment. Based on the same rationale, Article 300 allows the court to change the indicted charges as long as the changes are within the factual boundaries of the original indictment. The primary purpose of the single case doctrine is to promote efficiency by allowing judges to resolve all related disputes in one single procedure, but doing so reinforce the court's ability to create a single narrative.

Another mechanism supporting the objective truth approach is the limitation of prosecutorial discretion. Prior to 2002, Taiwanese prosecutors were legally obligated to indict a suspect if there was sufficient evidence that they had committed a crime. The only exception to this obligation came from Article 253, which allowed prosecutors to not indict if the crime was deemed so minor that it did not warrant prosecution. In 2002, the rules of deferred prosecution were passed. Relevantly, Article 253-1 stipulates that if a defendant is not facing the death penalty, life imprisonment, or a prison sentence of three years or more, the prosecutor may, after considering all circumstances regarding the defendant and public interest, impose a deferred prosecution decision. The deferred period shall be determined as one to three years. If a deferred prosecution decision is granted, Article 253-2 stipulates that the defendant may be required to perform specific actions, such as apologizing to the victim, paying compensation, paying to the public treasury, or providing community service. They may also be ordered to undergo treatment or take steps to prevent future offenses. Deferred prosecutions are widely used by prosecutors (Lewis, 2009). In 2021, the average number of defendants receiving deferred prosecution was 34,235, and the total number of cases deemed to have sufficient evidence to prosecute was 246,664. The deferred prosecution rate was 13.9% (Ministry of Justice, 2022).

The use of deferred prosecution has not operated without controversy. In 2017, the owner of a well-known tech company was accused of various charges, including providing false financial statements, which violated the Taiwan Securities and Exchange Act. After an investigation, the Hsinchu Prosecutor's Office offered the defendant a deferred prosecution decision, taking into account the public interest and the fact that the defendant had no criminal history and did not profit from the offense. The defendant was ordered to pay NTD 110 million to the public treasury (Hsinchu Prosecutor's Office, 2017). This decision caused a public outcry. Indeed, some rumors suggested that prosecutors at Hsinchu Prosecutor's Office obtained bribes from the defendant (Lin, 2017). Eventually, the prosecutors were compelled to reverse its decision and charge the defendant through an indictment. This example is one reflecting the tip of the iceberg, but it demonstrates the public lack of trust in 'alternative dispute resolutions' which do not reveal the objective truth of cases and the pressure on prosecutors to use such methods as a result.

One final example is the evidence exclusionary rule. Article 158-4 of the Code of Criminal Procedure provides that the admissibility of evidence obtained in violation of legal procedure by a law enforcement official in the course of criminal proceedings shall be determined by weighing the protection of human rights against the preservation of public interests, unless otherwise specified by law. The rule functions as a balancing test that obliges judges to examine the totality of circumstances when deciding on the admissibility of unlawfully obtained evidence. In practice, such ambiguous regulations provide judges with ample room to maneuver, making it easier for judges to construct their own narratives. However, recent laws such as Article 18-1 of the 2014 Communication Security and Surveillance Act mandate an absolute prohibition on the use of information acquired through illegal surveillance or if the content is not related to the purpose of the surveillance. These different models highlight the tension between the Code of Criminal Procedure's responsibility to seek the objective truth and its objective to safeguard individual rights (Lin et al., 2019).

In summary, Taiwan's judicial tradition grants judges exclusive control over case narratives, building a legal culture whereby judicial intervention is encouraged and expected. Any mechanism which undermines this narrative monopoly is interpreted as diminishing the impartial discovery of truth. This is especially so for plea bargaining which represents a clear procedural departure from this judicial tradition.

Cultural Resistance to Plea Bargain

Researchers have highlighted that the legal community in Taiwan harbors doubts about the plea bargain system. Under the inquisitorial tradition of searching for the objective truth, plea bargains have always been criticized as 'buying and selling justice' because justice is compromised through a negotiation process similar to buying and selling products in the marketplace (Wang, 2008). Some prosecutors have expressed ethical concerns about the negotiation aspect of the plea bargain process, as many people still believe that justice is non-negotiable (Lin, 2004; Su, 2022; Sun, 2007, 2008; Tu, 2007). In a qualitative study, prosecutors reported reluctance to use plea bargains because they fear defendants will plead guilty to avoid more serious charges (Wang, 2008). More specifically, they do not wish to waste investigative resources or evidence gathered through investigations. It follows that prosecutors tend to believe that defendants should plead guilty during the investigation rather than the trial. Some prosecutors are also concerned that pursuing a plea bargain could upset their colleagues in the investigation office, or that taking into consideration the victims' feelings as part of the plea bargain process may result in a lenient sentence. Others feel that the limitation on appealing plea bargains is too strong in its restriction of appeal mechanisms. Finally, some high-level officials in the prosecution system worry about public pressure and believe that the public will see prosecutors who use plea bargains as ignoring justice (Wang, 2008).

Although judges have expressed their support for plea bargains, this by itself does not overcome the culture of reluctance within the prosecutor's office. Indeed, high-ranking officials in the prosecution system actively discourage its use, and internal regulations make the procedure more complex (Wang, 2008). For instance, prosecutors must first seek the investigative prosecutor's opinion to initiate a plea bargain and obtain approval from multiple superiors. Some regulations even require prosecutors to obtain the victim's approval first (Wang, 2008).

According to the Ministry of Justice, while conducting plea bargain negotiations, prosecutors 'shall' (instead of 'may') inquire about the victim's opinion, as required by the law. Although the Ministry's orders are not legally binding, most prosecutors comply (Sun, 2008). Judges have also noted that victims' opinions often play a significant role in whether a case can be resolved through plea bargain. In effect, where the victim does not agree to settle or refuses to resolve the case through a plea bargain, prosecutors and judges are less likely to follow the plea bargain option (Wang, 2008).

Research has shown that at least some judges and prosecutors understand that a trial may not necessarily reveal the truth, as the concept of truth itself is ambiguous and subjective (Wang, 2008). The truth from the evidence may only be one version to reflect the state of the evidence. In contrast, defense lawyers almost unanimously support plea bargains, perhaps because they are not tethered to establishing the objective truth as the other parties, and doubt that this can be established through a regular trial in any event (Wang, 2008).

The perception within the legal professional community to plea bargaining may, to some extent, merely mirror the prevailing public sentiment. It is important to note that the judiciary in Taiwan has lacked sufficient public support for a long time. According to relevant public opinion polls conducted over the years, the percentage of people who trust the judiciary is less than 40%. Additionally, those who believe that the court is unfair usually outnumber those who believe that the court is fair (Chang, 2014). As a result, when the legal professional community faces public questioning, it is challenging to counteract public doubts about the fairness of the judicial system. Indeed, the decline in judicial legitimacy can explain why the prosecutor community adopts a more skeptical attitude toward plea bargaining. When the general public starts to question the process, prosecutors often find themselves at the forefront facing criticism. As a result, they may be cautious and hesitant about embracing a mechanism that is already met with cynicism, fearing that their actions could be further scrutinized and tarnish their public image.

The reason for the public's distrust of the judiciary in Taiwan is not fully understood. Some scholars have suggested that this distrust may be due to the regime's past authoritarian regime, which still casts a shadow over the judiciary (Liao & Chen, 2019). Another study highlighted that the height of distrust toward the judiciary occurred in 2010, following the exposure of a series of judicial bribery scandals and controversial court rulings related to child sexual abuse that caused public outrage (Su, 2017). During her speech at the judicial reform meeting in 2016, President Ing-wen Tsai mentioned her expectation that judges should not practice a 'rich acquittal, poor conviction' 「有錢判生, 無錢判死」 approach. Such remarks sparked strong criticism from the Judges Association at the time, who believed that the President had sentenced the judiciary to death (Chen, 2016). However, the President's words did, to some extent, reflect the general public's perception of the judiciary. Other studies, including one that surveyed 1006 respondents, concluded that governmental performance, such as the handling of unemployment rates, crime, ethnic conflicts, and citizens' right to access government information, had a significant impact on the level of trust in Taiwan's judiciary (Wong et al., 2009).

Regardless of where the general public's lack of trust in the judiciary stems from, implementing plea bargaining becomes challenging when the judiciary lacks sufficient legitimacy. Even a comprehensive and lengthy public trial would face skepticism, let alone private negotiations between a politically sensitive prosecutor and a defendant.

Other research observed that the public often have unrealistic expectations of prosecutors, believing prosecutors have the resources to uncover the truth (Su, 2022). They expect the judicial system to invest significant resources in resolving even minor disputes without realizing that judicial resources are limited.

Following on from this, there is a prevailing belief that reducing investment in resources will compromise justice. When a case draws public attention or concerns an issue that society is worried about, such as drunk driving, if the outcome of the negotiated sentence between the prosecutor and the defendant does not meet public expectations, the prosecutor may face public suspicion of having exchanged conditions or colluded with the defendant. Under these circumstances, the practical approach for prosecutors is, unsurprisingly, to reject plea bargains and amplify the victim's opinions (Su, 2022).

This phenomenon to some extent reflects the attitude of Taiwanese society toward government officials. Taiwanese people often hold government officials to excessively high standards, expecting them not only to fulfill their job duties but also to go above and beyond, even to the point of complete self-sacrifice. Although there is no empirical evidence to support this, it is reasonable to speculate that this tendency might be related to Taiwan's authoritarian past when government officials were often supporters of the ruling party and may not have earned the people's recognition by way of qualifications or hard dedication. These impressions seem to have been retained into the present, making them particularly sensitive to the notion of government officials 'slacking off' or being lazy. With these attitudes in mind, plea bargaining may be perceived as a way for the judicial system to take shortcuts.

Tendency to Use Summary Procedures Instead of Plea Bargain

The rules for summary judgment have always provided a fast-track mechanism for resolving minor cases. When the code of criminal procedure was first passed by the legislature in 1928, simplified trials were limited to offenses that carried no more than six months of imprisonment, detention, or a fine. In 1967, the code was amended to cover circumstances that were 'minor and appeared to be forgivable' and expanded to include offenses that carried no more than three years of imprisonment, detention, or a fine, including specific offenses such as theft, embezzlement, fraud, breach of trust, extortion, and receiving stolen property.

In 1995, the element of 'minor and appeared to be forgivable' was removed, and the list was expanded to include all offenses that could not be appealed to the third instance. In 1997, all limitations on offenses were removed, and the rule mandated that a simplified trial could only result in probation, imprisonment, or detention that is convertible to a fine or detention. In 2003, the procedural element requiring the court to hold a hearing before conviction was removed. Thus, summary judgments are usually completed without a hearing (Chang, 2018).

Moreover, under the current code, a simplified trial can be processed by a single judge, who does not need to provide a complete written verdict. Similar to plea bargains, judges are only required to provide the facts, a list of evidence, and applicable rules; they need not provide their reasoning for a verdict. The development of these rules reflects the judicial system's efforts to expedite its resolution of a backlog of cases. Over the years, limitations have been removed, and the applicable offenses have been expanded to broaden the scope of application for summary procedures.

Compared to the low utilization of plea bargains, the summary judgment procedure has been used extensively by the judicial system. Between 2017 and 2021, the average number of people sentenced annually through summary judgment was 104,473. Almost 60% of all cases were resolved by summary judgment (Ministry of Justice, 2022). Summary judgments have emerged as a significant means of diverting criminal cases and reducing the justice system's workload.

The simplified trial procedure, introduced in 2003 as a supplement to the summary judgment option, provides a second fast-track option for resolving non-serious criminal cases. According to Article 273-1 of the Code of Criminal Procedure, this procedure is only applicable to crimes that do not carry a sentence of death, life imprisonment, or a minimum sentence of three years and are not within the jurisdiction of a higher court as the court of first instance. Defendants charged with non-serious crimes may be informed of this procedure during the preparatory procedure. If the facts of the case are clear and the case is simple, the presiding judge may decide to proceed with the simplified trial procedure after hearing the opinions of the defendant and the prosecutor.

The simplified and regular trial procedures differ critically. First, simplified trials can be decided by a single judge instead of a panel of three judges, as provided by Article 284-1 of the Code of Criminal Procedure. Second, the procedure for investigating evidence can be simplified, as outlined in Article 273-2. Since the simplified trial procedure is valued for its efficiency and convenience, the presiding judge has discretion in investigating the evidence and is not strictly bound by the rules of 'strict proof', allowing the inclusion of hearsay and cross-examination procedures. Lastly, as per Article 310-2 of the Code of Criminal Procedure, guilty verdicts rendered under the simplified trial procedure apply to the same rules as the summary judgment, allowing the written verdict to be simplified.

A study suggests that judges and prosecutors prefer summary judgment or simplified trial procedures over plea bargains to resolve cases (Su, 2022). Although significant overlap exists in the types of cases eligible for these options, summary judgments and simplified trial procedures have unique advantages. For example, investigative prosecutors can independently resolve cases using summary judgments without seeking internal approval from their colleagues or superiors. In addition, summary judgments and simplified trial procedures save more time than plea bargains, which require communication with the victim and the defendant. Furthermore, summary judgments do not require court hearings, while plea bargains require at least two court dates: one to initiate negotiations and another to confirm the deal after obtaining internal approval. Finally, either prosecutors or judges can initiate summary judgments, while judges initiate simplified trial procedures. However, judges have no power to initiate plea bargains.

Even so, scholars have highlighted the unique advantages of plea bargaining over summary judgment and simplified trial procedures, despite its lowest utilization rate among Taiwan's three expedited procedures (Su, 2022; Tu, 2007). Defendants seeking a plea bargain can negotiate with prosecutors and potentially receive a reduced sentence or other benefits, making the process more predictable than summary judgment or simplified trial procedures, which rely on judges or prosecutors making decisions without input from the defendant. Additionally, plea bargains have clear rules and procedures for judicial review that protect defendants from making false admissions.

In contrast, summary judgment procedures do not have such rules, and as they can be conducted without a court hearing, they may have a lower level of judicial scrutiny. There have been instances where prosecutors have misunderstood defendants' words and processed cases through summary judgment, only to discover their mistakes after the defendants received summary judgment rulings from the court and tried to challenge them through appeals (Chang, 2015). Finally, compared to simplified trial procedures requiring a full trial, plea bargains offer a better balance between efficiency and procedural protection in Taiwan's criminal justice system.

Therefore, the plea bargain process is arguably a better case handling mechanism than the summary procedures. However, due to various legal constraints and cultural factors mentioned above, plea bargaining is only sparingly utilized in Taiwan. Instead, a large number of cases are diverted to summary procedures which may resemble a trial on the surface but lack the substantive essence of one. Ironically, the differences between summary procedures and a full trial have not garnered attention in the same way that the obvious distinction between the plea bargain system and a trial have. As a result, the potential risks of following summary procedures in lieu of a full trial remain unrealized and unaddressed in public forums. One can argue that the summary procedure is, to some extent, a sleight of hand devised by legal professionals to discourage considering the option of pursuing plea bargaining. This is so where summary procedures are often resorted and preferred to address the issue of caseload.

New Opportunities and the Future of Plea Bargain

In response to calls for judicial reform, the Taiwan Judicial Yuan enacted the Citizen Judge Act, which introduces lay participation in the criminal justice system. From January 2023, citizen judge courts will try crimes resulting in death due to intent. By 2026, the scope of trials will be expanded to include crimes with a minimum sentence of more than ten years of imprisonment.

Citizen Judge Courts are a type of mixed court composed of three professional judges and six lay judges. In addition to determining the facts, the mixed court also determines sentencing. Guilt or innocence is decided by a two-thirds (six votes) majority, while sentencing involves arranging all members' decisions in ascending order of severity and starting from the most severe punishment. The final sentence gets to be passed when the accumulated votes reach more than half of the total votes. The majority must also receive at least one vote from a professional judge to confirm the sentence (Chin, 2019).

The Citizen Judge Act is expected to further increase the workload of the judicial system. To avoid information discrepancies between lay and professional judges, and considering that lay jurors may not be proficient in reading case files, Article 43 explicitly prohibits prosecutors from providing case files to the presiding professional and citizen judges. Instead, in a way similar to the US jury system, prosecutors and defense attorneys must first complete discovery procedures to exchange information and conduct opening statements, before presenting evidence, cross-examination, and closing arguments in the courtroom during the trial (Chin, 2019). Such a process renders the trial process no longer merely supplementary in formalizing the procedure, thereby increasing pressure on the court. Courtroom activities will become the focus of the trial process instead of the mere exchange of documents (Chin, 2019).

Since no Citizen Judge Courts have conducted trials at the time of writing this chapter, how long a case will take before it concludes remains unclear. However, based on simulated court experiences from the past few years, it would not be surprising for a case to take a week to conclude if full-day hearings are held daily. Complex cases may even take up to two weeks or more. Preparation time may take several months or even a year or more. Indeed, further delays may occur as preparation and trial times may become even longer considering the unfamiliarity of judges, prosecutors, and lawyers with the procedures.

Courts and prosecutors will inevitably need to dedicate more resources on trials to carry out the citizen judge system. Taiwan's current judicial system has not proposed any effective solutions to address this impact. In fact, a review of all the judicial reform issues and directions in Taiwan reveals that they have all been focused on increasing the rigor of procedures and making significant progress toward protecting human rights in the process. However, such changes are not sustainable without corresponding measures, given the legal system's limited resources (Chin & Su, 2022). Therefore, perhaps now is a suitable opportunity for existing expedited procedures to come into play to address this imminent issue.

From the defendant's perspective, engaging in plea bargaining in citizen judges eligible cases is attractive. This is partly because the approach of a lay judge to sentencing would be more uncertain than that of a traditional professional judge, and the possibility of a successful appeal from such a decision is limited because appellate courts would be more reluctant to reverse decisions made by citizen judges. Furthermore, the legal professional community is anticipated to embrace the plea bargain system in the context of the citizen judges system, as it provides a chance to effectively tackle the issue of overwhelming caseloads. This, in turn, allows judicial resources to be concentrated on genuinely disputed cases.

Nonetheless, even if the plea bargain mechanism is viewed as a sensible complementary approach to the citizen judge system concerning judicial resources and defendants' rights, and even if it has garnered support from the legal professionals, it ultimately needs to withstand scrutiny from the general public. The citizen judge system represents an enhanced version of a full trial, with increased resources, additional procedures, and enhanced transparency to earn the public's trust. Conversely, the plea bargain mechanism operates essentially in the opposite direction. No matter how theoretically or practically sound the plea bargain mechanism may be, and no matter the endorsement it receives from the legal community, if the public's perception of the judicial system remains unchanged, it is unlikely to gain the people's support. Perhaps this is also why substantial resources have been invested in rebuilding judicial trust through the implementation of the citizen judge system first even when the system is already overburdened by the caseloads, as this would lay the fundamental basis for the success of all other alternative procedures.

Among the three expedited procedures discussed above, the summary and simplified trial procedures have shortcomings. The former lacks procedural safeguards for defendants, while the latter expends resources for non-serious crimes. Only the plea bargain procedure, which has not reached its potential, has seemingly struck a balance between procedural protection and judicial resources. Based on existing research, there are at least two directions in which the plea bargain procedure can be improved to make it more attractive and favored by legal practitioners.

First, the plea bargain system must establish its position and distinguish itself from other expedited procedures. This system's most significant advantage is settling cases early during the investigation stage through plea bargains, which prevents prosecutors from investing resources in outcomes where there is no guilty verdict, or even after obtaining a guilty verdict, incurring huge costs and extending the litigation to the second and third instances.

Due to Taiwan's tradition of pursuing objective truth, the current plea bargain system does not permit prosecutors to negotiate before filing an indictment. However, the decision to prosecute indicates that the investigation is well-developed, and the prosecutor is confident of securing a guilty verdict. Consequently, prosecutors lack the motivation to incur additional administrative expenses by seeking approval from their colleagues and superiors and negotiating with defendants and victims. However, in cases where the prosecutor has already met the evidence required for filing an indictment, this study posits that plea bargains may not be an appropriate method to balance the pursuit of objective truth. More refined standards for such cases could be established through internal best practice guidelines or ethical rules within the prosecutor system.

Expanding the range of charges eligible for plea bargain is another crucial aspect of this reform proposal. Currently, the law only allows plea bargains for minor offenses that substantially overlap with other expedited procedures. Cases of such minor nature do not require prosecutors to devote significant resources to settling such cases. However, prosecutors may opt out of plea bargains when the prosecution is not deemed burdensome. Hence, a plea bargain is better suited for highly complicated cases, where prosecutors may consider reducing the expenditure of investigative resources through negotiation, thus allowing for the conservation of judicial resources and prompt compensation for victims by avoiding prolonged and unpredictable trials. However, expanding the scope of applicable charges should also be subject to restrictions. If the charge carries the death penalty or life imprisonment, the prosecutor may hold excessive bargaining power, and the defendant may be coerced into making a false confession due to the overwhelming pressure of avoiding the death penalty or life imprisonment, resulting in a wrongful conviction. These circumstances should not fall within the scope of plea bargains.

In addition to expanding the applicable scope, legislators can consider other supplementary measures. For example, a certain degree of information parity is required for a plea bargain to succeed. Although the current law allows defendants to be assisted by defense counsel and indeed defense attorneys help the defendants understand the reasonableness of the plea bargaining sentence, Taiwan currently lacks clear sentencing guidelines. Judges mostly rely on past experiences and consider the overall circumstances of the case to make independent judgments. As a result of this unpredictability, the guidance and advice that defense attorneys can provide are very limited. Naturally, the availability of any information about past decisions on similar crimes can encourage more informed and quicker decision-making. This creates more reassurance and encourages better decision-making for defendants who are currently oblivious to possible outcomes under the current system. In addition, if the bargaining process advances to the investigation stage, defendants should be provided with comprehensive legal defense resources so that they can engage in substantive bargaining with prosecutors. As one scholar has pointed out, the key issue is not which aspects can or cannot be negotiated, but rather the implementation of systematic safeguards to prevent the abuse of the plea bargain system (Chen, 2004). Finally, other alternative dispute resolution methods can be used in conjunction with plea bargains. For example, cases that may be subject to bargaining can be referred to mediation, allowing professional mediators to try to reach a compromise between the victim and the defendant. Regardless of whether mediation is successful, it can serve as a reference for prosecutors to initiate subsequent bargaining procedures where cases are straightforward, thereby increasing the chances of successful bargaining.

Conclusion

Over the past 20 years, Taiwan's criminal procedure has been in the process of transitioning from an inquisitorial system to an adversarial system. The first wave of reform occurred two decades ago, granting both parties some control over the presentation of evidence and incorporating cross-examination into the criminal procedure, awarding parties the central role in presenting and reviewing evidence. The most recent reform was the Citizen Judge Act, which grants even more control to the opposing parties over the procedure and encouraging increased activity in the courtroom. Nevertheless, adopting the adversarial system will continue to affect the inquisitorial ideology of pursuing objective truth at a deeper level. Although more practitioners are gradually accepting the adversarial system, many still adhere to the intuitive pursuit of objective truth. Greater consensus among legal practitioners will be necessary for the plea bargain system to become more well-known and accepted by the general public. However, it is anticipated that this change may take more time to be fully accepted, as most of the empirical evidence reviewed in this chapter indicates that the general public has not embraced this method of dispute resolution yet.

References

Chang, T. Y. (2015, June 7). *The Problems of Summary Judgment and Its Direction of Reform* (conference transcript). Seminar on the Head Account Case: Judicial Issues Behind High Conviction Rates, Taipei, Taiwan. https://www.jrf.org.tw/articles/784 (in Chinese).

Chang, T. Y. (2018). The Current Summary Judgment and Its Direction of Reform: Comparing to the Japanese "Simplified Order." *Taiwan Jurist, 194*, 35–50 (in Chinese).

Chang, W. C. (2014). Courts and Judicial Reform in Taiwan: Gradual Transformations Towards the Guardian of Constitutionalism and Rule of Law from Part I—Courts in Advanced Economies. In J. Yeh & W.-C. Chang (Eds.), *Asian Courts in Context* (pp. 143–182). Cambridge University Press.

Chen, Y. (2016, November 30). Tsai Ing-wen Expressed her Expectation to Avoid a "Rich Acquittal, Poor Conviction" Approach, but the Judges Association Criticized it, Interpreting it as a Verdict of "Judicial Death" for Taiwan's Judiciary. Storm Media. https://www.storm.mg/article/195932 (in Chinese).

Chen, Y. T. (2004). The Lights and Shadows of the Plea Bargain System. *The Taiwan Law Review, 110*, 230–248 (in Chinese).

Chin, M. H. (2019). Lay Participation in Taiwan: Observations from Mock Trials. *Asian Journal of Law and Society, 6*, 181–207.

Chin, M. H., & Su, Y. J. (2022). A Study on the Plea-Bargain System in the United States and How Can Taiwan Learn from Its Experiences. *Taipei University Law Review, 122*, 205–258 (in Chinese).

Henning, P. J., Feller, L., & Henning K. M. (2016). *Criminal Pretrial Advocacy*. West Academic.

Lewis, M. K. (2009). Taiwan's New Adversarial System and the Overlooked Challenge of Efficiency-Driven Reforms. *Virginia Journal of International Law, 49*, 651–726.

Liao, C. C., & Chen, Y. J. (2019). Transitional Justice in Taiwan: Changes and Challenges. *Washington International Law Journal, 28*, 619–644.

Lin, C. H. (2017, September 22). Hsinchu Prosecutors Give Light Punishment to Tech Prodigy, and Rumors Emerge of Judicial Officials Buying Stocks to Protect Him. Mirror Media. https://www.mirrormedia.mg/story/20170920inv001/

Lin, L. Y. (2004). A Few Opinions on the Plea Bargain System. *Law Forum, 29*, 32–37 (in Chinese).

Lin, Y. H., Wang, S. F., Chen, C. Y., Tsai, T. C., & Tsai, C. M. (2019). The Potential to Secure a Fair Trial Through Evidence Exclusion: A Taiwanese Perspective. In S. Gless & T. Richter (Eds.), *Do Exclusionary Rules Ensure a Fair Trial?* (pp. 131–162). Springer.

Liu, P. J. (2004). A Review of the Newly Adopted Criminal Plea Bargain Procedure. *Law Forum, 28*, 51–61 (in Chinese).

Ministry of Justice (Taiwan). (2022). Judicial Statistics Annual Report 2021. https://www.rjsd.moj.gov.tw/RJSDWeb/book/Book_Detail.aspx?book_id=555

Su, K. P. (2017). Criminal Court Reform in Taiwan: A Case of Fragmented Reform in a Not-Fragmented Court System. *Washington International Law Journal, 27*, 203–240.

Su, Y. J. (2022). *Improving Taiwan's Plea-Bargain System—A Lesson from the U.S. Law* [Master's Thesis, National Yang Ming Chiao Tung University School of Law] (in Chinese).

Sun, C. C. (2007). Plea Bargain in Practice I. *Judicial Weekly, 1333*, 2–3 (in Chinese).

Sun, C. C. (2008). Study of Plea Bargain Procedure [Master's Thesis, National Kaohsiung University Department of Law. NDLTD] (in Chinese).

Tsai, C. Y. (2004). Criminal Plea Bargain in Practice. *Judicial Weekly, 1194*, 2–3 (in Chinese).

Tsai, S. H. (1998). Let the Prosecutor Who Originally Investigated the Case Personally Appear in Court to Present the Accusation. *Judicial Reform Magazine, 15*, 25–26 (in Chinese).

Tu, Y. T. (2007). *Empirical Study of Criminal Plea Bargain—A Case Study of Kaohsiung District Court in Taiwan* [Master's Thesis, National Kaohsiung University Department of Law] (in Chinese).

Wang, H. Y. (2008). Plea Bargaining in Legal Sociological Perspective: The Case of Taiwan Criminal Judicial Reform. *NTU Law Journal, 37*(4), 65–113 (in Chinese).

Wen, T. T. (2018). Prosecutorial Discretion Review—Analyzing the US Legal System to Discuss the Future Direction of Regulation in Taiwan. *Tunghai University Law Review, 53*, 31–89 (in Chinese).

Wong, T., Hsiao, H., & Wan, P. (2009). Comparing Political Trust in Hong Kong and Taiwan: Levels, Determinants, and Implications. *Japanese Journal of Political Science, 10*(2), 147–174.

Wu, X. L. (2003). Should Taiwan Expand Plea Bargain to Provide Relief to the Judicial Caseload? *Taiwan Law Journal, 50*, 91–108 (in Chinese).

Judicial Paternalism and the Stagnant Bargaining Process in Taiwan

Mao-hong Lin

Introduction

Over the past few decades, plea bargaining or comparable plea-based mechanisms which are designed to achieve a conviction without formal trial proceedings have been widely established around the world in both common law and civil law countries (Langer, 2004, 2021). Nevertheless, this trend has come relatively late to the East Asian region. South Korea does not have this type of plea-based procedure in its criminal justice system (Langer, 2021, p. 381). Japan introduced an agreement-based mechanism in 2018, which entails cooperation from defendants on evidence collection instead of their guilty pleas (Abe, 2023). After a two-year pilot program in some cities, the People's Republic of China (hereinafter the PRC) officially incorporated a plea-based mechanism into its criminal justice system in 2018, the plea leniency system, which provides simplified and fast-track procedures for those defendants who plead guilty and accept sentencing recommendations from the procuratorate as well as the means of implementation (Li, 2022). Taiwan was an early adopter of this procedure and implemented a plea-based mechanism

M. Lin (✉)
National Taipei University, Taipei, Taiwan
e-mail: mhlin@gm.ntpu.edu.tw

E. Li et al. (eds.), *Criminal Case Dispositions through Pleas in Greater China*, https://doi.org/10.1007/978-981-97-1856-6_7

in 2004, the bargaining process, which allows prosecutors and defendants who plead guilty to negotiate over the sentence and other dispositions (Wang, 2011).

Unlike counterparts in the United States, where plea bargain accounted for 98% of criminal cases filed in the federal courts in 2018 (Gramlich, 2019), or the PRC, where more than 85% of criminal cases were ended via the plea leniency system in 2020 (Li, 2022, p. 77), the bargaining process in Taiwan has attracted little attention from the legal practice. It usually makes up 3.5% of the entire caseload every year on average. The share of criminal cases in the courts resolved through the bargaining process looks to have waned, from as high as 6% in 2008 to 2.4% in 2019. Why is the bargaining process strongly underutilized in Taiwan? Prior study shows that there are other similar abridged tracks in the criminal procedure, such as deferred prosecution,[1] summary procedure,[2] and simplified trial procedure,[3] and the bargaining process does not have the institutional advantages needed to outweigh these alternatives (Chin & Su, 2022; Huang, 2016). Also, for prosecutors, the bargaining process itself is not as efficient as originally anticipated (Lewis, 2009). Therefore, there are less incentives for prosecutors to take advantage of the process in lieu of other conventional tools to dispose of cases. Further, previous research also shows that there are concerns about the process including the deep-rooted doubt about the legitimacy of such a negotiation-based mechanism, which may displease victims and even the general public as it allows prosecutors to sell justice rather than to preserve it (Wang, 2008). However, research also shows that judges are more positive about the addition of a bargaining process into the criminal justice system, with respect to its strength when compared with alternatives, ability to conclude a case in a more efficient way, or the legitimacy of the process (Wang, 2008).

The extant research has developed a comprehensive discussion on the reason why prosecutors would rather opt for other trial-avoiding conviction mechanisms (Langer, 2021) instead of the bargaining process. This chapter moves further to explore the question why there are conflicting views on the bargaining process between prosecutors and judges. By

[1] Article 253-1 of the Code of Criminal Procedure.

[2] Article 449 of the Code of Criminal Procedure.

[3] Article 273-1 of the Code of Criminal Procedure.

exploring and explaining why prosecutors and judges have clashing views, this chapter argues that the hesitancy of prosecutors to take advantage of the bargaining process comes from its court-centric rationale. The court-centric bargaining process takes a paternalistic view, allowing judges to intervene regardless of the agreement between parties. This chapter also specifies two forms of the court's paternalistic role in the process: the court as a guardian of the defendant and as an enforcer of moral discipline. The former is set to protect defendants irrespective of their will. The latter is to ensure that defendants repent for their wrongdoing. Finally, this chapter spells out that the origin of judicial paternalism comes from the inquisitorial legacy of courts in the criminal procedure and criminal court's function in civilization.

The remainder of the chapter will proceed as follows. Section "Taiwan's Bargaining Process" proffers a historical overview of Taiwan's bargaining process and its features that make the process distinctive among its peers around the world. Section "Crisis, Challenges, and Conflicting Views About the Bargaining Process" lays out the crisis and the challenges confronted by the bargaining process and the conflicting views toward it between prosecutors and judges. Section "The Paternalistic Role of the Court in the Bargaining Process" is the main structure of the chapter. It introduces the idea of judicial paternalism, disassembles the paternalistic role of courts in Taiwan's bargaining process, explains why such paternalistic design dissuades prosecutors from making use of the process, and traces the origins of this judicial paternalism. Section "Conclusion" is the conclusion of the chapter.

Taiwan's Bargaining Process

Historical Overview

Since the enactment of the Code of Criminal Procedure in 1935, the criminal justice system of Taiwan has adhered to the civil law tradition. The inquisitorial and active role of courts during trial proceedings, and the capacities of the prosecutorial and defense parties have been quite restricted when judges presided over the trial. In an attempt to grapple with the bulky caseload in criminal courts, three new amendments to the summary procedure were passed in 1990 to encourage prosecutors to make more use of the summary procedure instead of formal trial procedure (Wang, 2002). Summary procedure is instituted for minor offenses

(Kennedy, 2003, pp. 115–116). The scope of punishment rendered via summary procedure is limited to probation, a fixed-term imprisonment that is convertible to community service, short-term detention, or a fine.[4] The judge in a summary proceeding may make decisions solely based on paper files without hearings (Kennedy & Shen, 2005; Lewis, 2009) and a summary judgment may be written in a brief manner or quote the texts directly from the indictment.

Application of the three new amendments passed in 1990 is preconditioned on a guilty plea from the defendant. The first amendment is Section 4 of Article 451, which allows a defendant who pleads guilty during investigation to petition the prosecutor to file a motion for summary procedure. The second is Article 451-1, which grants a defendant who pleads guilty during investigation the ability to convey to the prosecutor or the court the range of sentence the defendant would like to serve, and the prosecutor will accordingly make a suggestion to the court if they agree with the defendant's request. The last is Article 455-1, which curtails the right to appeal in the summary procedure. A normal summary judgment can be appealed to the court of second instance but cannot be appealed to the court of third instance. Moreover, if the summary judgment is made in accordance with Article 451-1, it is not appealable.

Article 451-1 is a predecessor of Taiwan's bargaining process (Chin & Su, 2022; Wang, 2008). Despite this, the provision does not explicitly allow the defense and prosecution to negotiate. The trade-off between a defendant's guilty plea and the sentence imposed in the provision has demonstrated the core value of negotiation in the later-enacted official bargaining process. Subsequently in 1997, three new elements were added in Article 451-1. First, defendants with a guilty plea may request probation and the prosecutor can also suggest the court grant probation to the defendant. Second, with the consent of the victim, the prosecutor may order the defendant to apologize to or compensate the victim before suggesting a sentence to the court. Third, the court must impose a sentence on the defendant within the scope suggested by the prosecutor unless they find the case does not qualify for a summary judgment, there exists a factual error that renders the sentence inappropriate, the defendant is to be acquitted or the case is terminated on procedural grounds

[4] See Article 449 of the Code of Criminal Procedure.

rather than on its merit, or the prosecutor's suggestion of sentence is tellingly improper or unfair.

Based on the resolution of the National Judicial Reform Conference in 1999, criminal procedure would be redirected from the traditional inquisitorial track toward a "reformed" adversarial one (Su, 2017, pp. 206–207). This newly revised criminal procedure was meant to incorporate some typical aspects of the American-style adversarial proceeding while maintaining a few fundamental characteristics of the inquisitorial tradition, for instance, judges are still afforded an investigatory power/responsibility under certain circumstances (Lewis, 2018).[5] One typical adversarial feature brought into Taiwan's criminal procedure is "cross examination," which was introduced in 2003. Also since 2003, every criminal case in the court of first instance shall be presided over by a collegial panel of three judges, except cases in the summary procedure, simplified trial procedure or those unappealable to the court of third instance which can be tried by a single judge.[6] Combining the two new requirements together indicates that a formal criminal trial would cost an immense amount of time, money, and work. This made the heavy workload suffered by the criminal courts even heavier.

Consequently, the chapter on the bargaining process[7] was enacted in April 2004 as an alternative to the formal trial proceedings after a fierce debate among government officials, legislators, judges, prosecutors, lawyers, and legal scholars (Wang, 2011). It was the first time that Taiwan officially introduced a plea-based process that allows defendants to offer their guilty pleas for "sale"[8] in exchange for better outcomes in their cases. This negotiation-based process is also viewed as a typical attribute of the US style adversarial system (Yang, 2004a, p. 84). The final version of the bargaining process is a compromised one among

[5] As per Section 2 of Article 163 of the Code of Criminal Procedure, the court "may" take further investigatory actions by its discretion for discovering the truth, and the court "must" take further investigatory actions for the purpose of maintaining fairness and justice or discovering the facts that are critical to the interest of the defendant.

[6] Article 284-1 of the Code of Criminal Procedure.

[7] It includes Articles 455-2 through 455-11 of the Code of Criminal Procedure.

[8] Plea bargain is considered as a sale of justice by some judges in Taiwan. See Kennedy and Shen (2005). In the United States, some situates plea bargain on the basis of contract theory. See, e.g., Scott and Stuntz (1991).

divergent interest groups (Wang, 2008) and hence possesses some distinctive features which do not resemble the American form. The bargaining process was expected to relieve the bulky backlog of cases in the criminal courts so that judges have more time and energy to deal with the cases in formal trial proceedings (Lewis, 2009).

Distinctive Features of the Process

There are six features rendering Taiwan's bargaining process distinct from the American-style plea bargain. The first one is related to the scope of cases eligible for bargaining. Unlike the United States, Taiwan allows only non-serious crimes to be managed through the bargaining process (Wang, 2011). In other words, crimes punishable by the death penalty, life imprisonment, imprisonment of no less than three years, or cases over which the court of appeal has jurisdiction of the first instance,[9] are excluded from the bargaining process.[10]

The second and third features are related to the timing and the content of the negotiation between the defense and the prosecution. Negotiation begins only after the case is indicted to the court and before the court of first instance makes a judgment.[11] In the original draft bill of the bargaining process proposed by the Judicial Yuan, the highest office of the judicial branch in Taiwan, parties are allowed to negotiate as early as in the investigation proceedings, but this design was highly criticized because it hollows out the core value of Taiwan's criminal procedure to discover an objective truth rather than a truth entirely manufactured by the parties (Lewis, 2009; Yang, 2004a). The timing for beginning a bargaining process is thus put off until the defendant is indicted. Unlike the practice in some common law countries where charges or counts of offense may be negotiated, such as the United States, Australia, Canada, England, and New Zealand (Brook et al, 2016), Taiwan only allows parties to make a trade-off between the guilty plea and the sentence together with other conditions like an apology to the victim, compensation to the victim, or donation of a certain amount of money to the

[9] As per Article 4 of the Code of Criminal Procedure, they are the cases involved with offenses against the internal security of the State, against the external security of the State, and of interference with foreign relations with other States.

[10] Section 1 of Article 455-2 of the Code of Criminal Procedure.

[11] *Id.*

government treasury.[12] Charges and counts of offense are not negotiable during the bargaining process (Chin & Su, 2022; Su, 2017; Wang, 2008). The sentencing options are confined to probation, imprisonment of less than two years, detention, or a fine.[13] The range of confiscation is also negotiable.[14] One more thing to be noted is that the consent of the victim is suggested as a prerequisite to entering into a bargaining process[15] and is required before bargaining with the defendant on whether to make an apology or compensation to the victim.[16]

The fourth and fifth features are concerned with other participants in the bargaining process. Also different from the practice in the United States, judges in Taiwan play a passive yet decisive role in the bargaining process. Judges are not allowed to take part in the negotiation process, but the agreement reached by the parties must be reviewed and approved by the court before it takes effect. Judges must wait until the prosecution motions for a bargaining judgment after the agreement is reached.[17] The agreement will be reviewed by the court. A bargaining judgment will be rendered on the basis of the agreement if the court approves it (Su, 2017; Wang, 2008; Yang, 2004a).[18] Moreover, the assistance of counsel is not mandatory in the bargaining process. Instead, defendants may communicate with the prosecution about the plea agreement without representation. If the court finds that the sentence of imprisonment accepted by the defendant is higher than six months without probation and the defendant has no support from any lawyers, the court has to appoint a public defender or a lawyer to the defendant to provide the necessary legal assistance. Once retained, the defense attorney may express opinions of law and facts that are not contrary to the defendant's expressed thoughts.[19] Clearly the function of legal assistance throughout the bargaining process is rather limited (Huang, 2016).

[12] *Id.*

[13] Section 2 of Article 455-4 of the Code of Criminal Procedure.

[14] Section 1 of Article 455-2 of the Code of Criminal Procedure.

[15] *Id.*

[16] Subsections 2 and 3 of Section 1 and Section 2 of Article 455-2 of the Code of Criminal Procedure.

[17] Section 1 of Article 455-2 of the Code of Criminal Procedure.

[18] Article 455-4 of the Code of Criminal Procedure.

[19] Article 455-5 of the Code of Criminal Procedure.

The last aspect concerns the remedy in the case of a bargaining judgment. After the court makes a bargaining judgment aligned with the agreement reached by the parties, apart from some exceptions the judgment is not appealable. This limitation is grounded both theoretically on the doctrine of estoppel and pragmatically on the idea of lowering the workload of the court of second instance (Wang, 2008). A bargaining judgment may be brought to the appellate court under some exceptional circumstances. These include where the agreement is withdrawn or revoked by one of the parties before the bargaining judgment is made, the agreement is not made of the defendant's free will, the offense admitted by the defendant is not eligible for a bargaining process, the defendant may receive a harsher sentence because of their other offenses in the same course of action, the defendant's punishment is to be remitted, the case is exempted from prosecution or dismissed, or the sentence imposed on the defendant goes beyond the limitation of Section 2 of Article 455-4 (Wang, 2008).[20]

The above features of the bargaining process have a similar institutional design to its prototype, the trade-off mechanism in Article 451-1 in the summary procedure. They are both applicable to a limited scope of non-serious cases. The parties are allowed to confer on the sentence and compensating measures like apology or restitution to the victim, but not on charges or counts of offense. Consent of the victim plays a pivotal role in both procedures. The agreement reached by parties in both procedures is under the supervision of the court. The assistance of counsel is either non-mandatory or substantially limited and the remedy for the judgments out of these procedures is highly restrained. It has been more than thirty years since Article 451-1 was passed and almost two decades since the enactment of the bargaining process. Why do the shared features persist for such a long time without any change, despite other parts of the criminal procedure being revised or amended around thirty times during the same period? This inquiry will be addressed in section "The Paternalistic Role of the Court in the Bargaining Process".

[20] Section 1 of Article 455-10 of the Code of Criminal Procedure.

Crisis, Challenges, and Conflicting Views About the Bargaining Process

The Vanishing Bargaining Cases

Contrary to a prior study that predicted the use of the bargaining process in the future would rise (Wang, 2011, p. 13), the research outlined in Table 1 below as well as other studies (Huang, 2016, pp. 51–53; Wang, 2008, pp. 83–84) have already highlighted that the use of the bargaining process is declining, and bargaining cases only make up a small portion of the entire caseload every year, ranging from 2.2% to 6%, with a yearly average of 3.5%. There was indeed a rise in the early years since its introduction, though still only small, but during the last decade its use has decreased significantly, dropping by almost half from 4.6% in 2012 to 2.4% in 2019. On the contrary, the entire backlog of criminal cases in the district courts each year has been rising from around 125,000 in 2004 to more than 207,000 in 2019. The bargaining process is gradually vanishing from the criminal courts.

Table 1 clearly illustrates the decline in the use of the bargaining process. The meager numbers of bargaining cases and the declining trend in its usage have drawn attention from academia. Three major challenges confronted by the bargaining process are specified by prior research (Wang, 2008, pp. 87–100). The first is about the competing mechanisms that marginalize the bargaining process. The second is related to the inefficient nature of the process itself. The third concerns the perennial doubt about the legitimacy of such a negotiation-based scheme in criminal justice.

Comparative Weakness in the Institutional Design

Whether to commence a bargaining process depends on what the prosecutor decides. If an agreement has been reached by the prosecutor and the defendant, then the prosecutor may file a motion to the court to embark on a bargaining process.[21] If they do not make a deal, the original proceeding may continue, or other alternative procedures may take over. As prior research has already indicated (Huang, 2016, pp. 54–56), there exist other mechanisms in criminal procedure which can dispose of

[21] Section 1 of Article 455-2 of the Code of Criminal Procedure.

Table 1 The number of bargaining cases and its share of the entire caseload in the district courts by year

	Bargaining Cases (A)[a]	*Entire Caseload (B)*[b]	*Percentage (A/B)*	*Note*
2004	1535	125,816	1.2%	About 9 months[c]
2005	5182	136,276	3.8%	
2006	6174	159,537	3.9%	
2007	8968	186,991	4.8%	
2008	12,132	203,843	6.0%	
2009	8775	193,133	4.5%	
2010	5911	189,261	3.1%	
2011	8061	185,810	4.3%	
2012	8218	180,520	4.6%	
2013	6789	182,327	3.7%	
2014	5685	200,111	2.8%	
2015	4549	204,465	2.2%	
2016	4688	208,478	2.2%	
2017	4781	218,623	2.2%	
2018	5424	216,017	2.5%	
2019	4935	207,851	2.4%	
2020	4106	202,744	2.0%	COVID-19[d]
2021	2092	163,879	1.3%	
2022	2323	196,951	1.2%	
			3.5% on average (2005–2019)	

Sources Judicial Statistical Yearbook

[a]The number of cases solved via the bargaining process in all district courts of the year

[b]The number of criminal cases solved in all district courts in that year. Cases concluded through the summary procedure are not included

[c]The bargaining process took effect on April 9, 2004, so the number of bargaining cases of the year covers a span of about nine months

[d]The COVID-19 pandemic has caused immense negative impacts on interpersonal activities around the globe, including those happening in court proceedings, so the numbers of the three years are for reference only and cannot be interpreted in the same way as the numbers of other years

criminal cases in an expedient way such as deferred prosecution, simplified trial procedure, and summary procedure. Previous research using the interview data of prosecutors also confirms that the bargaining process is disfavored by prosecutors because of its institutional deficiencies (Wang, 2008).

The three types of abridged process have their own institutional superiority over the bargaining process. For example, prosecutors possess the full discretion to determine whether to grant a deferred prosecution to the defendant, but the bargaining process, once initiated, is under the control of the court and subject to its discretion. Simplified trial procedure, which omits the complicated and time-consuming rules of evidence like hearsay or cross examination to accelerate the process, allows both parties to appeal to higher courts (Lewis, 2009, p. 672), whereas a bargaining judgment is in general non-appealable. Research has shown that even after the enactment of the bargaining process in 2004, still more than 40% of cases in the district courts were concluded via a simplified trial procedure (Wang, 2008, p. 84). As for the summary procedure, one of its features is that the process can be conducted entirely with paperwork without holding any hearings (Lewis, 2009, p. 640). Therefore, summary procedure spares prosecutors time and energy because they neither negotiate with the defendant nor go to the court in person. Chart 1 demonstrates that, although the use of the bargaining process has waned, the number of cases finished with a summary judgment substantially increased from about 80,000 in 2004 to more than 130,000 since 2014.

Taiwan's bargaining process lacks the institutional advantages that would convince prosecutors that its use may preserve their discretionary power (compared with deferred prosecution), opportunity to appeal (compared with simplified trial procedure), or time and energy (compared

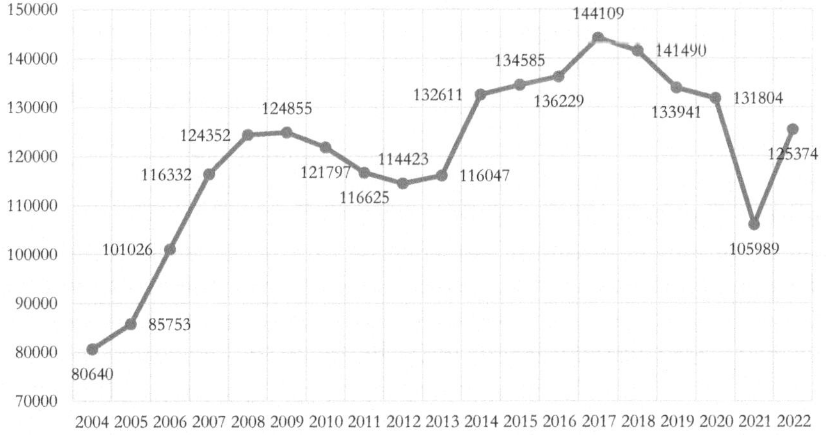

Chart 1 The number of criminal cases solved through the summary procedure by year (*Sources* Judicial Statistical Yearbook)

with summary procedure). Therefore, there are less incentives for prosecutors to resort to the bargaining process in place of other competing mechanisms when dealing with cases. The comparative weaknesses surely frustrate the expected function of the bargaining process so that this ambitious and contentious institution is marginalized over time.

In contrast with prosecutors, judges view the institutional design of the bargaining process more positively (Wang, 2008, pp. 91–93). During the negotiation, judges and prosecutors are not the only participants. Defendants may also feel respected by being able to take part in the process more actively, rather than passively waiting for a judgment as they would normally do in other expedient procedures. Moreover, the process provides victims with a chance to express their thoughts and feelings in exchange for an apology and compensation from defendants. This is what restorative justice is looking for. Lastly and practically, the heavy caseload for the entire judiciary could be relieved because it is more difficult for defendants to appeal a bargaining judgment which is made on the basis of the agreement between the defendant and the prosecutor. These attributes make the bargaining process more valuable than and different from its competing alternatives.

Cost-Ineffectiveness

In addition to the comparative advantages of alternative mechanisms, the design of the bargaining process itself is also not as cost-effective. The current version of the bargaining process allows parties to negotiate only after the case is indicted to the court. In other words, bargaining during the stage of investigation is prohibited. The rationale behind such a design is "quick decision for clear cases, careful judgment for dubious cases" (Wang, 2008, p. 76). The investigation and indictment by the prosecutor together with a guilty plea from the defendant make the case a clear one, so it is cost-effective to deal with the case expediently, such as through a bargaining process. On the contrary, a defendant's guilty plea alone is not sufficient for a clear-cut case. If a case remains unclear, it needs more time and energy through conducting a thorough exploration.

This rationale totally contradicts what prosecutors deem cost-effective in two aspects (Wang, 2008, pp. 98–100). The first one is about the timing. If prosecutors have spent lots of time and energy on investigating and eventually indict the defendant and send the case to court, they would prefer to see their prior efforts result in a conviction. Conversely, only when a case is still under investigation would prosecutors be more willing to negotiate with defendants in exchange for their guilty pleas. Thus, it is not cost-effective for prosecutors to pay additional costs to negotiate with the defendant after the case has been investigated and indicted.

The second concern is about the clearness of a case. If the case is a clear one, as described by the rationale, it means the defendant will be more easily convicted and the prosecution has higher odds of winning the case. In these cases, there are few incentives for prosecutors to negotiate with the defendant to secure a guilty plea. On the contrary, when the details of a case are still unclear, prosecutors are motivated to settle the case through negotiation instead of investigation and prevent unnecessary costs. It is also not cost-effective for prosecutors to pay additional costs to negotiate with the defendant when the case is clear.

Interestingly, judges have different thoughts on the idea of cost-effectiveness (Wang, 2008, pp. 91–93). First, just like the summary judgment, a bargaining judgment can be written in a brief way or quote text directly from the indictment.[22] This can considerably alleviate the burden on judges. Second, a bargaining judgment is appealable only under certain exceptions and it is less possible for defendants to appeal a bargaining judgment because it is made upon the defendant's agreement with the prosecutor. Limited chance to appeal means fewer cases for the appellate courts. Third, the prosecutor's idea of cost-effectiveness is at the cost of the defendant's voice, which is opposed to the core values of such a negotiation-based process. On the contrary, the bargaining process abates not only the costs of the prosecutor and the judge, but also the defendant's costs for traditional trial procedure like retaining a defense counsel, anxiety incurred by the uncertainty of court decision, or mandatory appearances in court. This is truly cost-effective and has no hidden costs.

Legitimacy in Doubt

The legitimacy of the bargaining process is of serious concern to prosecutors in Taiwan. Prosecutors believe that the foundation of criminal justice is based on evidence and facts, not on the agreement between

[22] Articles 455-8 and 455-9 of the Code of Criminal Procedure.

parties. That is, justice is about truth, rather than compromise. Therefore, there are understandable reasons for prosecutors to oppose the use of the bargaining process (Wang, 2008). First, to prevent defendants from pleading guilty to minor offenses in exchange for not being investigated for more serious ones. Second, defendants usually get a lighter sentence than they arguably deserve for the crime they committed. Third, victims may be hurt again if the prosecutor reaches a deal on the sentence with the defendant. Fourth, prosecutors are worried that they may lose the trust of the general public as they are likely to be viewed as selling justice rather than preserving it.

Due to distrust of the bargaining process, some internal rules have formed to lower the willingness of prosecutors to use it (Wang, 2008). These include setting up a maximum number of cases that can be processed in the bargaining process, trial prosecutors waiting to obtain the investigating prosecutor's consent before entering an agreement with the defendant,[23] the agreement needing to be reviewed by the chief prosecutor or other managing prosecutors before the trial prosecutor files a motion to the court for a bargaining process,[24] and consulting with the victim before filing a motion for a bargaining process[25] despite the fact that the victim's consent is not legally required. All these internal rules employed by prosecutors' offices are intended to increase the difficulty and complexity of reaching an agreement. These internal rules have tellingly demonstrated the non-cooperative attitude of prosecutors toward the bargaining process.

Contrary to strong criticism and non-cooperation from the prosecution, judges have different ideas about the legitimacy of the bargaining process. Generally, judges possess a wider view on the nature of criminal justice. First, they don't think the legitimacy of criminal justice comes only from facts and evidence. Sometimes a criminal may be acquitted because

[23] Section 3 of Point 138 of the Directions for Prosecutors When Dealing with Criminal Litigation Cases. There are two major types of prosecutors in Taiwan: investigation prosecutor and trial prosecutor. As their names have implied, the former is responsible for the investigation of crime. Once the defendant is indicted, the latter takes over the case and advocates in court. See Kennedy (2007, pp. 136–138) for the introduction to Taiwan's prosecutorial system.

[24] Section 3 of Point 138 and Sections 3 and 5 of Point 141 of the Directions for Prosecutors When Dealing with Criminal Litigation Cases.

[25] Section 1 of Point 138 of the Directions for Prosecutors When Dealing with Criminal Litigation Cases.

the incriminating evidence is excluded according to the laws of evidence. This is also justice, procedurally. Second, they think justice can be served through negotiation. Restorative justice is a persuasive example in this sense. Third, justice based on facts and evidence, namely the pursuit of truth based on facts and evidence has its limits in the aspects of time, money, and manpower. It is not feasible to seek truth at all costs. Fourth, there is no such thing as intact truth. In effect, what we know is only part of the whole truth (Wang, 2008).

The Paternalistic Role of the Court in the Bargaining Process

Court-Centric Rationale

As the previous section has indicated, the reluctance of prosecutors to utilize the bargaining process is the main reason for its declining usage over time. Three justifications have been pinpointed for this hesitancy: the comparative weakness of the process with competing alternatives, the process not being as cost-effective as touted, and the legitimacy of the process being highly questionable. Judges, however, take a different stance. They think the process has its own institutional strengths and the interpretation of both cost-effectiveness and the legitimacy of criminal justice should be more inclusive and pluralist.

The future of the bargaining process and the conflicting views of the prosecution and the court arouse two important questions: (1) what causes the dichotomous standpoint on the process between prosecutors and judges and (2) why have there not been any statutory changes to the bargaining process since its inception in 2004 to address its low usage and the strong criticism from prosecutors.

The rationale of the bargaining process, that is, quick decision for clear cases and careful judgment for dubious cases, answers the first question. As discussed before, for prosecutors, there is no reason to negotiate with defendants in clear cases because that creates additional costs to convict a defendant who is easy to convict. Conversely, only in dubious cases which have uncertainty in their outcome will negotiation be a rational choice for prosecutors to bargain with defendants. For judges, however, it is a different story. Clear cases relieve judges from the role of fact finder. The present version of bargaining gives judges the opportunity to preside over each participant in the process: prosecutors (by reviewing the motions for bargaining judgment from the prosecution), defendants (via the procedure of questioning and informing defendants after receiving the prosecutor's motion),[26] and victims (by requesting that the prosecution show proof that the victim's consent has been secured if one of the conditions in the agreement is that the defendant has to make an apology or compensate the victim). Also, it allows judges to apply different types of justice during the process: substantive, procedural, and restorative.

The rationale of the bargaining process is not party-centric but court-centric. This is why there are clashing views between prosecutors and judges: comparative weakness becomes institutional strength, cost-ineffectiveness becomes cost-effective for every participant, and the accusation of selling justice becomes a pluralist view of justice. The first question about what causes the dichotomous viewpoints on the bargaining process between prosecutors and judges is hence addressed. Realizing the rationale is court-centric is only the first step. We must keep examining why a negotiation-based mechanism is court-centric which leads us to consider the paternalistic nature of the bargaining process.

Paternalism and Law

Paternalism is a concept that has been widely debated and possesses multiple definitions (Dworkin, 2015; Husak, 2005; van Boom & Agus, 2010). It is in general defined as the practice of those in positions of authority or power making decisions for others based on the belief that they are acting in the best interest of those individuals (Zamir, 1998). In a paternalistic relationship, one person assumes responsibility for the well-being of another, limiting the choices that the subordinate can make. Paternalism is sometimes used as a means of curtailing individual freedom with the assurance of promoting better results or social welfare. However, it has been criticized for infringing on individual freedoms, autonomy, and may lead to further inequality (King, 2004).

A new theoretical exploration of paternalism called libertarian paternalism has emerged recently (Sunstein & Thaler, 2003). It is a concept that suggests that people can be guided toward making better choices by providing them with nudges or gentle pushes in the right direction. It is a way of encouraging people to make decisions that are in their

[26] Article 455-3 of the Code of Criminal Procedure.

best interests while still allowing them the freedom to make their own choices. Nudges are small changes that are designed to encourage people to make better decisions. In the context of libertarian paternalism, nudges are seen as a way of encouraging people to make choices that are good for them without being overly intrusive. Libertarian paternalism aims to strike a balance between promoting good behavior and respecting individual freedom (Sunstein, 2014). But the idea of libertarian paternalism is not completely new. It shares the theoretical foundation of libertarianism with legal paternalism (Feinberg, 1971; Hospers, 1980) but has some modifications, like the notion of "nudging."[27]

Paternalism has been employed to analyze legal questions in certain areas, such as criminal law (Tur, 1985), contract (Kronman, 1983), divorce (Bridge, 1999), copyright (Nahmias, 2019), mental health (Whelan, 2021), insurance (Schwarcz, 2010), and consumer protection (Bar-Gill & Ferrari, 2010). There are also studies exploring paternalism in interdisciplinary fields, such as legal history (Winkel, 2010) and gender studies (Daly, 1989). Moreover, paternalism can be used to understand not only a specific area of law, but also an entire system. Foote (1992), for example, describes the criminal justice of Japan in the 1990s as benevolently paternalistic as it granted government officials the power to interfere with a suspect's personal freedom to the degree considered necessary to understand their behavior and decide on the most effective way to reform them.

The Paternalistic Design of the Bargaining Process

In theory, a negotiation-based procedure must be centered around the parties because their bargaining and agreement are the main structure of the procedure. In Taiwan, however, the bargaining process is rather court-centric. The inconsistency here can be explained via the notion of paternalism, by which we can unveil the judicial-paternalistic nature of the bargaining process in two ways. First, the court acts as the guardian

[27] The idea of libertarian paternalism, to wit, nudge, also has incurred some criticism on its definitional side, such as it is still a form of paternalism and not quite libertarian (Hausman & Welch, 2010; Mitchell, 2005); and on its normative side, like it contradicts with the requirement of transparency in democratic societies (Oliver, 2013) and education is a better option than nudge (Gigerenzer, 2015).

of the defendant most of the time during the bargaining process. Second, sometimes the court also acts as an enforcer of moral discipline.

As elucidated before, once the parties reach an agreement, the prosecutor will file a motion for a bargaining process. If a bargaining process is commenced, the first thing the court needs to do is to make sure that the defendant makes the rational choice of pleading guilty and reaching an agreement with the prosecution. Within ten days after the motion is received, the court is required to commence a proceeding to question and inform the defendant of the rights waived, the offense admitted, and the punishment that might be imposed if a bargaining judgment is made pursuant to the agreement. If the defendant changes their mind, they may withdraw from the agreement without giving any reason by the end of the proceeding (Wang, 2011). On the contrary, the prosecutor may revoke the agreement only if the defendant disobeys the agreement.[28] After the duty to inform is completed, the court will check whether to approve the agreement and make a bargaining judgment. There are seven circumstances under which a bargaining judgment cannot be entered. They are all concerned with the defendant in the following ways where: (1) the defendant has withdrawn from the agreement, (2) the defendant's consent is not made with free will, (3) the agreement is inappropriate or unfair, such as the defendant is innocent but has consented to a guilty plea (Yang, 2004b), (4) the offense admitted by the defendant is not eligible for a bargaining judgment, (5) the facts found by the court are different from the facts agreed, (6) the defendant may receive a harsher sentence because of their other offenses in the same course of action, and (7) the defendant's punishment is to be remitted or the case is to be exempted from prosecution or dismissed.[29] Despite the fact that a bargaining judgment is in principle not appealable, the above circumstances (1), (2), (4), (6), (7) can be grounds for an appellate review.

There are other procedural requirements for the court. The court must appoint a public defender or a lawyer to the defendant if finding the sentence of imprisonment agreed by the defendant is higher than six months without probation and the defendant has no support from any lawyers.[30] This requirement exists to make sure the defendant's rights are

[28] Article 455-3 of the Code of Criminal Procedure.

[29] Section 1 of Article 455-4 of the Code of Criminal Procedure.

[30] Section 1 of Article 455-5 of the Code of Criminal Procedure.

not compromised because of the power imbalance between the parties (Yang, 2004a). If a bargaining judgment is not entered, the statements by the defendant, their agent, or defense attorney during the bargaining process cannot be used by courts as evidence against the defendant or other co-defendants in later trials.[31] This institutional design exists to make sure the defendant can give their voice more freely (Yang, 2004a).

Consequently, throughout the entire bargaining process, the court is institutionally designed to act as the guardian of the defendant most of the time. The court is heavily involved in the decision-making of the defendant. As per the stipulations, the court has the duties to question and inform the defendant, to assign them an attorney, and to exclude the statements during negotiation from evidence if a bargaining judgment is not entered. Also, the court may set aside what the defendant agrees, admits, or accepts. In other words, what law deems appropriate can outweigh what the defendant personally prefers, and such legal rules are interpreted and applied by the court in specific cases. Therefore, defendants' choices are subject to the court's discretion. The appropriateness or fairness of the agreement, the offense or the facts admitted by the defendant, or the punishment accepted by the defendant, are all subject to review by the court. In most scenarios, decisions of the court are advantageous to the defendant, but in some situations, they are not, at least in the literal meaning. This is due to another aspect of the paternalistic role of the court: court as an enforcer of moral discipline (Kuo & Chen, 2019).

As already expounded, the victim is treated as an important participant in the bargaining process by judges. Even though victims' consent is only advisory and is not required by the law, judges usually won't hand down a bargaining judgment without the victim's consent (Wang, 2008). Whether the victim will consent usually hinges on the atonement of the defendant. In a more formal sense, atonement denotes the defendant's apology and compensation. Therefore, if the defendant desires a bargaining judgment, to manifest their repentance by apologizing and making compensation to the victim is a must. Furthermore, the compensation promised by the defendant can be enforced by the court compulsorily if the defendant fails to perform it.[32] Consequently,

[31] Article 455-7 of the Code of Criminal Procedure.

[32] Section 4 of Article 455-5 of the Code of Criminal Procedure.

through the bargaining process, the court also becomes an enforcer of moral discipline, making sure that the defendant has demonstrated contrition by making an apology and giving restitution to the victim. After this, the court may deem the defendant a person who deserves a lenient disposition. Otherwise, a bargaining judgment is not possible. Again, a bargaining judgment is not contingent on the agreement reached by the parties, but on the penitence of the defendant in an expressive manner.

The Origin of Judicial Paternalism in Taiwan

The previous section has disclosed the two forms of judicial paternalism in the bargaining process: the court as a guardian of the defendant and the court as an enforcer of moral discipline. But where does judicial paternalism come from? It can be traced to the inquisitorial legacy of courts in the criminal procedure and criminal courts function in civilization.

The origin of judicial paternalism is the inquisitorial legacy. When the bargaining process was still under discussion before its enactment, some suggested to adopt the US mode. That is, to allow parties to bargain before indictment. But this suggestion was not eventually accepted because it contradicts the core value of Taiwan's criminal procedure by depriving the court of the function to discover objective truth based on evidence and replacing it with a negotiated truth. Instead, the present mode of bargaining in Taiwan was learned from Italy (Chin & Su, 2022; Heron, 2020; Huang, 2016). This origin is evidence that the inquisitorial legacy of Taiwan's traditional mode of justice remains influential in the criminal procedure (Huang, 2016). Plus, the rationale of the bargaining process is court-centric rather than party-centric. A negotiation-based mechanism stuffed with an inquisitorial soul is what Taiwan's bargaining process now looks like.

In addition, studies on the relationship between death penalty and criminal courts in Taiwan find that Taiwan's criminal courts also have a function in civilization (Kuo & Chen, 2019). The International Covenant on Civil and Political Rights limits the use of the death penalty to only the cases of most serious crimes, but Taiwan's criminal courts read this requirement together with the domestic legal idea of rehabilitation to determine whether a defendant is 'reformable' and thus worthy of life. The "most serious crimes" requirement is hence rendered instrumental to estimate the value of the defendant's life. In this sense, the court not only interprets legal rules, but also acts as a civilizer, determining whose life is more valuable based on the rehabilitation of defendants in each case. This trait of Taiwan's criminal courts echoes their role as an enforcer of moral discipline in the bargaining process. Consequently, judicial paternalism in the bargaining process is rooted in criminal court's function in civilization.

Conclusion

Taiwan introduced the bargaining process into its criminal procedure in 2004 as an alternative to the ordinary trial proceedings to alleviate the heavy workload of courts entering the era of the adversarial system. The bargaining process, however, has been barely utilized since its installment. Prior research shows that prosecutors are reluctant to use the process because of its comparative weakness in its institutional design, cost-ineffectiveness, and questionable legitimacy. However, judges have opposite opinions about the process in the three aspects. By exploring and explaining why prosecutors and judges have conflicting views, this chapter argues that the hesitancy of prosecutors to take advantage of the bargaining process comes from the court-centric rationale of the process, which causes the dichotomous standpoint between prosecutors and judges. The court-centric bargaining process takes a paternalistic view, allowing judges to intervene in the process regardless of the agreement between parties. This chapter also specifies two forms of the court's paternalistic role in the process: the court as a guardian of the defendant and the court as an enforcer of moral discipline. The former is set to protect defendants irrespective of their will. The latter is to make sure that defendants repent. Finally, this chapter spells out that the origin of judicial paternalism comes from the inquisitorial legacy of courts in the criminal procedure and criminal court's function in civilization. This answers why there have not been any statutory changes to the process despite its low usage by and high criticism from prosecutors. Moreover, existing studies on judicial paternalism address mostly the issues of substantive rights. This chapter makes a theoretical addition to the literature by pointing out the procedural aspects of judicial paternalism.

References

Abe, H. (2023). The Japanese Cooperation Agreement System in Practice: Derived from the US Plea Bargaining System but Different. *Global Journal of Comparative Law, 12*(1), 1–35.

Bar-Gill, O., & Ferrari, F. (2010). Informing Consumers about Themselves. *Erasmus Law Review, 3*, 93–119.

Bridge, S. (1999). Judicial Paternalism and Private Ordering on Divorce. *The Cambridge Law Journal, 58*(3), 495–497.

Brook, C. A., Fiannaca, B., Harvey, D., & Marcus, P. (2016). A Comparative Look at Plea Bargaining in Australia, Canada, England, New Zealand, and the United States. *William & Mary Law Review, 57*, 1147–1224.

Chin, M.-H., & Su, Y.-J. (2022). A Study on the Plea-Bargain System in the United States and How Can Taiwan Learn from Its Experiences. *Taipei University Law Review, 122*, 205–257.

Daly, K. (1989). Rethinking Judicial Paternalism: Gender, Work-Family Relations, and Sentencing. *Gender & Society, 3*(1), 9–36.

Dworkin, G. (2015). Defining Paternalism. In T. Schramme (Ed.), *New Perspectives on Paternalism and Health Care* (pp. 17–29). Springer.

Feinberg, J. (1971). Legal Paternalism. *Canadian Journal of Philosophy, 1*(1), 105–124.

Foote, D. H. (1992). The Benevolent Paternalism of Japanese Criminal Justice. *California Law Review, 80*, 317–390.

Gigerenzer, G. (2015). On the Supposed Evidence for Libertarian Paternalism. *Review of Philosophy and Psychology, 6*(3), 361–383.

Gramlich, J. (2019). *Only 2% of Federal Criminal Defendants Go to Trial, and Most Who Do Are Found Guilty*. Retrieved from Pew Research Center: https://www.pewresearch.org/fact-tank/2019/06/11/only-2-of-federal-criminal-defendants-go-to-trial-and-most-who-do-are-found-guilty/

Hausman, D., & Welch, B. (2010). Debate: To Nudge or Not to Nudge. *The Journal of Political Philosophy, 18*(1), 123–136.

Heron, C. A. (2020). How to Sue an Asue? Closing the Racial Wealth Gap Through the Transplantation of a Cultural Institution. *Michigan Journal of Race & Law, 26*(1), 171–203.

Hospers, J. (1980). Libertarianism and Legal Paternalism. *Journal of Libertarian Studies, 4*(3), 255–265.

Huang, T.-H. (2016). The Deconstruction and Reconstruction of Plea Bargaining. *China Law Journal, 242*, 25–70.

Husak, D. N. (2005). Legal Paternalism. In H. LaFollette (Ed.), *The Oxford Handbook of Practical Ethics* (pp. 387–412). Oxford University Press.

Kennedy, B. L. (2003). Walking the Fine Line in Taiwan's New Criminal Code. *American Journal of Chinese Studies, 10*(2), 111–117.

Kennedy, B. L. (2007). Long Hot Summer for Taiwan's Prosecutors. *American Journal of Chinese Studies, 14*(2), 135–152.

Kennedy, B. L., & Shen, C.-L. (2005). The Best of Times and the Worst of Times; Criminal Law Reform in Taiwan. *American Journal of Chinese Studies, 12*(2), 107–137.

King, E. (2004). Paternalism and the Law: Taking a Closer Look. *University College Dublin Law Review, 4*, 134–151.

Kronman, A. T. (1983). Paternalism and the Law of Contracts. *The Yale Law Journal, 92*(5), 763–798.

Kuo, M.-S., & Chen, H.-W. (2019). Killing in Your Name: Pathology of Judicial Paternalism and the Mutation of the "Most Serious Crimes" Requirement in Taiwan. In J. A. Cohen, W. P. Alford, & C.-F. Lo (Eds.), *Taiwan and International Human Rights: A Story of Transformation* (pp. 331–348). Springer.

Langer, M. (2004). From Legal Transplants to Legal Translations: The Globalization of Plea Bargaining and the Americanization Thesis in Criminal Procedure. *Harvard International Law Journal, 45*, 1–64.

Langer, M. (2021). Plea Bargaining, Conviction Without Trial, and the Global Administratization of Criminal Convictions. *Annual Review of Criminology, 4*, 377–411.

Lewis, M. K. (2009). Taiwan's New Adversarial System and the Overlooked Challenge of Efficiency-Driven Reforms. *Virginia Journal of International Law, 49*(3), 651–726.

Lewis, M. K. (2018). Forging Taiwan's Legal Identity. *Brooklyn Journal of International Law, 44*(2), 489–562.

Li, E. (2022). Haste Makes Waste: Why China's New Plea Leniency System Is Doomed to Fail. *Asian Journal of Comparative Law, 17*(1), 76–105.

Mitchell, G. (2005). Libertarian Paternalism Is an Oxymoron. *Northwestern University Law Review, 99*(3), 1245–1259.

Nahmias, Y. (2019). The Limitations of Information: Rethinking Soft Paternalistic Interventions in Copyright Law. *Cardozo Arts & Entertainment Law Journal, 37*(2), 373–413.

Oliver, A. (2013). From Nudging to Budging: Using Behavioural Economics to Inform Public Sector Policy. *Journal of Social Policy, 42*(4), 685–700.

Schwarcz, D. (2010). Regulating Consumers Demand in Insurance Markets. *Erasmus Law Review, 3*, 23–45.

Scott, R. E., & Stuntz, W. J. (1991). Plea Bargaining as Contract. *Yale Law Journal, 101*, 1909–1968.

Sunstein, C. R. (2014). *Why Nudge?: The Politics of Libertarian Paternalism.* Yale University Press.

Sunstein, C. R., & Thaler, R. H. (2003). Libertarian Paternalism Is Not an Oxymoron. *The University of Chicago Law Review, 70*(4), 1159–1202.

Su, K.-P. (2017). Criminal Court Reform in Taiwan: A Case of Fragmented Reform in a Not-fragmented Court System. *Washington International Law Journal, 27*(1), 203–240.

Tur, R. (1985). Paternalism and the Criminal Law. *Journal of Applied Philosophy, 2*(2), 173–189.

van Boom, W. H., & Ogus, A. (2010). Introducing, Defining and Balancing Autonomy v. Paternalism. *Erasmus Law Review, 3*(1), 1–5.

Wang, H.-Y. (2008). Plea Bargaining in Legal Sociological Perspective: The Case of Taiwan Criminal Judicial Reform. *National Taiwan University Law Journal, 37*(4), 65–113.

Wang, J.-P. (2011). The Evolution and Revolution of Taiwan's Criminal Justice. *Taiwan in Comparative Perspective, 3*, 8–29.

Wang, T.-S. (2002). The Legal Development of Taiwan in the 20th Century: Toward a Liberal and Democratic Country. *Pacific Rim Law and Policy Journal, 11*, 531–559.

Whelan, D. (2021). Application of the Paternalism Principle to Constitutional Rights: Mental Health Case-Law in Ireland. *European Journal of Health Law, 28*(3), 223–243.

Winkel, L. (2010). Forms of Imposed Protection in Legal History, Especially in Roman Law. *Fundamina: A Journal of Legal History, 16*(1), 578–587.

Yang, Y.-H. (2004a). Discussion on the Newly Added Bargaining Process in the Criminal Procedure (I). *Taiwan Jurist, 20*, 83–90.

Yang, Y.-H. (2004b). Discussion on the Newly Added Bargaining Process in the Criminal Procedure (II). *Taiwan Jurist, 21*, 98–107.

Zamir, E. (1998). The Efficiency of Paternalism. *Virginia Law Review, 84*(2), 229–286.

The Courts, the Prosecution, and the Defence in Plea-Based Case Dispositions in Hong Kong

Kevin Kwok-yin Cheng

Introduction

Hong Kong is the only common law jurisdiction in China. This is a legacy of British colonial rule in Hong Kong and the continuation of Hong Kong's legal system after the resumption of the exercise of sovereignty by the People's Republic of China (PRC) on 1 July 1997.[1] Currently Hong Kong is a special administrative region of the PRC, operating under the framework of 'one country, two systems',[2] meaning that while Hong Kong is a part of the PRC, it has a distinct legal system compared with the rest of the country.[3] One key distinction, as mentioned, is the continuation of the common law system. Article 8 of the Basic Law states: 'The laws previously in force in Hong Kong, that is, the common law, rules of equity, ordinances, subordinate legislation and customary law shall be

[1] Paragraph 1 of the Sino-British Joint Declaration.

[2] Preamble of the Basic Law of the Hong Kong Special Administrative Region of the People's Republic of China (hereafter 'Basic Law').

[3] The Macao Special Administrative Region also has a distinct legal system.

K. K. Cheng (✉)
Faculty of Law, The Chinese University of Hong Kong, Shatin, Hong Kong
e-mail: kevincheng@cuhk.edu.hk

E. Li et al. (eds.), *Criminal Case Dispositions through Pleas in Greater China*, https://doi.org/10.1007/978-981-97-1856-6_8

maintained, except for any that contravene this Law, and subject to any amendment by the legislature of the Hong Kong Special Administrative Region'. Likewise, the common law courts of Hong Kong have continued after the handover.[4]

Another distinction is the adversarial system for court trials in Hong Kong, which is typical of common law jurisdictions, differing from the inquisitorial system that is the practice in the PRC. In criminal cases in Hong Kong, the prosecution bears the burden of proof against the defendant. At the same time, there is a presumption of innocence in favour of the defendant. The presumption of innocence is encapsulated in the seminal English House of Lords case of *Woolmington v. DPP* (1935, pp. 481–482), which referred to the presumption of innocence as the 'golden thread' of English criminal law and the burden on the prosecution to prove the defendant's guilt as part of the common law of England.[5] This common law right also extends to Hong Kong. The presumption of innocence is moreover enshrined in Hong Kong's Basic Law. Article 87 of the Basic Law states: 'In criminal or civil proceedings in the Hong Kong Special Administrative Region, the principles previously applied in Hong Kong and the rights previously enjoyed by parties to proceedings shall be maintained'. It continues: 'Anyone who is lawfully arrested shall have the right to a fair trial by the judicial organs without delay and shall be presumed innocent until convicted by the judicial organs'. The Hong Kong Bill of Rights Ordinance (Cap. 383), which incorporated the provisions of the International Covenant on Civil and Political Rights (ICCPR) into domestic law,[6] also enshrines this presumption. Article 11(1) of the Hong Kong Bill of Rights Ordinance states:

[4] Article 81 of the Basic Law states: 'The judicial system previously practised in Hong Kong shall be maintained except for those changes consequent upon the establishment of the Court of Final Appeal of the Hong Kong Special Administrative Region'. The Court of Final Appeal replaced the Privy Council as Hong Kong's highest court post-handover.

[5] (1935) A.C. 462 at 481–482.

[6] Article 39 of the Basic Law states: 'The provisions of the International Covenant on Civil and Political Rights, the International Covenant on Economic, Social and Cultural Rights, and international labour conventions as applied to Hong Kong shall remain in force and shall be implemented through the laws of the Hong Kong Special Administrative Region. The rights and freedoms enjoyed by Hong Kong residents shall not be restricted unless as prescribed by law. Such restrictions shall not contravene the provisions of the preceding paragraph of this Article'. The Hong Kong Bill of Rights Ordinance (Cap. 383) came into force in 1991, six years before the handover.

'Everyone charged with a criminal offence shall have the right to be presumed innocent until proved guilty according to law'. Given all these provisions, it is clear that the presumption of innocence is meant to be a core feature of Hong Kong's justice system.

However, like other common law jurisdictions, although the adversarial trial is seemingly the method of criminal case dispositions, in reality, it is guilty pleas that play a significant role in resolving criminal cases before the courts. When a defendant pleads guilty, the prosecution need not prove its case in trial. The defendant will be convicted upon their own plea and will be sentenced accordingly. This chapter argues that while that law in Hong Kong protects the rights of defendants including the presumption of innocence, the right to legal counsel, and voluntariness of guilty pleas, the way that plea-based dispositions are structured in the criminal process gives a lot of power and leverage to judges, the prosecution, and even defence lawyers to encourage defendants into pleading guilty—and doing so as early as possible.

A Voluntary Guilty Plea

Under Hong Kong law, a guilty plea entered by the defendant must be voluntary. Hong Kong continues to follow the principles that are set out in the English case of *R v Turner* (1970).[7] In this case, the counsel for the defendant, after visiting the trial judge's chambers with the prosecutor, gave the defendant (Turner) advice regarding his plea decision. The defence counsel conveyed that if he pleaded guilty, then the sentence may be non-custodial, but if he were to contest his case at trial and lose, then his criminal record would be exposed and he would face the prospect of imprisonment. Although the defence counsel had maintained that the defendant had the final say in his plea decision, it was held that the defence counsel had given the defendant the impression that this was the judge's views, and consequently, the defendant was deemed to not have freedom of choice in his plea decision.

The Court held that while access between defence counsel and the judge must be maintained, these discussions must take place with the

[7] *R v Turner* (1970) 2 QB 321.

prosecution present and perhaps with the defence's solicitor present.[8] Any discussions between defence counsel and the judge that occurred should be disclosed to the defendant. Moreover, defence counsel must be free to give their clients the best legal advice that they can and may give such legal advice 'in strong terms'[9] (*R v Turner*, 1970, p. 327), including the advice that a guilty plea is a mitigating factor which may lead to a lesser sentence. The judge should not indicate the sentence that would be imposed following a guilty plea and that a harsher sentence would be imposed following a conviction post-trial. This may be seen as undue pressure on the defendant to plead guilty. The only exception is that the judge may indicate that a sentence will not take a certain form, such as a custodial sentence, regardless of whether the defendant pleads guilty or not guilty. It is maintained that the defendant, after considering legal advice, must be free to choose their own plea decision. If a guilty plea is found to not have resulted from the defendant's free choice, then it should be treated as a nullity. This position is reiterated by the Hong Kong courts. For example, *Lam Yin* (1995, p. 20) states:

> It is axiomatic that a plea of guilty should be entered voluntarily. If, at the time a defendant is required to plead, he is subjected to such pressure that he does not genuinely have a free choice between pleading guilty and not guilty, his plea is a nullity. The same is true if the defendant pleads guilty only because the true facts have been seriously misrepresented to him.[10]

When the defendant is called for a plea arraignment, the charge is read to the defendant and the defendant will be asked by the court whether the charge is understood. If the defendant answers in the affirmative, then the defendant is asked for their plea decision. The indictment may be explained, if necessary, by the magistrate, the Registrar, or the interpreter of the court.[11] If the defendant is represented, then it is their solicitor's responsibility to ensure that they understand the charge. The guilty plea must come from the defendant's own mouth and the defendant must clearly answer by stating the words 'guilty' or 'not guilty'. A nod or shake

[8] Hong Kong, like England and Wales, maintains the split legal profession between barristers and solicitors.

[9] *Turner* at 327.

[10] *R v Lam Yin* (1995) 2 HKCLR 124 at 20.

[11] Section 49(2) of the Criminal Procedure Ordinance (Cap. 221).

of the head by the defendant is not acceptable. Likewise, a long ramble by the defendant is not acceptable. A legal representative for the defendant must not enter a guilty plea on behalf of the individual defendant (So, 2022, p. 191).[12] If a clear plea has not been made, then the court may enter a plea of not guilty on the defendant's behalf. If there is an equivocal plea made by the defendant—that is, if the defendant adds a qualification to the guilty plea, which if found to be true might show that the defendant was not guilty of the offence charged—then the court must not accept it. The court has no discretion in this matter and must refuse an equivocal guilty plea. If an unequivocal guilty plea has been made, then until sentence is passed, the court has the discretion to permit the change of the guilty plea into a not guilty plea. This discretion is not to be exercised lightly, but rather only in 'clear cases and very sparingly' (*HKSAR v Chan Chi Ho Lincoln*, 2018, p. 40).[13] The facts upon which the conviction is based on should also be read out in open court to the defendant and acknowledged by the defendant as being true (*R v Siu Kwong-Wing*, 1993).[14]

Hong Kong arguably adopts a more conservative position in maintaining that defendants must be prevented from undue pressure in their plea decisions compared to England and Wales. In England and Wales, the defence can seek an indication from the judge and judges can indicate the maximum sentence that would be imposed if the defendant pleads guilty at that stage in the proceedings. The indication should be given in open court. The judge, however, may refuse to give an indication when asked or reserve their position to give it at a later time, and the judge must refrain from indicating a maximum possible sentence following a conviction after trial. Generally, once a sentence indication is given, it is binding on the presiding judge and subsequent judges who handle the case for a reasonable period of time (*R v Goodyear*, 2005).[15] Such advanced sentence indications, referred to as *Goodyear indications*, have not been adopted in Hong Kong. Hong Kong courts are keen not to have an appearance that the defendant makes a 'bargain' with the court.

[12] So, S. (2022). *Knight and Upham: Criminal Litigation in Hong Kong, Fourth Edition*. Hong Kong: Sweet & Maxwell, p. 191.

[13] *HKSAR v Chan Chi Ho Lincoln* (2018) 21 HKCFAR 588 at 40.

[14] *R v Siu Kwong-Wing* (1993) 2 HKCLR 94.

[15] *R v Goodyear* (2005) 3 All ER 117.

This is best exemplified by the statement made by Silke JA in the case of *Scales* (1987, pp. 587–588):

> It is of major importance that there be no appearance of a defendant striking a bargain with the court ... we take to mean an indication from a trial judge that if a man pleads guilty he will get one sentence and if he does not, and is convicted after trial, he will get another and more severe one. Anything of that nature would be quite wrong.[16]

It is true that the sentencing judge would not in each case tell the defendant, or the defence lawyer, that if the defendant pleads guilty, he or she would receive one sentence, whereas if he or she pleads not guilty but is eventually convicted after trial, he or she would receive a more severe sentence. Nonetheless, as a general rule, the reduction in sentence defendants who plead guilty would receive is referred to as a sentence discount. So, in this sense, defendants who plead guilty would receive a more lenient sentence than they otherwise would have had they opted for trial but ultimately lost.

Sentence Discounts for Guilty Pleas

A guilty plea at the first available opportunity would likely lead to a one-third sentence discount. This would mean that a defendant who pleaded guilty at the first available opportunity would generally receive a sentence that is one-third less than he or she would otherwise receive had they been convicted after trial. A one-third sentence discount is not insignificant, especially in criminal cases that would attract long years of imprisonment. Take the offence of trafficking in dangerous drugs for example, if a defendant is convicted of trafficking 400–600 grammes of heroin contrary to section 4 of the Dangerous Drugs Ordinance (Cap. 134), the sentencing guidelines indicate that the customary sentence for 400–600 grammes of heroin corresponds with 15–20 years of imprisonment (*R v Lau Tak-ming & Ors*, 1990).[17] Even taking the low end of the spectrum, the starting point of a sentence would be 15 years for 400 grammes of heroin.

[16] *R v Scales* (1987) HKLR 583, (1987) HKCU 179 at pp. 587–588.

[17] *R v Lau Tak-ming and Ors* (1990) 2 HKLR 370, (1990) HKCU 399.

Removing any other considerations of aggravating or mitigating factors,[18] this would mean that if a defendant pleads guilty at the first opportunity, he or she would face 10 years imprisonment. If the defendant decides to go to trial but still loses, then the defendant faces 15 years imprisonment. That is a difference of 5 years based on the one decision by the defendant to plead guilty or not. If the trafficked amount of heroin is even higher, say from 4000 grammes to 15,000 grammes (which corresponds with an imprisonment range of 26–30 years) (*HKSAR v Abdallah Anwar Abbas*, 2009),[19] and if this time the high end of the spectrum is taken, namely 15,000 grammes, a one-third sentence discount could mean the difference of 10 years imprisonment![20]

Scholars have criticised such a substantial plea-trial difference as a 'trial penalty' on defendants who exercise their constitutional right to a fair trial (Johnson, 2019; Kim, 2015; Tata & Gormley, 2020).[21] As noted above, in Hong Kong, 'Anyone who is lawfully arrested shall have the right to a fair trial by the judicial organs'.[22] However, in exercising the right to a fair trial and putting the state's case to the test before the courts, defendants face the prospect of a more severe sentence if they are convicted post-trial. Welsh, Skinns, and Sanders, although writing in the context of the English criminal justice system, puts it more bluntly by stating that: 'The most naked attempt to persuade defendants to plead guilty lies in the sentencing principle established by the courts that defendants

[18] Aggravating factors are factors which may inflate a sentence whereas mitigating factors are factors which may reduce the sentence. In Hong Kong, a guilty plea is a potent mitigating factor.

[19] *HKSAR v Abdallah Anwar Abbas* (2009) 2 HKLRD 437, (2009) 2 HKC 197.

[20] The sentence discount is not limited to imprisonment but is applicable to fines as well.

[21] B. D. Johnson, 'Trials and tribulations: the trial tax and the process of punishment' (2019) 48 *Crime and Justice*, 313–63; A. C. Kim, 'Underestimating the trial penalty: an empirical analysis of the federal trial penalty and critique of the Abrams study' (2015) 84 *Mississippi Law Review*, 1195–256; C. Tata and J. Gormley, 'To plead or not to plead? "Guilt" is the question: rethinking sentencing and plea-decision making in Anglo American countries', in C. Spohn and P. K. Brennan (eds), *Handbook on Sentencing Policies and Practices in the 21st Century* (New York, NY: Routledge, 2020).

[22] Article 87 of the Basic Law.

pleading guilty…should receive a lighter sentence than those convicted after a contested trial' (Welsh et al., 2021, p. 358).[23]

Indeed, the sentence discount is to be communicated to defendants in Hong Kong. The sentencing court should always indicate the starting point adopted for a sentence with precision and how and on what basis that it is reducing that sentence (Cross & Cheung, 2022).[24] It would not be correct for a judge to simply indicate the starting point of a sentence by way of a range. This would make it difficult to ascertain the actual amount of the sentence discount that was given (Cross & Cheung, 2022).[25] Where a sentencing judge is providing a lesser sentence discount than the customary one-third sentence discount, then the judge must provide reasons for why this is the case (*HKSAR v Shaer Chun-keung*, 1998).[26] At the same time, it has been said by the courts that the one-third sentence discount is a 'high watermark', and in only exceptional cases where a sentence discount would exceed one-third for a timely guilty plea (*HKSAR v Chow Yuen Fai*, 2010).[27] In other words, the one-third sentence discount is known and expected for a guilty plea. By making the starting point of sentence and the sentence discount explicit, the courts in essence are communicating to all defendants that upon a timely guilty plea, there will be a reduced sentence.

Although, as previously discussed, Hong Kong courts are hesitant to appear that they are influencing the plea decisions of defendants by indicating that there will be a particular sentence if he or she pleads guilty but upon a conviction post-trial he or she would receive another more severe sentence, in effect, the customary sentence discount does exactly this—a lesser sentence for those who plead guilty and a more severe sentence most likely for those who do not. The only difference is that this plea-trial difference is not communicated to each defendant separately before they make their plea decisions, and that defendants would not know the exact sentence that he or she would ultimately receive, i.e.

[23] L. Welsh, L. Skinns, and A. Sanders. *Sanders & Young's Criminal Justice*, 5th edn (Oxford: Oxford University Press, 2021), p. 358.

[24] G. Cross and P. S. W. Cheung, *Sentencing in Hong Kong*, 10th edn (Hong Kong: LexisNexis, 2022).

[25] Ibid.

[26] *HKSAR v Shaer Chun-keung* (1998) 1 HKLRD 348.

[27] *HKSAR v Chow Yuen Fai* (2010) 1 HKLRD 354, (2010) 1 HKC 181 at 31.

there are not two clear and distinct alternative sentences on the table. However, defendants know that a guilty plea would most likely result in a more lenient sentence because the customary sentence discount is made publicly known, whether this is by sentencing remarks in open court or read in court judgments, or even—as will be discussed later—made known by criminal defence lawyers.

Previously, a defendant would receive a one-third sentence discount from the first available opportunity where the plea is taken up until the day of trial. Nowadays, the timing of when a guilty plea is entered takes on extra importance as it corresponds directly to the amount of sentence discount that is awarded. The change is reflected in the cases of *Ngo Van Nam* (2016) and *Abdou Maikido Abdoulkarim* (2016), which were heard jointly.[28] A one-third sentence discount is retained if the defendant pleads guilty at the first available opportunity such as during the plea arraignment in the Magistrates' Courts, the plea day in the District Court, or in the committal proceedings prior if the case is committed to the Court of First Instance. The Magistrates' Courts are the lowest criminal courts in Hong Kong. It can hear summary offences and offences triable either summarily or by indictment, if the prosecution elects for the case to be tried summarily. It can impose a maximum sentence of two years imprisonment, up to three in some special circumstances, and a maximum fine of HK$100,000.[29] All criminal cases start in the Magistrates' Courts even if the cases are more serious. These cases would just be transferred or committed to the other courts. The District Court can try indictable offences and can impose a maximum sentence of seven years imprisonment.[30] The Court of First Instance hears the most serious criminal cases and has unlimited criminal jurisdiction to try cases on indictment.[31]

However, according to *Ngo Van Nam* (2016),[32] if a trial date has already been fixed and but before the first day of trial, then the sentence discount is reduced to one-quarter. This would mean that the defendant initially pleaded not guilty and then changed the plea to one of

[28] *HKSAR v Ngo Van Nam; HKSAR v Abdou Maikido Abdoulkarim* (2016) 5 HKLRD 1; (2016) HKCA 397.

[29] Section 92 of the Magistrates Ordinance (Cap. 227).

[30] Section 82 of the District Court Ordinance (Cap. 336).

[31] Section 3(2) of the High Court Ordinance (Cap. 4).

[32] (2016) 5 HKLRD 1; (2016) HKCA 397.

guilty. If the defendant waits until the first day of trial and then pleads guilty, then the sentence discount is reduced to one-fifth. If the trial has already commenced and then the defendant pleads guilty, then the sentence discount is to be less than one-fifth. The sentencing judge has overriding discretion, but it is clear from the sentencing guidelines that the timing of guilty pleas matter, where the earlier the defendant pleads guilty, the greater the sentence discount the defendant will most likely get (Cheng, 2023; Ri & Cheng, 2022).[33] If the defendant wants to retain the one-third sentence discount, then the defendant should plead guilty as soon as possible.

This approach that was adopted by Hong Kong's Court of Appeal in 2016, which will be referred to a sliding scale of sentence discounts, follows the approach that is adopted in England and Wales. In its 2007 definitive guideline on sentence reductions for guilty pleas by the then Sentencing Guidelines Council, a one-third sentence discount is to be given when a guilty plea is indicated at the first reasonable opportunity. The sentence discount is reduced to one-quarter is admitted after the first reasonable opportunity but before a trial date has been fixed. When the guilty plea is indicated at the 'door of the court' or after the trial has already begun, then the sentence discount is to be reduced to one-tenth (Sentence Council, 2007).[34] The Sentence Council for England and Wales, succeeding the Sentencing Guidelines Council, issued a new definitive guideline that took effect in 2017. The approach is similar: if the defendant pleads guilty at the first stage of the proceedings, a one-third sentence discount is retained. After the first stage of proceedings, the sentence discount is reduced to one-quarter. If the guilty plea is indicated on the first day of trial, then the sentence discount is further reduced to one-tenth. If the guilty plea is made after the trial has begun, then the

[33] Although in *Ngo Van Nam*, it is emphasised that the sentencing judge or magistrate has overriding discretion, empirical evidence in Hong Kong suggests that sentencing judges adhere quite closely to the prescribed sliding scale of sentence discounts for guilty pleas. See K. K. Cheng, *The Timing of Guilty Pleas: Lessons from Common Law Jurisdictions* (Cambridge: Cambridge University Press, in press); S. Ri, & K. K. Cheng, 'Plea discounts deviations: A mechanism for gender disparities in Hong Kong', (2022) *17 Asian Journal of Criminology*, 237–261.

[34] Sentencing Guidelines Council, *Reduction in Sentence for Guilty Plea: Definitive Guideline* (London: Sentencing Guidelines Secretariat, 2007).

sentence discount is reduced further or there may even be no sentence discount (Sentence Council, 2017).[35]

It should be noted that Hong Kong does not possess the equivalent of a Sentencing Council. Therefore, the guidelines for the sliding scale of sentence discount are made by the Hong Kong Court of Appeal.[36] Indeed, in the case of *Ngo Van Nam* (2016, p. 198), the Court of Appeal made references to the sentencing guidelines in England and Wales. The Court stated: 'There is no doubt that the utilitarian value of a plea of guilty is greater the earlier the plea of guilty is intimated or tendered. The authorities to which we have referred speak with one voice in that respect'.[37] The authorities cited include the Sentencing Guidelines Council's definitive guideline for sentence reductions for guilty pleas and related English court cases, as well as cases from other jurisdictions such as Scotland and Australia.[38]

The Court of Appeal touted the utilitarian benefits of encouraging earlier guilty pleas. This echoes previous Hong Kong court cases. For instance, Bokhary JA remarked in *Chan* Chi-sing (1995, p. 326): 'For one thing, a guilty plea removes the question of guilt or innocence from the consideration of the courts whether at trial or on appeal...And even a very late plea does save some time even if not as much as it would have saved had it come earlier'.[39] This also echoes the statement of purpose in the 2007 English Sentencing Guideline Council's (2007, paragraph 2.2) definitive guideline, which stated:

> A reduction in sentence is appropriate because a guilty plea avoids the need for a trial (thus enabling other cases to be disposed of more expeditiously), shortens the gap between charge and sentence, saves considerable cost, and, in the case of an early plea, saves victims and witnesses from the concern about having to give evidence. The reduction principle derives

[35] Sentencing Council, *Reduction in Sentence for Guilty Plea: Definitive Guideline* (London: Sentencing Council, 2017).

[36] The main role of the Sentencing Council for England and Wales is to issue sentencing guidelines, which the courts must follow. The Sentencing Council is part of the United Kingdom's Ministry of Justice arm's-length bodies.

[37] *HKSAR v Ngo Van Nam; HKSAR v Abdou Maikido Abdoulkarim* (2016) 5 HKLRD 1; (2016) HKCA 397 at 198.

[38] E.g. *R v Caley* (2013) 2 Cr App R (S) 305.

[39] *R v Chan Chi-sing* (1995) 3 HKC 325 at p. 326.

from the need for the *effective administration of justice* and not as an aspect of mitigation (Emphasis added).[40]

If every defendant opts to have the state's case against them tested in trial, then it is believed that the courts would simply be unable to cope with the volume of matters which needs to be heard. After all, a contested trial, where witnesses are called and cross-examined, takes time, whereas a guilty plea is a much quicker process. In short, the sentence discount and, in particular, the sliding scale of sentence discounts for guilty pleas, operate with the aim of saving costs and encouraging defendants to plead guilty as early as possible (Cheng, 2023; Cheng et al., 2018).[41]

It is interesting to note that while Hong Kong followed the framework of a 'quantified' sliding scale of sentence discounts set up by England and Wales, other common law jurisdictions have resisted such an approach. For instance, the Supreme Court of New Zealand in the seminal case of *Hessell* (2010)[42] overturned the New Zealand Court of Appeal's decision to set out a sliding scale of sentence discounts for guilty pleas much like the sliding scale of sentence discounts that England, Wales and Hong Kong currently possess. The New Zealand Supreme Court was concerned that such encouragement to get defendants to plead guilty as early as possible would serve pressure on innocent defendants to plead guilty to crimes that they had not committed (*Hessell v R*, 2010, p. 60; Cheng, 2013).[43] This is not to say that the timing of guilty pleas does not matter in New Zealand. Rather, it is preferred that all circumstances of the case be taken into account instead of placing the main emphasis on just the stage of when the defendant pleaded guilty.

[40] Sentencing Guidelines Council, *Reduction in Sentence for Guilty Plea: Definitive Guideline* (London: Sentencing Guidelines Secretariat, 2007), paragraph 2.2.

[41] K. K. Cheng, *The Timing of Guilty Pleas: Lessons from Common Law Jurisdictions* (Cambridge: Cambridge University Press, in press); K. K. Cheng, W. H. Chui, S. N. M. Young, & R. Ong, 'Why do criminal trials "crack"? An empirical investigation of late guilty pleas in Hong Kong' (2018) *13 Asian Journal of Comparative Law*, 1–25.

[42] *Hessell v R* (2010) NZSC 135.

[43] Ibid. at 60. See also K. K. Cheng, 'Pressures to plead guilty: Factors affecting plea decisions in Hong Kong's Magistrates' Courts', (2013) *53 British Journal of Criminology*, 257–275.

The Prosecution

Article 63 of the Basic Law states: 'The Department of Justice of the Hong Kong Special Administrative Region shall control criminal prosecutions, free from any interference'. The decision to prosecute or not, and what charges against the defendant should proceed, is an important decision that the prosecution must make. This decision is so paramount that the Basic Law guarantees that the Department of Justice is to control criminal prosecutions free from any interference. This means that the Government of the Hong Kong Special Administrative Region or the courts of Hong Kong shall not interfere. According to the Prosecution Code issued by the Hong Kong Department of Justice, the decision to prosecution involves the two-tiered test of sufficiency of evidence and the public interest.

When determining whether there is sufficient evidence to support a prosecution, the prosecutor must decide whether the evidence demonstrates a reasonable prospect of conviction. Prospective judgements need to be made about matters including: the evidence available; any challenge that may be made to the admissibility or the reliability of such evidence; the availability, competence, and credibility of witnesses, and how the court will likely assess the witness; contrary evidence that may reasonably be anticipated; likely defences that may be raised by the defence; and the way that the court will likely act after weighing all the evidence raised and arguments made in the case.[44] In relation to witnesses, the prosecutor will need to consider other matters such as: the reliability of the witness's memory; any favourable or unfavourable association with the defendant; any motive for not telling the truth; any exaggeration in their statements; their availability to attend trial; and their vulnerability to attack by the defence.[45] After all, if the case goes to trial, it will be an adversarial trial.

Where there is deemed to be sufficient evidence for a reasonable prospect of conviction, the prosecutor must then consider whether the prosecution is in the public interest. It is noted that there can be no exhaustive definition for what constitutes the public interest. However, the Prosecution Code provides a number of factors for prosecutors to consider. They include: the nature and circumstances of the offence; the seriousness of the offence, where the more serious the offence, or more

[44] Paragraph 5.5 of the Prosecution Code.

[45] Paragraph 5.6 of the Prosecution Code.

serious the harm caused, then the more likely that prosecution serves the public interest; any delays in the proceeding with the prosecution and its causes; any cooperation with law enforcement agencies from the suspect, where the public interest may be served by not prosecuting suspects that have cooperated with law enforcement in the prosecution of others; the attitude, the nature, or physical or psychological condition of the suspect, a witness, and/or the victim; and the prevalence of the offence in question and potential deterrent effect that a prosecution may bring.[46] The public interest test is based on the Criminal Procedure Ordinance (Cap. 221) which states that the Secretary for Justice, who is the head of the Hong Kong Department of Justice, shall not be bound to prosecute a defendant in any case which, in his or her opinion, the public interest does not require him or her to interfere.[47] This provision extends to the Director of Public Prosecutions, who is the head of the Prosecutions Division of the Department of Justice,[48] and to prosecutors who are acting on behalf of the Secretary for Justice.

Although Hong Kong operates an adversarial system or accusatorial litigation system, this does not mean the prosecutor should be seeking to 'win' the case or obtain a conviction at all costs. Rather, in litigation, the prosecutor's role is to have all relevant and credible evidence placed fully and intelligibly before the court; assist the court with an accurate and complete submissions of the law; refrain from expressing any personal opinion especially towards the guilt of the defendant; and if it becomes reasonably apparent that there is no longer a reasonable prospect of conviction, invite the courts to stop the proceedings.[49] A prosecutor in a contested trial is still, however, entitled to advocate firmly and, if need be, attack the position of the defence or evidence raised by the defence.[50] The proper role of the prosecutor is to act on behalf of the community

46 Paragraph 5.9 of the Prosecution Code.

47 Section 15(1) of the Criminal Procedure Ordinance (Cap. 221).

48 The Prosecutions Division is the largest division in the Department of Justice. Other divisions include the Law Drafting Division, Civil Division, and International Law Division.

49 Paragraph 3.5 of the Prosecution Code.

50 Paragraph 3.3 of the Prosecution Code.

and fairly and objectively assist the court in arriving at the truth to do justice. The prosecutor's role is that of a 'minister of justice'.[51]

As mentioned above, it is the prosecution that bears the burden of proof in criminal cases. The standard of proof is beyond a reasonable doubt. The standard of proof of beyond a reasonable doubt has been described in this way in the classic case of Miller v Minister of Pensions (1947)[52]:

> It need not reach certainty, but it must carry a high degree of probability. Proof beyond reasonable doubt does not mean proof beyond the shadow of a doubt. The law would fail to protect the community if it admitted fanciful possibilities to deflect the course of justice. If the evidence is so strong against a man as to leave only a remote possibility in his favour which can be dismissed with the sentence 'of course it is possible, but not in the least probable', the case is proved beyond reasonable doubt, but nothing short of that will suffice. (*Miller v Minister of Pensions*, 1947, p. 373)[53]

Proof beyond a reasonable doubt is a higher standard than the standard of proof in civil cases, where the standard of proof is 'on a balance of probabilities' which has been described to mean: 'If the evidence is such that the tribunal can say: "We think it more probable than not," the burden is discharged, but, if the probabilities are equal, it is not' (*Miller v Minister of Pensions*, 1947: 374).[54]

The prosecution's decision to prosecute and its decision on what charges to proceed with is inexorably linked with the defendant's decision to plead guilty or not. The Prosecution Code, under the heading 'Plea Negotiation and Agreement', states that the prosecution may be invited by the defence to resolve the case where the defendant agrees to plead guilty to lesser charges or fewer charges that have been laid against the defendant.[55] For instance, this could mean the prosecution dropping certain charges in a multiple charge case in return for the defendant pleading guilty to the remaining charges. This practice is what scholars

[51] Paragraph 3.1 of the Prosecution Code.

[52] (1947) 2 All ER 372.

[53] Ibid. at p. 373.

[54] Ibid. at p. 374.

[55] Paragraph 13.1 of the Prosecution Code.

refer to as charge bargaining (Welsh et al., 2021).[56] To proceed, the prosecutor must be satisfied that: there is admissible evidence to prove the charges against the defendant regarding the charges to which pleas of guilty have been offered; the charges adequately reflect the criminality of the defendant's alleged conduct; and the charges provide the court with adequate scope to impose sentences that are appropriate in addressing the criminality of the defendant.[57] Plea negotiations, however, must not be accepted by the prosecution if the defendant maintains his/her innocence against the charges.[58]

Where there are plea negotiations that are being discussed by the defence and the prosecution, the prosecutor should consult, if appropriate, the investigator in charge of the case, or if any, the victim of the crime. The prosecutor may take the views of the investigator or the victim into account. Investigations are conducted by law enforcement agencies in Hong Kong, such as by the Hong Kong Police Force, the Immigration Department, and the Independent Commission against Corruption. However, the decision regarding accepting guilty pleas is still for the prosecution to make.[59] In no way should the investigator or victim give 'instructions' to the prosecution. The relationship between the prosecution and the investigators differs from a lawyer-client relationship, meaning that investigators are not the 'clients' of the prosecution.[60] Investigators in Hong Kong gather the evidence and other materials upon which the prosecution relies. The investigative and prosecutorial functions are separate and distinct.[61] Though, that is not to say that there are no consultations and cooperation between the two. Indeed, in practice there are continuous consultations between investigators and prosecutors. Prosecutors may request further investigations be conducted by the investigators. What the prosecution in Hong Kong cannot do is to take charge and directly lead the investigation. On a similar vein, investigators receive advice from the prosecution with respect to the law and evidence.

[56] L. Welsh, L. Skinns, and A. Sanders. *Sanders & Young's Criminal Justice*, 5th edn (Oxford: Oxford University Press, 2021).

[57] Paragraph 13.1 of the Prosecution Code.

[58] Paragraph 13.4 of the Prosecution Code.

[59] Paragraph 13.5 of the Prosecution Code.

[60] Paragraph 4.1 of the Prosecution Code.

[61] Paragraph 4.2 of the Prosecution Code.

The prosecution may advise on matters such as the appropriateness of the charges, the admissibility of evidence, the present state of the law, and the appropriate venue for trial.[62]

Although, the prosecutor's role is that of a 'minister of justice' and bears the higher standard of proof of beyond a reasonable doubt, if the defendant pleads guilty—whether resulting from plea negotiations or not—the prosecution need not prove its case in trial. The justification for accepting pleas from the prosecution's point of view, as stipulated in the Prosecution Code, is that time and expenses can be saved, victims and other witnesses are spared from needing to testify in court, and the criminal justice process operates more efficiently.[63]

Defence Lawyers

Article 35 of the Basic Law states that: 'Hong Kong residents shall have the right to confidential legal advice, access to the courts, choice of lawyers for timely protection of their lawful rights and interests or for representation in the courts, and to judicial remedies'. Having legal advice and legal representation in court proceedings are certainly important in protecting the rights and interests of defendants. Where defendants are unable to afford legal representation, Hong Kong provides publicly funded defence lawyers. This is in accordance with Article 11(2)(d) of the Hong Kong Bill of Rights Ordinance (Cap. 383), which states that everyone charged with a criminal offence is entitled:

> ...to defend himself in person or through legal assistance of his own choosing; to be informed, if he does not have legal assistance, of this right; and to have legal assistance assigned to him, in any case where the interests of justice so require, and without payment by him in any such case if he does not have sufficient means to pay for it.

If the defendant does not have sufficient means and where the interests of justice require, then publicly funded defence lawyers may be assigned to assist and represent such indigent defendants.

Legal aid for criminal cases is provided for by the Legal Aid Department in Hong Kong. A publicly funded solicitor and, if necessary, a

[62] Paragraph 4.3 of the Prosecution Code.

[63] Paragraph 13.3 of the Prosecution Code.

barrister is provided to represent the defendant in the District Court, the Court of First Instance, and all criminal appeals. Representation by a legal aid lawyer is not available for Magistrates' Court cases except for committal proceedings in the Magistrates' Courts: that is, where serious criminal cases are being committed to the Court of First Instance from the Magistrates' Court for hearing. Hong Kong continues to maintain the split profession of solicitors and barristers like that of England and Wales (Ip, 2017).[64] Applicants who pass both a means test and a merits test are eligible to receive legal aid. The means test is determined by the applicant's financial resources, where it does not exceed the financial eligibility limit set by the Legal Aid Department.[65] The merits test provides that, for trials in the District Court or Court of First Instance, legal aid will be granted if it is desirable in the interests of justice to do so. For appeal cases, legal aid will likewise be granted if it is in the interests of justice to do so and there are reasonable grounds for appeal.

Publicly funded lawyers in the Magistrates' Courts are provided for by the Duty Lawyer Service through the Duty Lawyer Scheme. The Scheme covers around three hundred statutory and common law offences. Defendants can approach the Court Liaison Office situated in each Magistrates' Courts. For defendants remanded in custody, they will be approached by a staff member of the Court Liaison Office on the day of their first court appearance. Defendants charged with an offence covered by the Scheme are provided with legal representation if they wish for their first court appearance without any means testing. There is then a means test or a financial eligibility test for subsequent appearances.[66] After passing the means test, applicants are only required to pay a one-off handling fee and they will be provided with legal representation no matter how long the trial lasts.

64 See E. C. Ip, 'Legal profession and representation' in W. H. Chui and T. W. Lo (eds) *Understanding Criminal Justice in Hong Kong*, 2nd edn (London: Routledge, 2017).

65 The eligibility limit may be waived by the Director of Legal Aid if the Director is satisfied that it is in the interests of justice to do so and where the applicant will be subject to higher contribution rates.

66 The Administrator of the Duty Lawyer Service has the discretion to waive the means test of a defendant if the Administrator considers that it is in the interest of justice to do so.

Although publicly funded lawyers for the Duty Lawyer Scheme and many legal aid lawyers are drawn from private practice, there is a perception by defendants in Hong Kong that they are on the side of the state and publicly funded lawyers are useful only to suggest to the court mitigation factors in order to receive a more lenient sentence after pleading guilty. In interviews with defendants in Hong Kong, past studies found that there is a degree of mistrust between defendants and publicly funded lawyers from the Duty Lawyer Scheme where the former regards the latter as government employees. There is a sense that publicly funded lawyers' questioning of their clients resembles that of police officers or prosecutors, leading to animosity from both sides. Moreover, defendants felt that publicly funded lawyers were not primarily concerned with securing an acquittal for them, rather more focused on explaining the benefits of a sentence discount for a guilty plea. However, defendants revealed that seeking legal representation from publicly funded lawyers was still useful because the lawyers can assist them in plea mitigation to the courts. If the defendant pleads guilty, then a publicly funded lawyer is sufficient, but if the defendant seeks to contest the prosecution's case in trial, they are better off seeking a private lawyer (Cheng et al., 2015, 2018).[67]

It is the duty of defence lawyers to advise their clients about guilty plea decisions regardless of whether they are privately instructed or acting as a publicly funded lawyer. Under the Bar Code of Conduct published by the Hong Kong Bar Association, barristers in Hong Kong must advise their clients about their plea decisions. While it is stressed that the client has the responsibility for and the complete freedom of choice in making the plea decision, barristers are 'entitled to refer to all aspects of the case and where appropriate he may advise his client in *strong terms* that he is unlikely to escape conviction and that a plea of guilty is generally regarded by the Court as a mitigating factor (emphasis added)'.[68] Proper legal advice entails stating to clients in strong terms the consequences of not pleading guilty, namely the unlikelihood of acquittal. Additionally, the notion that guilty pleas are regarded as a mitigating factor refers to the

[67] K. K. Cheng, W. H. Chui, and R. Ong, 'Providing justice for low-income youths: Publicly funded lawyers and youth clients in Hong Kong', (2015) *24 Social & Legal Studies*, 577–593; K. K. Cheng, W. H. Chui, S. N. M. Young, & R. Ong, 'Why do criminal trials "crack"? An empirical investigation of late guilty pleas in Hong Kong' (2018) *13 Asian Journal of Comparative Law*, 1–25.

[68] 10.56(a) of the Bar Code of Conduct of the Hong Kong Bar Association.

sentence discount for guilty pleas. It is the duty of the barrister to make it known to their clients and advise them about the sentence discount. There is a similar duty on solicitors in Hong Kong as well. Under the Hong Kong Solicitors' Guide to Professional Conduct published by the Law Society of Hong Kong, 'Advice may be given in a *strong and persuasive manner* but the client must be left with the clear understanding that he has the right to choose how to plead and whether to give evidence (emphasis added)'.[69] Although it is emphasised in the respective professional codes of conduct and in case law that the decision to plead guilty is ultimately one for the defendant to make, Tata acutely observed that the lawyer-client relationship is often not an equal one in terms of knowledge and information, and lay clients will not commonly question their legal representative's legal advice (Tata, 2007).[70]

Past studies in England and Wales and in Hong Kong have found defence lawyers to be a main, if not the most vital influence, in defendants pleading guilty (Baldwin & McConville, 1977; Cheng et al., 2018; McConville et al., 1994; Newman, 2013).[71] In interviews with criminal defence lawyers in Hong Kong, whether they be barristers or solicitors, the lawyers have touted the benefits of guilty pleas and plea bargaining. Defence lawyers pointed to the undesirability of contested trials, where the outcome is less certain, and how guilty pleas and plea bargaining allows the case to be dealt with as expediently as possible, which is desirable for both the criminal justice system and for defendants. The defendant can save on legal costs, the stress on having to face a criminal conviction, and perhaps time spent remanded in custody if denied bail. Moreover, although the Hong Kong courts do not explicitly promote the use of plea bargaining, it is understood by criminal defence lawyers

[69] Commentary 2 on Rule 10.16 of the Hong Kong Solicitors' Guide to Professional Conduct, vol. 1.

[70] C. Tata 'In the interests of clients or commerce? Legal aid, supply, demand, and "ethical indeterminacy" in criminal defence work' (2007) *34 Journal of Law and Society*, 489–519.

[71] E.g. D. Newman, *Legal Aid Lawyers and the Quest for Justice* (Oxford: Hart Publishing, 2013); J. Baldwin and M. McConville, *Negotiated Justice: Pressures to Plead Guilty* (London: Martin Robertson, 1977); K. K. Cheng et al., 'Why do criminal trials "crack"? An empirical investigation of late guilty pleas in Hong Kong' (2018) 13 *Asian Journal of Comparative Law*, 1–25; M. McConville et al., *Standing Accused: The Organisation and Practices of Criminal Defence Lawyers in Britain* (Oxford: Clarendon Press, 1994).

to be implicitly tolerated. It is rare for a magistrate or a judge to refuse a plea bargain that has been agreed upon between the prosecution and the defence (Cheng, 2014).[72]

Conclusion

Although Hong Kong's criminal justice system touts its adversariness, the voluntariness of the defendant's plea decision, and the presumption of innocence in favour of the defendant, it can be seen that key actors in the criminal justice system, namely that of judges and magistrates, prosecutors and even defence lawyers, have considerable leverage over defendants to encourage them to plead guilty as early as possible. For the courts, the sentence discount is a powerful factor that encourages defendants to plead guilty. A one-third sentence discount, or even a one-quarter or one-fifth sentence discount can be a considerable reduction in the length of time served behind bars. Prosecutors make the powerful decision of whether to prosecute and which criminal charges to proceed with. They can also engage in 'plea negotiations and agreements' with the defence over the charges. While sentencing remains with the courts, the charge(s) can already give a good indication of the likely outcome, as a less serious charge will most likely result in a more lenient sentence compared with a more serious charge. Defence lawyers, who owe a duty to their clients,[73] also have a duty to the courts to ensure court resources are used efficiently.[74] They are to advise their clients about plea, including the sentence discount for guilty pleas, and to do so in 'strong terms' if necessary.

Hong Kong's adversarial system is supposedly structured in a way where the defendant is presumed to be innocent, the prosecution has the burden to prove the defendant's guilt beyond a reasonable doubt, and the court, being a neutral arbitrator, determines the outcome after hearing all the evidence and arguments in law. The defence theoretically need only raise reasonable doubt. Yet, there is also a guilty plea system, where the prosecution and defence can negotiate charge(s), the defence

[72] K. K. Cheng, 'The practice and justifications of plea bargaining by Hong Kong criminal defence lawyers' (2014) 1 *Asian Journal of Law and Society*, 395–412.

[73] E.g. 10.13 of the Bar Code of Conduct of the Hong Kong Bar Association.

[74] E.g. 10.36 of the Bar Code of Conduct of the Hong Kong Bar Association.

lawyer advises his or her client about sentencing discounts, and the courts provide reduced sentences in return for timely guilty pleas. Although the plea decision is supposedly voluntary, there are serious consequences that the defendant must consider when contemplating a not guilty plea, while all three legal actors emphasise the benefits of pleading guilty.

References

Baldwin, J., & McConville, M. (1977). *Negotiated Justice: Pressures to Plead Guilty*. Martin Robertson.

Cheng, K. K. (2013). Pressures to Plead Guilty: Factors Affecting Plea Decisions in Hong Kong's Magistrates' Courts. *British Journal of Criminology, 53*, 257–275.

Cheng, K. K. (2014). The Practice and Justifications of Plea Bargaining by Hong Kong Criminal Defence Lawyers. *Asian Journal of Law and Society, 1*, 395–412.

Cheng, K. K. (2023). *The Timing of Guilty Pleas: Lessons from Common Law Jurisdictions*. Cambridge University Press. in press.

Cheng, K. K., Chui, W. H., & Ong, R. (2015). Providing Justice for Low-Income Youths: Publicly Funded Lawyers and Youth Clients in Hong Kong. *Social & Legal Studies, 24*, 577–593.

Cheng, K. K., Chui, W. H., Young, S. N. M., & Ong, R. (2018). Why Do Criminal Trials 'Crack'? An Empirical Investigation of Late Guilty Pleas in Hong Kong. *Asian Journal of Comparative Law, 13*, 1–25.

Cross, G., & Cheung, P. S. W. (2022). *Sentencing in Hong Kong* (10th ed.). LexisNexis.

Ip, E. C. (2017). Legal Profession and Representation. In W. H. Chui & T. W. Lo (Eds.), *Understanding Criminal Justice in Hong Kong* (2nd ed.). Routledge.

Johnson, B. D. (2019). Trials and Tribulations: The Trial Tax and the Process of Punishment. *Crime and Justice, 48*, 313–363.

Kim, A. C. (2015). Underestimating the Trial Penalty: An Empirical Analysis of the Federal Trial Penalty and Critique of the Abrams Study. *Mississippi Law Review, 84*, 1195–1256.

McConville, L., et al. (1994). *Standing Accused: The Organisation and Practices of Criminal Defence Lawyers in Britain*. Clarendon Press.

Newman, D. (2013). *Legal Aid Lawyers and the Quest for Justice*. Hart Publishing.

Ri, S., & Cheng, K. K. (2022). Plea Discounts Deviations: A Mechanism for Gender Disparities in Hong Kong. *Asian Journal of Criminology, 17*, 237–261.

Sentencing Council. (2017). *Reduction in Sentence for Guilty Plea: Definitive Guideline*. Sentencing Council.

Sentencing Guidelines Council. (2007). *Reduction in Sentence for Guilty Plea: Definitive Guideline*. Sentencing Guidelines Secretariat.

So, S. (2022). *Knight and Upham: Criminal Litigation in Hong Kong* (4th ed.). Sweet & Maxwell.

Spohn, C., & Brennan, P. K. (Eds.). (2020). *Handbook on Sentencing Policies and Practices in the 21st Century*. Routledge.

Tata, C. (2007). In the Interests of Clients or Commerce? Legal aid, Supply, Demand, and "Ethical Indeterminacy" in Criminal Defence Work. *Journal of Law and Society, 34*, 489–519.

Tata, C., & Gormley, J. (2020). To Plead or Not to Plead? "Guilt" Is the Question: Rethinking Sentencing and Plea-Decision Making in Anglo American Countries. In *Handbook on Sentencing Policies and Practices in the 21st Century* (pp. 208–234). Routledge.

Welsh, L., Skinns, L., & Sanders, A. (2021). *Sanders & Young's Criminal Justice* (5th ed.). Oxford University Press.

Cases

Hessell v R (2010) NZSC 135.

HKCA (2016) 397 at 198.

HKSAR v Abdallah Anwar Abbas (2009) 2 HKLRD 437, (2009) 2 HKC 197.

HKSAR v Abdou Maikido Abdoulkarim (2016) 5 HKLRD 1;

HKSAR v Chan Chi Ho Lincoln (2018) 21 HKCFAR 588 at 40.

HKSAR v Chow Yuen Fai (2010) 1 HKLRD 354, (2010) 1 HKC 181 at 31.

HKSAR v Ngo Van Nam; HKSAR v Abdou Maikido Abdoulkarim (2016) 5 HKLRD 1; (2016) HKCA 397.

HKSAR v Shaer Chun-keung (1998) 1 HKLRD 348.

Miller v Minister of Pensions (1947) 2 All ER 372.

R v Caley (2013) 2 Cr App R (S) 305.

R v Chan Chi-sing (1995) 3 HKC 325 at p. 326.

R v Goodyear (2005) 3 All ER 117.

R v Lam Yin (1995) 2 HKCLR 124 at 20.

R v Lau Tak-ming and Ors (1990) 2 HKLR 370, (1990) HKCU 399.

R v Scales (1987) HKLR 583, (1987) HKCU 179 at pp. 587–588.

R v Siu Kwong-Wing (1993) 2 HKCLR 94.

R v Turner (1970) 2 QB 321.

Woolmington v. DPP, (1935) A.C. 462 at 481–482.

Pressuring Defendants to Plead Guilty? A Comparative Analysis of Plea-Based Justice in Mainland China and Hong Kong

Chengchen He and Jingwei Liu

Introduction

In Mainland China (hereafter 'China'), the criminal justice system is suffering the crisis of heavy caseloads, particularly the mounting number of minor cases awaiting processing in basic courts (Supreme People's Procuratorate, 2022). The reasons for the proliferation of court cases in contemporary China are twofold. First, in 2013 China abolished its Re-education through Labor system, which previously relied on administrative detention to sanction people who committed minor offenses. As a result, offenders of minor offenses are shifted to be managed under the prosecutorial discretionary power, flooding the criminal court system with an influx of low-level offenses (Biddulph et al., 2017). Cases resulting in lengthy jail terms of three years or less have risen from 53.9% in 2000 to 77.4% in 2020 (Supreme People's Procuratorate, 2021). Second, a

C. He · J. Liu (✉)
The Chinese University of Hong Kong, Shatin, Hong Kong, People's Republic of China
e-mail: JingweiLiew@link.cuhk.edu.hk

C. He
e-mail: cecilia.hcc@link.cuhk.edu.hk

E. Li et al. (eds.), *Criminal Case Dispositions through Pleas in Greater China*, https://doi.org/10.1007/978-981-97-1856-6_9

judge quota system was established in 2014, which attempted to shape a professional and elite court system by admitting a fairly limited number of personnel to become judges and assigning administrative work to other personnel (Li, 2016). This judge quota system has exacerbated the onerous caseloads for judges as the number of judges has decreased while caseloads are increasing (He, 2021). Therefore, in order to help the criminal justice system handle minor or straightforward cases in a more efficient manner, China established its own version of a guilty plea system (Wu, 2020a).

The guilty plea is the primary mode of case disposition in common law jurisdictions (Sanders et al., 2010). As a special administrative region of the People's Republic of China, Hong Kong maintained its common law system under the framework of 'one country, two systems' after the 1997 handover (Lo et al., 2019). The guilty plea system in Hong Kong is an essential component of the criminal justice process, allowing defendants to admit guilt in exchange for potential benefits such as reduced sentences. The crucial rationale underlying the Hong Kong guilty plea system is utilitarianism since Hong Kong courts are encountering the predicament of huge caseloads in routine justice processing (Department of Justice, 2022). Offenders receive a 'benefit' of a sentence reduction in exchange for saving the state's costs of pursuing a trial, shielding victims and witnesses from being required to testify, and facilitating a swift completion of the case. In this regard, benefits are thus maximized for all parties involved.

Although Mainland China and Hong Kong possess distinct legal systems, both jurisdictions have operated a guilty plea process to tackle common challenges in criminal justice such as promoting efficiency. Nonetheless, concerns have emerged regarding the fairness of the system and the potential for innocent defendants to plead guilty due to fear or pressure, which could lead to wrongful convictions. In this chapter, we argue that, irrespective of the legal system differences, the principles of due process and fairness are compromised. The inherently punitive nature of the criminal justice system exerts pressure on defendants to reach a compromise, particularly in cases where the specifics of the crime are unclear and the evidence is inadequate, and thus the defendant is more likely to be innocent. This chapter presents the first study that provides a comparative analysis of the similarities and differences in how suspects and defendants experience pressure to plead guilty during pre-trial stages across these two jurisdictions. It is structured into a series of pre-trial stages that chronologically follow suspects and defendants as they navigate the criminal justice system.

A Snapshot of the Guilty Plea System in Mainland China and Hong Kong

In 2016, China formally introduced the guilty plea system with an official name of 'plea leniency' (*renzui renfa congkuan zhidu* 认罪认罚从宽制度), generally referring to acknowledging guilt and accepting penalties for leniency, with the introduction of an abridged process, known as the expedited procedure (*jianyi chengxu* 简易程序). This expedited procedure has accelerated the handling of cases, not only at trial, but faster police investigation and prosecutorial case review as well (Baum, 2021). Different from most western jurisdictions, this plea leniency process can take place throughout the entire criminal process from the police investigation to court adjudication.

The police, prosecutors, and judges view an offender's willingness to admit guilt as an indication of remorse (Bowers, 2007; Cross et al., 2011) and confessing guilt is regarded as the potential to obtain a more lenient sentence. It also can be regarded as an indication that the offender is more receptive to the possibility of rehabilitation and, therefore, would provide benefit to the offender in the form of a reduced sentence (Dobinson, 2013). In fact, the concept of affording leniency for those who admit their crimes is not new since 'leniency for those who confess, severity for those who resist' (*tanbaicongkuan, kangjucongyan* 坦白从宽，抗拒从严) is enshrined in the Chinese criminal justice system, echoing with the principle of 'balancing of leniency and harshness'. This principle, which came to prominence in the mid-2000s, is most notably championed by the Supreme People's Court (Biddulph et al., 2017). After a two-year pilot program in 18 cities, the plea leniency system was enacted in the 2018 Criminal Procedure Law (CPL), and has since accounted for nearly 90 percent of filed criminal cases (Dai, 2022).

The preamble of the *Guiding Opinions on the Application of the Plea Leniency System* (2019) lucidly proclaimed that the official goal of the plea leniency system in China is to punish crime and strengthen human rights protection in a timely and effective way. Some believe that this bourgeoning scheme has effectively contributed to managing judges' large caseloads. For example, Wu's research (2020b) suggests that the overall depositional time taken to complete case disposition was shortened and the appeal rate dropped significantly after the adoption of the guilty plea system.

The guilty plea system in Hong Kong is designed to enhance the overall efficiency of the criminal justice system by alleviating the burden on courts and expediting the resolution of criminal cases. This approach has the potential to conserve valuable resources and ensure the timely delivery of justice. In compliance with Hong Kong law, a defendant's guilty plea must be voluntary. Hong Kong adheres to the principles established in the English case of *Turner*,[1] which mandate that defendants have the freedom to choose between pleading guilty or not guilty. Judges are prohibited from suggesting to the defense that a more lenient sentence would be imposed if the defendant pleads guilty, and a harsher sentence if the defendant is convicted after trial. Defendants previously could receive a one-third sentence discount for pleading guilty from the initial plea arrangement up until the day of trial. However, in 2016, after the cases of *Ngo Van Nam* and *Abdou Maikido Abdoulkarim*, Hong Kong's Court of Appeal introduced a sliding scale of sentence discounts to encourage earlier guilty pleas to avoid cracked trials—where a defendant pleads guilty after a trial date has been set, which squanders public resources (Cheng, 2018). This new scheme means that:

> *In Hong Kong, a one-third discount should be given the when the defendant pleads guilty or gives an indication to plead guilty when asked, such as on or at the committal proceedings in the Magistrates' Courts and before a trial date the Plea Day has been fixed. The discount is reduced to one-quarter or one-fifth after the trial dates are scheduled but the plea is indicated or entered before the first day of trial. If the guilty plea is entered in the first day of trial, then the sentence discount is reduced to one-fifth.* (Cheng, 2018: 140)

The sentence discount system, particularly the sliding scale of sentence discounts for guilty pleas, seeks to achieve cost savings and incentivize defendants to enter guilty pleas at the earliest opportunity (Cheng, 2023).

[1] *R v Turner* [1970] 2 QB 321.

The Pressure in the Pre-trial Stages

Confession

Research has shown that Chinese police have cultivated a culture of presumption of guilt (Cohen, 2013). Rather than respecting the defendant's right to the presumption of innocence incorporated in the Criminal Procedural Law, Chinese police tend to focus exclusively on gathering inculpatory evidence (Shytov & Duff, 2019). For the police, confession is a straightforward form of evidence to be collected when other evidence is insufficient to prove the crime. It is regarded as the 'king of evidence' (McConville, 2011, p. 350) and confessing to crimes is almost seen as obligatory for the suspects. During interrogations, suspects enjoy no right to silence; instead, they must answer the questions truthfully. Previous research found that nearly 92 percent of suspects made full confessions, 5 percent of suspects made partial confessions, and only 3 percent of suspects denied involvement (McConville, 2011). This over-reliance on confessions has developed an ethos of encouraging coerced guilty pleas through torture and other illegal means (Belkin, 2013).

Despite the enactment of numerous laws and regulations prohibiting torture in China, it persists in practice (Jiang, 2018). Worse, the police tend to use other techniques to induce suspects to confess. For example, they may exploit suspects' vulnerabilities, such as their personal relationships, hopes for an uncertain future, and memories of past experiences, to induce confessions (Mou, 2022). In Mou's research, she recorded how the police induced a suspect to admit to a crime, which is illustrated by a police officer's words:

> Police: *If you don't tell us the details, you will be kept in the cell for a long time. Think about your old mother and your young kid. You have a responsibility to look after your family—be a filial son and a caring father. Your family needs you. Otherwise, you will be detained for another few months. You cooperate and go home earlier.* (Mou, 2022: 6)

In addition, in China there is little to gain in reversing a confession but much to lose (He, 2023). This is because the main function of Chinese criminal trials is seen as reviewing and confirming what has already been established in the pre-trial stages, rarely challenging it. Consequently, the Chinese criminal justice system has a conviction rate that exceeds 99.9% (China Law Society, 2018). Although the general trend in criminal justice reforms has been to reduce reliance on confessions, which are seen as a major cause of wrongful convictions, the plea leniency system is almost entirely based on confessions. This reliance may embolden the police to become even more assertive in obtaining early guilty pleas under pressure (Li, 2022b). Therefore, the plea leniency system has the potential to undermine the already limited protections afforded to China's criminal suspects and risks encouraging false confessions.

In Hong Kong, one of the powers of the police derived from the Police Force Ordinance (Cap.232) is questioning suspects to detect crimes. The interviews conducted by the police should be recorded in writing or by mechanical means.[2] During the interview, reasonable arrangements, such as refreshments, should be made for the comfort of the suspects, and suspects may choose to confess. A confession occurs when a defendant makes a declaration against their self-interest (So, 2020).

Typically, the confession is made to the police after a caution—you are not obliged to say anything unless you wish to do so, but what you say may be put into writing and given in evidence.[3] However, it shows that the majority of suspects have given oral evidence without a sufficient explanation of the purpose and consequences of this caution (Chiu, 2009). In addition, if the suspects confess in the interview, the contents of the record of the interview would not be put before the magistrate or judge for further scrutiny, which may cause the problem that the police might push the suspects to confess because no further investigation has to be conducted (Chiu, 2009; The Law Reform Commission of Hong Kong, 2023).

Once a confession is obtained, suspects are more likely to plead guilty. This is because the strength of evidence is a key factor relevant to the decision to plead guilty: a confession offers the prosecution tremendous leverage against the defendant in effectively proving its case. Consequently, it can be leveraged to force a guilty plea, even though the defense lawyer can question the confession at trial.

In a criminal trial, the defense lawyer can challenge the admissibility of the confession in a *voir dire*.[4] During this process, the presiding judge or

[2] Rules and Directions for the Questioning of Suspects and the Taking of the Statement.

[3] Rules and Directions for the Questioning of Suspects and the Taking of the Statement.

[4] A trial within a trial where the admissibility of the evidence is determined by the judge away from the jury.

magistrate will determine whether the statement is made voluntarily by the defendant and whether it can be introduced as evidence against him or her. This seems fair since the defense lawyer can challenge the confession in court. However, in reality, excluding guilty pleas, the conviction rate after contested trials remains high as well (generally ranged between 60 and 70%) in Hong Kong (Research Office Legislative Council Secretariat, 2021). Challenging a confession proves difficult since the police conduct interviews according to rules and standards stipulated in the *Rules and Directions for the Questioning of Suspects and the Taking of Statements*. As illustrated in Cheng (2013b)'s study, barristers indicated that it was very difficult to prove the police did something inappropriate unless special circumstances, such as a mismatched timeline or evidence of physical abuse.

Taken together, in both Mainland China and Hong Kong, the criminal justice systems exhibit a strong reliance on guilty pleas, which can lead to false confessions. In Mainland China, the presumption of guilt is pervasive, and police focus on collecting confessions as the 'king of evidence'. Legal prohibitions, torture, and other manipulative techniques are often employed to extract confessions. The plea leniency system, which is largely based on confessions, risks promoting false confessions and undermining the already limited protections for criminal suspects in Mainland China. In Hong Kong, confessions are typically made after a caution, but many suspects provide oral evidence without comprehending the potential consequences. When a suspect confesses, their interview record is not subject to further scrutiny, possibly incentivizing the police to pressure suspects to confess. Therefore, early pressures to make incriminating statements during the police's interviews will undermine the chances of acquittals for defendants, and increase the likelihood of pleading guilty in most cases (Cheng, 2013b).

'Bargaining' with the Prosecutor

In China, 'if the police have remained the initiator of the criminal justice process, the procuratorates have become the terminator' (He, 2023: 454). Compared with the investigation stage, leniency promises can only be granted at the prosecutorial phase by the prosecutor. The prosecutor has the power to initiate charges, determine detention periods and conditions, and decide whether or not there is culpability and recommend sentences.

China's inquisitorial criminal procedure and legal culture make plea bargaining in China distinct from common law jurisdictions. Under the inquisitorial model, the prosecutor represents the state interest rather than pursuing the narrow interests of the victim (Soubise, 2018). Therefore, the idea that case outcomes can be negotiated between the prosecutor and the defendant is alien to the inquisitorial system (Wu, 2020a). In addition, as a socialist country, China's criminal justice system is deeply influenced by Soviet Union's legal tradition where the prosecutor's main target is to cooperate with the police and the court to crack down on crime (Mou, 2017). The power and resource imbalance between the prosecutor and defendant make the pleas involuntary in nature. In other words, defendants are not in a position to negotiate with prosecutors, and there is no 'bargaining'; it is a 'plea for leniency' (He, 2023: 460).

In the Chinese criminal justice system today, justice personnel are incentivized to take action that aligns with performance objectives and penalized for not meeting those targets at nearly every stage of the process. In practice, the rate of application of plea leniency is one of the metrics of work performance. For example, some procuratorates require the prosecutors to apply plea leniency in over 70% of the cases, and failing to achieve this rate will negatively affect prosecutor's promotion and remuneration (Yin, 2021). Moreover, the earlier the suspect pleads guilty, the faster a case can be solved by the prosecutor. Therefore, prosecutors prefer to apply this scheme as frequently and rapidly as possible. From Galanter's (1974) view, prosecutors are repeat players, with repeated involvement in similar cases in the criminal justice system, while defendants, who mostly are first-timers, are one-shooters in the process. This imbalanced justice system favoring the prosecutors (Zuo, 2017) pressures defendants to confess, and most defendants who have made confessions have no bargaining power to negotiate for a lighter or mitigated sentence (Biddulph et al., 2017; Li, 2015). Even a failure to express remorse, which is seen as resistance, not only precludes any reduction in the sentence but arguably may even increase it (Dobinson, 2013; He, 2023). From this perspective, many scholars consider plea leniency to be a one-sided and restrictive process—legal authorities determine which charges to bring based on established facts and sufficient evidence, and then assess a limited discount range if the defendant chooses to plead guilty (Wu, 2020a; Xiong, 2020).

In Hong Kong, although the Court of Appeal had declared that plea bargaining does not exist, negotiations between the defense lawyer and prosecutors on dropping charges or charging with a lesser offense are permitted (Young, 2009). In practice, prosecutors possess considerable discretion in how they prosecute crimes. They can drop certain charges or charge with a lesser offense in return for the defendant pleading guilty. In other words, they can base their choice of charges on the evidence they are confident they can prove. In particular, this can occur in cases where there are multiple charges. In that, defendants can plead guilty to the charges with the most unfavorable evidence against them in exchange for the prosecutor dropping other charges. For example, the prosecution may agree to drop the fourth and fifth charges if the defendant pleads guilty to three charges. However, this gives prosecutors an advantage—if the prosecution's evidence is weak, they can overcharge and see whether the defendant would charge bargain, thus potentially securing a conviction for the lesser charge with weak evidence (Cheng, 2013a). In addition, prosecutors can reduce a charge to a lesser offense. Most criminal offenses can be placed on a spectrum according to their degree of seriousness, and prosecutors have a great degree of discretion in deciding which offense to charge. For example, they can initiate a charge and change it from child molesting (a more serious offense) to assault (a less serious offense) if the defendant pleads guilty to the lesser offense of assault (Inciardi, 1993). This increases the danger that an innocent person, fearing the final result of being found guilty and receiving a harsh sentence if the case goes to trial, may plead guilty when he or she is told that a guilty plea will result in lighter treatment (Young, 2009).

To summarize, prosecutors in both Mainland China and Hong Kong enjoy great discretion. In Mainland China, the inquisitorial criminal justice system, influenced by the Soviet Union's legal tradition, grants prosecutors significant power in determining charges, detention conditions, and recommended sentences. The power imbalance between prosecutors and defendants often pressures defendants into involuntary confessions. Failure to express remorse can lead to harsher sentences. Conversely, Hong Kong permits negotiations between defense lawyers and prosecutors to drop charges or charge with a lesser offense. Prosecutors have considerable discretion in charging decisions, which can result in overcharging and pressure on innocent defendants to plead guilty for lighter treatment.

Bail

Previous studies have identified pre-trial detention as a prior decision that can significantly influence the plea decisions: Dervan and Edkins (2013)'s experiment suggested that if an innocent person was detained and facing potential criminal punishment, he or she had a more than 50% chance of wrongfully pleading under pressure. While there are numerous ways in which a person can be released before trial, the most common includes bail, which refers to the release of a defendant from custody with a given set of conditions. In a substantial number of cases, bail plays a key role during pre-trial processes, determining whether, following arrest, defendants will be released or detained prior to trial (Menefee, 2018).

Unlike the common law jurisdiction where bail is the prima facie right of the suspects/defendants, pre-arrest detention (*Juliu* 拘留) and arrest (*Daibu* 逮捕) have long been the norm in the Chinese pre-trial process (Li, 2022b).[5] As a retributive and punitive society (Trevaskes, 2010), China may subject suspects to prolonged and pointless pre-trial imprisonment, which leads to frequent torture and inhumane incidents (Dobinson, 2013). Although the CPL's article 67 establishes a bail mechanism, suspects with less social recourses and status (e.g., rural migrants) are significantly more likely to be detained before trial (Dobinson, 2013; Xiong & Wei, 2017). According to article 67 of the CPL, one of the grounds for granting bail is the possible sentence. Nearly 90% of suspects, according to data from the case file analysis, do not even request bail (McConville, 2011, p. 62), and more than 85% of defendants are detained during pre-trial stages in practice (Xiong & Wei, 2017).

Under the plea leniency system, the procuratorates exercise their discretion to exert immense pressure on defendants. Prosecutors can grant bail, increase or shorten detention duration, and schedule earlier or later trial dates. The pressure on defendants to plead leniency is immense because their attitudes (such as their hesitation, reluctance, or eagerness) toward admitting guilt make a difference in the results (He, 2023). To be specific, when the defense 'works with' the prosecutors, the pleas made by the defense are more likely to be accepted; on the contrary, when the

[5] While investigating, the police can detain the suspect for two months, and the period may be extended by one month with the approval of the people's procuratorate (Article 156). The length of arrest can even be extended to seven months if the crimes are complex, grave, or extremely significant.

defense plays hardball (e.g., challenging the criminal charge by claiming innocence), their strategies would largely fail (Liang & He, 2014: 1246). While defendants who enter pleas may receive bail or be tried in a few days, those who refuse to plead guilty will likely be constrained to stay in custody at the detention center.

In Hong Kong, defendants enjoy the right to bail. The burden of proving to the court that bail should be rejected in a given case rests with the prosecution.[6] The court may also refuse bail if it has reason to believe that if the defendants are given bail—with or without conditions—they would not submit to the court's order for custody, would commit a crime while out on bail, would interfere with a witness, or would otherwise pervert or obstruct the administration of justice.[7] The nature and degree of the offense, the defendant's background and demeanor, their ties to the community, their financial situation, and their living situation are all factors that the court must take into account while making this decision.[8]

In general, it is not difficult for a defendant to obtain bail when there is no objection. However, in practice, judges often set the bail bonds too high for some defendants to afford, which leads them to be detained (Young, 2009). The harsh circumstances of detention centers pressure the suspects/defendants to plead guilty. Several studies in Hong Kong find that defendants who have been remanded in custody during pre-trial stages are much more likely to plead guilty because spending a long time in custody already outweighs the eventual punishment following conviction of many minor offenses (Cheng et al., 2018; Cheng, 2013b). More concretely, the grim conditions of detention facilities, such as overcrowding and poor sanitation, as well as the stress of confinement and the uncertainty surrounding criminal trials, make being held in custody challenging. Pre-trial detention, according to some detainees, is worse than jail, and getting a sentence provides the defendant with closure and, in many ways, promotes mental peace (Cheng & Leung, 2018).

[6] Article 5 of the Hong Kong Bill of Rights Ordinance (Cap. 383) provides that: 'Everyone has the right to liberty and security of person. No one shall be subjected to arbitrary arrest or detention. No one shall be deprived of his liberty except on such grounds and in accordance with such procedures as are established by law'. See also section 9D (1) of the Criminal Procedure Ordinance (Cap. 221).

[7] Section 9D (3) of the Criminal Procedure Ordinance (Cap. 221).

[8] Section 9G of the Criminal Procedure Ordinance (Cap. 221).

For instance, in the case of *HKSAR v Singh Sukhman Preet Sanny*, the defendant was charged with assault occasioning actual bodily harm, robbery, and assault with the intent to rob. His defense counsel said that 'the defendant prefers to be sent to prison. He has been in custody for 17 months'.[9]

Moreover, the cost and loss of time in pre-trial detention also pressure the defendants to plead guilty. For example, a 50-year-old man convicted of theft and selling goods that infringed copyright, who had been in custody for over a month, lost his flat because he could not pay the rent (Cheng et al., 2018). Many defendants just want their cases to be over as rapidly as possible and get back to their normal lives (Cheng, 2013b). Thus, pleading guilty urgently is one of the quickest and easiest methods to achieving finality and certainty. Compared to prisoners on bail, defendants in pre-trial detention were more likely to plead guilty.

Taken together, numerous defendants under bail are pressured into guilty pleas in Mainland China and Hong Kong during the pre-trial stage. On the one hand, the harsh environment during pre-trial imprisonment not only causes physical suffering for most defendants but also pressures them to plead guilty to get out of this situation. On the other hand, there are different reasons why defendants under bail are pressured to plead guilty under the two distinct jurisdictions. In Mainland China, bail decisions are made by the prosecutors, while in Hong Kong such decisions are made by the judges. In particular, the plea leniency system introduced in recent years gives prosecutors more discretion in making bail decisions. Bail virtually works as a bargain between the prosecutors and the defendants. The defendants usually have to plead guilty if they want to be granted bail. In Hong Kong, the high cost of bail and the uncertainty during detention pressure defendants to plead guilty to get the case result and certainty more rapidly.

Sentencing Discounts

Another factor that influences defendants' mindsets in pleading procedures is the additional penalty discount that pleading procedures offer over regular criminal procedures. This also can be described as a sentencing differential or trial penalty (Tata & Gormley, 2016). That is,

[9] Section 9G of the Criminal Procedure Ordinance (Cap. 221).

the greater the disparities between sentences imposed following pleas of guilty and not guilty, the greater the risk that innocent defendants will plead guilty (Baldwin & McConville, 1978).

In China, it is not uncommon for the judge to accept the prosecutor's sentencing recommendations (Li, 2022b). Since 1949, China has been following the mode of prosecutorial review rather than judicial review in its criminal justice system, which is a holdover from the concept of Lenin-style procuratorial supervision (Lin et al., 2017). The people's procuratorates are sanctioned to exercise extensive legal supervision over criminal proceedings, including the right to make decisions about pre-trial detention and the right to supervise the legitimacy of the investigative and trial proceedings, as well as the correctness of the judgment. By recommending a sentence following the defendant's guilty plea, the prosecutor is not recommending a sentence that honors a bargain contract made with the defendant, but rather making a de facto judgment about the sentence.

According to the *Guiding Opinions of the People's Procuratorate on Sentencing Recommendations* and *the Guiding Opinions on Applying the Leniency System for Pleas of Guilty and Punishment*, procurators in China have two types of sentencing recommendations: specific recommendations and range recommendations. The specific recommendation has a set prison term, such as two years, whereas the range recommendation suggests a penalty zone sentence, such as from one to two years or under two years. A sentencing recommendation can be considered a legal promise by the prosecutor on behalf of the defendant. However, as mentioned above, compared with the prosecutor, the defendant has no bargaining power to argue, which puts inappropriate pressure on defendants and may force them to accept the procurators' recommendation (Lu, 2021).

Although a defendant has the right to enter a not-guilty plea and request the prosecution to prove its case, defendants who choose to plead not guilty are severely disadvantaged given potential sentencing discounts available to those who choose to plead guilty (Mackenzie, 2007). The Criminal Law stipulates the conditions for sentence discounts in China. While the construction of a law-based criminal justice system in China has advanced significantly, there are still many challenges facing the country's sentencing system, such as illogical and inconsistent sentencing outcomes as widely documented in the relevant literature (Chen, 2010). This indicates that the application of these sentence discount conditions is arbitrary and not uniform—in other words, the defendant may be given leniency, but it is unclear how much. As mentioned earlier, under the principle of providing leniency to those who confess and severity to those who resist, the resistance of those who do not confess will directly impact the sentence. A prior study has thus concluded that Chinese authorities tend to impose 'trial penalties' on defendants who opt to enter a full trial, which leads to a decreased probability of probation grants (Wu, 2020a: 480). Therefore, it is contended that a failure to plead guilty will make the offense more serious than it would otherwise have been (Blume & Helm, 2014).

Moreover, in numerous plea leniency cases, defendants have agreed and signed away the right to appeal in exchange for better penalty discounts (Lu, 2021). There are also cases in which defendants first trade a guilty plea for a lower penalty and then appeal to revisit the plea leniency deal, relying on the legal stipulation that 'no additional penalty should be imposed on appeal' (*Shanghsu bu Jiaxing* 上诉不加刑). While their intention might prove to be 'impure', it virtually puts defendants in a more difficult situation. On the one hand, the defendants' appeals are mostly dismissed due to the plea leniency agreement being 'voluntarily' entered. On the other hand, the defendants are more likely to face a harsher penalty should the prosecutors decide to withdraw the previous plea leniency agreement and propose a new one (He, 2023).

In Hong Kong, under the *Turner* guideline, the defendant must be free to choose whether to plead guilty. The indication made by the court on the difference between the sentence with the defendant pleading guilty and sentence without the defendant pleading guilty 'could be taken to be undue pressure on the accused, thus depriving him of that complete freedom of choice which is essential' (R v. Turner, 1970, p. 328). Following the strict criteria established in the famous *Turner* case, Hong Kong continues to take a cautious position regarding the disparities between the sentence with and without guilty pleas. More specifically, the amount of sentence discount is determined primarily based on the timing of the guilty plea, whereas other factors, such as the strength of the prosecution's case or the defendant's remorse, are dealt with separately or subsumed in the sentence discount for the guilty plea. As a result, when the defendant pleads guilty becomes the crucial factor that informs the judge's sentencing decisions (Cheng, 2023).

As such, Hong Kong courts provide sentence discounts for defendants, stating the policy in Hong Kong is that these discounts are given to encourage guilty defendants to plead guilty (Cheng, 2023). Before 2016, defendants who plead guilty could enjoy a one-third sentence discount from the time that they would spend in prison or the amount that they would be fined had they been convicted at trial. In 2016, Hong Kong courts adopted the quantified sliding scale of sentence discount for defendants who plead guilty, which is reflected in the cases of *Ngo Van Nam* and *Abdou Maikido Abdoulkarim*:

> *In the Court of First Instance, usually the opportunity to secure a one-third discount occurred when the defendant was given the opportunity to plead in the Magistrates' Court, pleaded guilty and was committed to the Court of First Instance for sentencing. If the defendant indicated to the court or prosecution that he wished to plead guilty after he had been committed to the Court of First Instance for trial, but up to and until dates were fixed for his trial by the Listing Judge, the appropriate discount for sentence was 25%. Then, the range of discount to be afforded to a defendant who indicated to the court or the prosecution that he intended to plead guilty after trial dates had been fixed but before the first day of trial, lay between the 25% discount to be afforded to a defendant who indicated that he wished to plead guilty up to and until dates were fixed for his trial by the Listing Judge and the 20% discount to be afforded to a defendant for a plea of guilty on the first day of trial. The discount to be afforded to a defendant who pleaded guilty after arraignment but during the trial itself would usually be less than the 20% afforded to the defendant who pleaded guilty on the first day of the trial and will reflect the circumstances in which the plea was tendered.*[10]

The implementation of this quantified sliding scale is considered to be utilitarian since the final sentence discount is based on when guilty pleas are entered. However, the pressure on defendants continues to increase with each passing day, and they eventually crack and choose to plead guilty since the discount gets lower and lower as defendants wait before pleading guilty (Cheng, 2023). The defendant might receive a lesser discount because he or she missed a particular waypoint. This is particularly the case when the time between a defendant's first appearance and trial may be relatively short for proceedings in the Magistrates'

[10] HKSAR v. Ngo Van Nam; HKSAR v. *Abdou Maikido Abdoulkarim* [2016] 5 HKLRD 1; [2016] HKCA 397.

Courts, and the defendant may not have enough time to make a proper decision on entering a guilty plea.[11]

In summary, sentence discounts can pressure defendants to plead guilty in Mainland China and Hong Kong. However, the reasons for this are distinct for each jurisdiction. In Mainland China, the prosecutor's sentencing recommendations can greatly influence the judge's decision. Moreover, following the introduction of the plea leniency system, prosecutors are given more discretion, which leads to defendants' guilty pleas becoming bargaining chips in exchange for lenient sentencing. In Hong Kong, the quantified sliding scale of sentence discounts is the essential player in pressuring the defendants to plead guilty. In particular, the final sentence discounts are based on when guilty pleas are entered, leading defendants to plead guilty earlier to get higher sentence discounts.

The Defense Lawyers in the Pre-trial Stages

As mentioned before, because of the great challenges faced by criminal defendants, even with defense lawyers behind them, imbalances between the defense and the prosecution are enormous. Persuading judges to adopt criminal lawyers' defense opinions is rarely successful due to the internal coordination among the 'iron triangle' of Chinese criminal justice, namely, the police, the procuracy, and the courts (Liu & Halliday, 2009, p. 925; 2016). The three apparatuses work together to achieve criminal beliefs rather than forming a triangular framework of checks and balances (He, 2021).

It is the prosecutor who controls the case sources and makes decisions that are nearly impossible to refute under the plea leniency scheme. Defense lawyers find themselves, in most cases, only be able to encourage and witness defendants' acceptance of plea agreements (Hu, 2018). The reason is the high dependence of lawyers on the state justice bureaus. More specifically, lawyers have to attach themselves to state power in order to gain advantageous positions in market competition (Liu, 2011). To survive, lawyers have to access the local professional networks and state bureaucracy to make a living—any belligerent, confrontative, or uncooperative behavior will only harm their interests or even sabotage their careers (Liu et al., 2014). Defense lawyers who question the state

[11] *HKSAR v. Ngo Van Nam; HKSAR v. Abdou Maikido Abdoulkarim* [2016] 5 HKLRD 1; [2016] HKCA 397 at 174.

authority face the risk of being charged and convicted of offenses such as obstruction of justice or even perjury. The high-profile case of Li Zhuang illustrated the dilemma of the criminal defense in China. Li, a criminal defense lawyer, was sentenced to one and a half years in prison for perjury and obstruction of justice for allegedly instructing his witness to lie. The Li case incited fierce controversy over criminal defense lawyers' concerns about the abusive use of Article 306 of the criminal code at that time,[12] which they argued was an approach of procuratorial retaliation against criminal defense lawyers. Some lawyers even argued that the prosecution of Li was a political vendetta which was caused by Li's opposition to the police, the procuratorate, the court, and the local government.[13] Furthermore, many lawyers concurred the outcome of Li's case would not only aggravate the difficulties in the representation of criminals at the pre-trial stage but also worsen the existing imbalance of power between defense lawyers and law enforcement agencies (Li, 2010). By contrast, with cooperation with prosecutors, they can earn extra discounts on charges and sentences for their clients (Li, 2022a) since the majority (96.85%) of prosecutors' sentencing recommendations have been accepted and enforced by the court (The Supreme People's Procuratorate, 2021).[14] Another survey that echoes this conclusion shows that 89% of lawyers acknowledge that the only thing they do is seek lenient sentencing outcomes (Hu,

[12] Art. 306 of the 1997 Chinese Criminal Law stipulates: If, in criminal proceedings, a defender or agent ad litem destroys or forges evidence, helps any of the parties destroy or forge evidence, or coerces the witness or entices him into changing his testimony in defiance of the facts or give false testimony, he shall be sentenced to fixed-term imprisonment of no more than three years or criminal detention; if the circumstances are serious, he shall be sentenced to fixed-term imprisonment of no less than three years but no more than seven years.

[13] Quoted from Austin Ramzy. China's Dark City: Behind Chongqing's Crime Crackdown, TIME, Mar. 15, 2010, https://content.time.com/time/subscriber/article/0,33009,1969642,00.html.

[14] The Criminal Procedural Law regulates that except for five circumstances, the courts shall confirm the prosecutor's sentencing recommendations. According to Article 201 of the Criminal Procedure Law, the five circumstances are: (1) The conduct of the defendant does not constitute a crime or the defender shall not be held criminally liable; (2) The defendant admits guilt and accepts punishment against his or her will; (3) The defendant denies the facts of the crime which he or she is charged with; (4) The charges filed are inconsistent with those determined at trial; (5) The fair trial of the case may be otherwise affected.

2018). Therefore, while bearing pressure from police and prosecutors, defendants cannot be fully represented during the pre-trial stages.

Even worse, many defendants who cannot afford private lawyers have no or only limited legal aid before they plead guilty. In China, it is a problem for many defendants who come from a lower socio-economic background to access legal representation during the pre-trial period, although the duty lawyer (*zhiban lvshi 值班律师*) system has been incorporated into the defense system as part of the 2018 CPL Amendment. For example, a study shows that, during detention, it is common for suspects to confess their crimes because of the lack of legal advice under prolonged custody (Dobinson, 2013).

In addition, duty lawyers frequently need a solid level of professionality, ability, and real feelings of loyalty and obligation in order to do their job well (Yang & Wu, 2020). In practice, however, only those who have recently obtained their practicing license or have little business are willing to do duty lawyers' work. An empirical study has found that reality is far removed from the expectation for the duty lawyer scheme: the duty lawyers were usually so overloaded with cases that they had no time to communicate with defendants or provide specific legal advice, which led to most of duty lawyers signing the recognizances without even meeting the defendants (Mou, 2020). The Legal Aid Law in 2021 further clarifies that duty lawyers are part of legal aid system. However, a past study provided empirical data that contrasted the work of legal aid lawyers with that of the privately retained lawyers, which showed that the latter largely outperformed the former and represented their clients more zealously and aggressively (Liang & He, 2014). In particular, compared to privately retained lawyers whose remuneration is discussed with the clients, the pay for duty lawyers is accounted for on a daily basis, which is meager for most of them.[15] Furthermore, due to the tremendous professional difficulties and personal danger faced by criminal defense lawyers, the majority of Chinese lawyers try to avoid criminal defense work as much as they can (Liu & Halliday, 2016). In addition, as discussed before, in order to build a solid working connection with the procuratorial organs, they find it difficult to provide efficient legal assistance and even overlook the true wishes of suspects and defendants (Chen, 2019). The unfortunate conclusion

[15] For example, a lawyer from Nanchang City pointed that 'Usually, the subsidy for the duty lawyers is about 200 yuan a day. And if the duty lawyer is directly sent by law firm, there is even no subsidy'. See Tu and Che (2021).

that flows from a careful examination of the duty lawyer system is simply that it can hardly ensure the voluntariness, truthfulness, and integrity of criminal defendants' confessions and punishment (Yang & Wu, 2020).

Contrarily, studies in Hong Kong have tested the vital influence of defense lawyers on defendants' guilty pleas (Cheng, 2018). To protect and guarantee defendants' right to legal advice and representation in courts, The Duty Lawyer Service in Hong Kong provides publicly funded defense lawyers through The Duty Lawyer Scheme to defendants who do not have access to legal representation in all Magistrates' Courts and Juvenile Courts. These lawyers may be assigned to help and represent defendants in need where the defendant lacks the necessary resources and where interests of justice so require. Moreover, the Legal Aid Department provides legal aid lawyers to represent criminal defendants in the District Court, the Court of First Instance, and all criminal appeals. There are requirements for defendants to apply for legal aid—they can only be provided with legal aid if they pass the means test[16] and the merits test.[17]

Whether they are serving a private client contract or working as a publicly funded lawyer, defense lawyers have a duty to advise their clients regarding decisions to enter guilty pleas. More specifically, although it is emphasized that the client has the responsibility for and complete freedom in making the plea decision, barristers are

> *entitled to refer to all aspects of the case and, where appropriate, he may advise his client in strong terms that he is nearly impossible to escape conviction and that a plea of guilty is generally regarded by the Court as a mitigating factor.*[18]

This means the decision to enter a guilty plea is ultimately up to the defendant, as is asserted in the relevant professional codes of conduct and

[16] The means test is determined by the applicant's financial resources, where it does not exceed the financial eligibility limit set by the Legal Aid Department. The eligibility limit may be waived by the Director of Legal Aid if the Director is satisfied that it is in the interests of justice to do so and where the applicant will be subject to higher contribution rates.

[17] The merits test is that for trials in the District Court or Court of First Instance, legal aid will be granted if it is desirable in the interests of justice to do so. For appeal cases, likewise legal aid will be granted if it is in the interests of justice to do so and that there are reasonable grounds for appeal.

[18] 10.56(a) of the Bar Code of Conduct of the Hong Kong Bar Association.

case law. A previous study on criminal defense in Hong Kong finds that the lawyer-client relationship is frequently not equal in terms of decision-making power, with lay clients not commonly challenging their legal lawyer's legal advice (Tata, 2007). A further study on the perceptions of fairness and satisfaction with lawyers in the Hong Kong justice system reveals that offenders who had private lawyers feel that they were treated more fairly by their legal representative and in turn are more satisfied in their interactions with their lawyers, compared to being represented by a duty lawyer (Chui & Cheng, 2017). Furthermore, even though many publicly funded lawyers from the Duty Lawyer Scheme and legal aid lawyers are drawn from private practice, there is a view among defendants in Hong Kong that these lawyers are on the side of the state and are only useful for mitigating judges' sentencing decisions after the defendant has already pleaded guilty. This also exacerbates the perception of publicly funded lawyers as government employees (Cheng et al., 2015).

Taken together, defense lawyers are essential players influencing defendants' guilty plea. Criminal defense lawyers in China work in a minefield filled with bureaucratic trenches and bombs, sometimes with their hands cuffed, meaning they rarely oppose guilty charges and instead tend to persuade defendants to plead guilty for more lenient sentences (Liu & Halliday, 2016). For the duty lawyers under the newly established legal aid scheme, reality is far removed from the expectation of ensuring that defendants can access legal advice and make informed decisions on whether or not to enter a guilty plea (Mou, 2020). In Hong Kong, pressures from their defense counsel are the main cause of defendants deciding to plead guilty. Moreover, legally aided defendants are usually hurried by their solicitors to plead guilty to receive a more lenient sentence. Thus, due to the dilemma of their professional environment and lenient sentences, criminal lawyers can barely compete with the incentives for their clients to enter guilty charges. Defendants are therefore not alleviated of the great pressure to plead guilty.

Conclusion

This chapter has sought to compare the pressures imposed on defendants to plead guilty during pre-trial processes in two legal systems—Mainland China and Hong Kong. Through a comparative analysis, the present study helps explain why guilty pleas are ubiquitous during each stage before trial, from the perspectives of confession, bargaining with prosecutors, bail, sentence discounts, and defense lawyers.

During the investigation stage, the principle of 'leniency to those who confess, severity to those who resist' has cultivated a notorious culture of encouraging defendants to confess to a crime in exchange for sentencing concessions in Mainland China. This pursuit of confessions stems from an inquisitorial culture of criminal justice wherein confession is perceived as a precursor to the 'objective truth' legal authorities aspire to find (Li, 2022a, p. 82). Confessions have always been considered the king of evidence, which primarily determines how the police go around solving crimes (McConville, 2011). Apparently, this over-reliance on confessions has also developed an ethos of encouraging coerced guilty pleas through torture and other illegal means (McConville, 2011). Despite the broader trend in criminal justice reforms in Mainland China to reduce dependence on confessions, considered a major cause of wrongful convictions, the plea leniency system is almost exclusively based on confessions. Likewise in Hong Kong, despite its adversarial system, the defendant's admission of guilt also plays a decisive role when identifying the evidence and even throughout the entire criminal justice process. Furthermore, confessions are usually made the police caution, which puts defendants under pressure from the police. These caution statements are difficult to challenge in Hong Kong, leading to a guilty plea in most cases.

In the common law world, the prosecutor's unconstrained discretion during plea bargaining may have been a cause of injustice (Hessick, 2021). Unfortunately, the unbridled discretion of the procuratorates can only get worse in Mainland China (He, 2023). When the case is transferred from the police to the prosecutor, the prosecution can easily reach an agreement with the defendants by altering the evidence. They can even manipulate the timeline of the pre-trial process by delaying the presentation of beneficial evidence until after a guilty plea. The defendants have minimal power during the plea bargains compared to the prosecutors, who are more skilled stakeholders in this system.

In terms of pre-trial detention, defendants remanded in custody are much more likely to plead guilty, which has been verified in Hong Kong and Mainland China. Most defendants are held in custody for considerable periods of time prior to their trials. The closed and harsh environment, the cost, and the loss during detention are indispensable reasons for the high rate of involuntary confessions and guilty pleas in pre-trial proceedings.

As another crucial factor for the defendants to plead guilty, the sentence discount disparities may put innocent defendants at significant risk of pleading guilty, which has also been tested in judicial practice in both Mainland China and Hong Kong. Under the prosecutor-centered plea leniency system, as a synthetic judgment about the potential sentence, recommending a penalty is never a result of bargain but rather an assumed premise for the prosecutor to consider when applying plea leniency. Despite their right to enter a not-guilty plea, defendants who choose to do so are severely disadvantaged and not given substantial sentence discounts. Worse, under the plea leniency system, any appeals made by defendants are considered to have impure motives—to receive a lesser sentence—in practice making the defendant almost completely lose the right of appeal. Similarly, in Hong Kong, the timing of entering a guilty plea makes a decisive impact on sentence discounts, which naturally increases the pressure on defendants to eventually crack and plead guilty as the discount continuously lowers as defendants wait before pleading guilty. Moreover, defense lawyers often cannot shoulder the task of ensuring effective defense; they have even become the 'second public prosecutor', and they often only act as witnesses to witness a criminal suspect and defendant signing a written confirmation of confession (Yang & Wu, 2020, p. 379).

Even though each defendant may have different reasons for pleading guilty ultimately, the pressures of the pre-trial stage on them to end their punishment as soon as possible are common. As Feeley indicates, 'it is this cost which shapes their [defendants'] subsequent course of action once they are entrapped by the system' (Feeley, 1979, p. 30). The stress and costs defendants go through during pre-trial proceedings have a significant bearing on decisions to plead guilty. Under this system, if an innocent person is wrongfully convicted, neither the police, the prosecutor, the judge, nor the defense lawyers in the criminal justice system will undertake responsibility since the defendant 'voluntarily' pleads guilty (He, 2023).

As for the particularity of the crime of confession and punishment, the guarantee of the voluntary truthfulness of the guilty suspect and defendant is the basis of the legitimacy of the system and the key to preventing miscarriage of justice. However, neither the emphasis on the importance of ensuring the defendant's freedom from improper pressure to plead guilty in Hong Kong nor the leniency system in Mainland China has worked to accommodate the defendants' interests which stand at the core of its operation. The operational dynamics of the plea leniency system are weighed heavily toward efficacy with little regard to the fundamental norms of due process and fairness, upon which the procedural legitimacy of this trial-avoiding initiative is grounded.

Pursuing judicial efficiency and safeguarding rights are competing values that have yet to be reconciled in Chinese and Hong Kong plea leniency systems. What we need to think about is how to keep the bottom line of procedural justice while improving efficiency. How to lessen the pressure on defendants should be an urgent and crucial goal when implementing this scheme. Lawyers should fully perform their functions, including providing legal advice for detainees, relieving the unease of detention and isolation, informing suspects and defendants of their legal rights and litigation procedure in a timely manner, and appealing or suing on behalf of defendants when a proceeding is found to be illegal. Furthermore, the waiting time before trial—the pre-trial detention period in particular—should be reduced. It is time to adopt the principle of presumption of innocence and to avoid unnecessary detention. The leniency system of pleading guilty and accepting the penalty should be justified from the procedure, fully protecting the defense rights of suspects and defendants and preventing the wrongful convictions from the source.

References

Baldwin, J., & McConville, M. (1978). Plea Bargaining and Plea Negotiation in England. *Law & Society Review, 13*(2), 287–308.

Baum, J. (2021). *A Plea for Greater Reform and Engagement*. Retrieved December 20, from https://www.chinalawtranslate.com/a-plea-for-greater-reform-and-engagement/#_ftn13

Belkin, I. (2013). China's Tortuous Path Toward Ending Torture in Criminal Investigations. In *Comparative Perspectives on Criminal Justice in China*. Edward Elgar Publishing.

Biddulph, S., Nesossi, E., & Trevaskes, S. (2017). Criminal Justice Reform in the Xi Jinping Era. *China Law and Society Review, 2*(1), 63–128.

Blume, J. H., & Helm, R. K. (2014). The Unexonerated: Factually Innocent Defendants Who Plead Guilty. *Cornell Law Review, 100*, 157.

Bowers, J. (2007). Punishing the Innocent. *University of Pennsylvania Law Review, 156*(5), 1117–1179.

Chen, R. (2019). Review and Prospect of Criminal Defense System in the Past 40 Years. *Tribune of Political Science and Law, 6*, 4–5.

Chen, X. (2010). The Chinese Sentencing Guideline: A Primary Analysis. *Federal Sentencing Reporter, 22*(4), 213–216.

Cheng, K. K. (2023). *The Timing of Guilty Pleas: Lessons from Common Law Jurisdictions*. Cambridge University Press.

Cheng, K. K. (2013a). The Guilty Plea Process in the Hong Kong Magistrates' Courts. *HKU Theses Online (HKUTO).*

Cheng, K. K. (2013b). Pressures to Plead Guilty: Factors Affecting Plea Decisions in Hong Kong's Magistrates' Courts. *British Journal of Criminology, 53*(2), 257–275.

Cheng, K. K. (2018). Navigating Through the Effects of 'Cracked Trials': How Hong Kong Legal Practitioners Deal with Late Guilty Pleas. *Common Law World Review, 47*(2), 136–149.

Cheng, K. K., & Leung, P. Y. (2018). Passing the Threshold of One Justice System to the Next: Challenges of Emerging Young Adults in Hong Kong's Adult Criminal Justice Process. *International Journal of Offender Therapy and Comparative Criminology, 62*(9), 2650–2668.

Cheng, K. K. Y., Chui, W. H., & Ong, R. (2015). Providing Justice for Low-Income Youths: Publicly Funded Lawyers and Youth Clients in Hong Kong. *Social & Legal Studies, 24*(4), 577–593.

Cheng, K. K., Chui, W. H., Young, S. N., & Rebecca, O. (2018). Why Do Criminal Trials 'Crack'? An Empirical Investigation of Late Guilty Pleas in Hong Kong. *Asian Journal of Comparative Law, 13*(1), 1–25.

China Law Society. (2018). *Law Yearbook of China*. The Press of Law Yearbook of China.

Chiu, J. W. K. (2009). Criminal Interrogation and the Right to Remain Silent—A Study of the Hong Kong Customs Service. *International Journal of Police Science & Management, 11*(2), 217–235.

Chui, W. H., & Cheng, K. K. Y. (2017). Perceptions of Fairness and Satisfaction in Lawyer–Client Interactions Among Young Offenders in Hong Kong. *Journal of Mixed Methods Research, 11*(2), 266–285.

Cohen, J. A. (2013). Introductory Reflections. In *Comparative Perspectives on Criminal Justice in China*. Edward Elgar Publishing.

Cross, I. G., Cheung, P. W., & Tsui, E. Y. (2011). *Sentencing in Hong Kong*. LexisNexis Butterworths.

Dai, J. (2022). *From January to September This Year, the Application Rate of the Leniency System for Guilty Pleas and Punishments Reached 90.5%.* Retrieved December 10, from https://www.chinacourt.org/article/detail/2022/10/id/6956970.shtml

Department of Justice. (2022). *Key Figures and Statistics*. Retrieved March 23, from https://www.doj.gov.hk/en/about/stat.html.

Dervan, L. E., & Edkins, V. A. (2013). The Innocent Defendant's Dilemma: An Innovative Empirical Study of Plea Bargaining's Innocence Problem. *The Journal of Criminal Law & Criminology, 103*(1), 1–48.

Dobinson, I. (2013). The Guilty Plea: An Australian/Chinese Comparison. In *Comparative Perspectives on Criminal Justice in China*. Edward Elgar Publishing.

Feeley, M. M. (1979). *The Process Is the Punishment: Handling Cases in a Lower Criminal Court*. Russell Sage Foundation.

Galanter, M. (1974). Why the Haves Come Out Ahead: Speculations on the Limits of Legal Change. *Law and Society Review, 85*(3), 575–640.

He, X. (2021). Pressures on Chinese Judges Under Xi. *The China Journal, 85*(1), 49–74.

He, X. (2023). *Plea Leniency and Prosecution-Centeredness in China's Criminal Process*. Retrieved December 20, from https://papers.ssrn.com/sol3/papers.cfm?abstract_id=4184653

Hessick, C. B. (2021). *Punishment Without Trial: Why Plea Bargaining Is a Bad Deal*. Abrams.

Hu, M. (2018). The Role of Counsel and Its Perfection in the System of Plea Leniency—An Empirical Analysis of City H in Z Province. *Criminal Science, 5*, 115–126.

Inciardi, J. A. (1993). *Criminal Justice*. Harcourt Brace Jovanovich College Publishers.

Jiang, N. (2018). Excluding Tortured Confessions in the People's Republic of China: A Long March Towards the Eventual Abolition of Torture? *International Journal of Law, Crime and Justice, 54*, 1–10.

Li, E. (2010). The Li Zhuang Case: Examining the Challenges Facing Criminal Defense Lawyers in China. *Columbia Journal of Asian Law, 24*(1), 129–170.

Li, A. H. (2016). Centralisation of Power in the Pursuit of Law-Based Governance: Legal Reform in China Under the Xi Administration. *China Perspectives, 2*, 63–68.

Li, E. (2022a). Chinese Courts' New Plea Leniency System: Scrutinizing the Efficacy of Mandatory Defense Counsel. *The China Journal, 88*(1), 78–99.

Li, E. (2022b). Haste Makes Waste: Why China's New Plea Leniency System Is Doomed to Fail. *Asian Journal of Comparative Law, 17*(1), 76–105.

Li, X. (2015). Confession Governance and Chinese Criminal Judicial Referee. *Social Science in China, 1*, 119–205.

Liang, B., & He, N. (2014). Criminal Defense in Chinese Courtrooms: An Empirical Inquiry. *International Journal of Offender Therapy and Comparative Criminology, 58*(10), 1230–1252.

Lin, X., Gu, Z., & Lin, X. (2017). The Gap Between Law and Practice: An Empirical Study on China's High Pretrial Detention Rate. *Hong Kong Law Journal, 47*, 525–553.

Liu, S., & Halliday, T. C. (2009). Recursivity in Legal Change: Lawyers and Reforms of China's Criminal Procedure Law. *Law & Social Inquiry, 34*(4), 911–950.

Liu, S. (2011). Lawyers, State Officials and Significant Others: Symbiotic Exchange in the Chinese Legal Services Market. *The China Quarterly, 206*, 276–293.

Liu, S., Liang, L., & Michelson, E. (2014). Migration and Social Structure: The Spatial Mobility of Chinese Lawyers. *Law & Policy, 36*(2), 165–194.

Liu, S., & Halliday, T. C. (2016). *Criminal Defense in China: The Politics of Lawyers at work*. Cambridge University Press.

Lo, S. H., Cheng, K.K.-Y., & Chui, W. H. (2019). *The Hong Kong Legal System*. Cambridge University Press.

Lu, Y. (2021). *Comparative Research of the Plea Leniency System of China* [Dissertation, Indiana University].

Mackenzie, G. (2007). The Guilty Plea Discount: Does Pragmatism Win Over Proportionality and Principle? *Southern Cross University Law Review, 11*, 205–223.

McConville, M. (2011). *Criminal Justice in China: An Empirical Inquiry*. Edward Elgar Publishing.

Menefee, M. R. (2018). The Role of Bail and Pretrial Detention in the Reproduction of Racial Inequalities. *Sociology Compass, 12*(5), e12576.

Mou, Y. (2017). Overseeing Criminal Justice: The Supervisory Role of the Public Prosecution Service in China. *Journal of Law and Society, 44*(4), 620–645.

Mou, Y. (2020). *The Construction of Guilt in China: An Empirical Account of Routine Chinese Injustice* (Vol. 17). Bloomsbury Publishing.

Mou, Y. (2022). Techniques to Exploit Vulnerabilities: Persuasion and Education in Chinese Police Interrogations. *The British Journal of Criminology, 62*(3), 734–750.

Research Office Legislative Council Secretariat. (2021). *Prosecutions and Convictions*. Retrieved February 10, from https://www.legco.gov.hk/research-publications/english/2021issh14-prosecutions-and-convictions-20210114-e.pdf

Sanders, A., Young, R., & Burton, M. (2010). *Criminal Justice*. Oxford University Press.

Shytov, A., & Duff, P. (2019). Truth and Procedural Fairness in Chinese Criminal Procedure Law. *The International Journal of Evidence & Proof, 23*(3), 299–315.

So, S. (2020). *Law of Evidence in Hong Kong*. Thomson Reuters Hong Kong Limited Trading as Sweet & Maxwell.

Soubise, L. (2018). Guilty Pleas in an Inquisitorial setting—An Empirical Study of France. *Journal of Law and Society, 45*(3), 398–426.

Supreme People's Procuratorate. (2022). *The Main Case-Handling Data of National Procuratorial Organs in 2021*. Retrieved March 25, from https://www.spp.gov.cn/spp/xwfbh/wsfbt/202203/t20220308_547904.shtml#1

Tata, C. (2007). In the Interests of Clients or Commerce? Legal Aid, Supply, Demand, and 'Ethical Indeterminacy' in Criminal Defence Work. *Journal of Law and Society, 34*(4), 489–519.

Tata, C., & Gormley, J. M. (2016). Sentencing and Plea Bargaining: Guilty Pleas Versus Trial Verdicts. In *Oxford Handbooks Online: Criminology & Criminal Justice*. Oxford University Press. https://doi.org/10.1093/oxfordhb/9780199935383.013.40

The Law Reform Commission of Hong Kong. (2023). *The Procedure Governing the Admissibility of Confession Statements in Criminal Proceedings*. The Law Reform Commission of Hong Kong. https://www.hkreform.gov.hk/en/docs/radmissibility-e.pdf

The Supreme People's Procuratorate. (2021). *Supreme People's Procuratorate Issues Guiding Opinions to Comprehensively Regulate Sentencing Suggestions for Pleas of Guilty and Punishment Cases*. Retrieved December 20, from https://www.spp.gov.cn/spp/xwfbh/wsfbt/202112/t20211220_539038.shtml#1

Trevaskes, S. (2010). The Shifting Sands of Punishment in China in the Era of "Harmonious Society." *Law & Policy, 32*(3), 332–361.

Tu, G., & Che, Y. (2021). The Dilemma and Way Out of the Duty Lawyer System Under the Leniency System. *Shangquan Xinbian*. https://mp.weixin.qq.com/s/xHQvaFtRnwIvmYt6mmsUeg

Wu, Y. (2020a). Is a Plea Really a Bargain? An Empirical Study of Six Cities in China. *Asian Journal of Criminology, 15*(3), 237–258.

Wu, Y. (2020b). On the Effect of the Chinese Version of Speedy Trial and Plea Bargaining Pilot Programs: Observation from DUI Cases in Fujian Province. *Crime, Law and Social Change, 74*(4), 457–484.

Xiong, M., & Wei, S. (2017). Unequal Treatment in Pretrial Detention in China. *British Journal of Criminology, 57*(6), 1398–1419.

Xiong, Q. (2020). The Sentencing Recommendation in the System of Plea Leniency. *Peking University Law Journal, 32*, 1168–1186.

Yang, H., & Wu, S. (2020). The Proper Orientation of China's Lawyer on Duty System—Discussion on the Leniency System of Pleading Guilty and Accepting Penalty. *Open Journal of Social Sciences, 8*(12), 388–399.

Yin, B. (2021). Impact and Restraint of Performance Appraisal Indexes upon Criminal Procedure. *Legal Forum, 36*(2), 143–151.

Young, S. (2009). Prosecutions Division of the Department of Justice. In M. Gaylord, D. Gittings, & H. Traver (Eds.), *Introduction to Crime, Law and Justice in Hong Kong* (pp. 111–130). Hong Kong University Press.

Zuo, W. (2017). Why Impose Leniency on Admission of Guilty and Acceptance of Punishment: Misunderstanding and Clarification. *Chinese Journal of Law, 3*, 160–175.

Prosecution or Mediation: Perpetrator-Victim Negotiation in Macau and the Way Forward

Zhe Li, Xueke Fan, and Heng Ut Wong

Introduction

The main sources of criminal law in Macau are the 'Penal Code', 'Penal Procedure Code', separate criminal law, accessory criminal law, and international treaty (de Figueiredo Dias, 2021).[1] The Penal Code of Macau was introduced on November 14, 1995 and went into effect on January

Z. Li (✉) · H. U. Wong
School of Law, University of Macau, Macau, China
e-mail: zheli@um.edu.mo

X. Fan
School of Law, City University of Macau, Macau, China

[1] Many separate criminal laws are being executed in Macau, such as 'Organized Crime Act', 'Prevention and Repression of Money Laundering Crimes', 'Prohibition of Illicit Production, Trafficking and Consumption of Narcotic Drugs and Psychotropic Substances', and 'Combat the Crime of Human Trafficking'. Meanwhile, there are many accessory criminal laws in effect, such as 'Road Traffic Act', 'Prevention, Control and Treatment of Infectious Diseases', 'Copyright and Related Rights System', and 'Domestic Violence Prevention and Combating Act'.

E. Li et al. (eds.), *Criminal Case Dispositions through Pleas in Greater China*, https://doi.org/10.1007/978-981-97-1856-6_10

1, 1996,[2] while the Penal Procedure Code of Macau was passed on September 2, 1996 and came into force on April 1, 1997.[3] After Macau's return to Mainland China on December 20, 1999, these two decrees have continued to take effect in Macau pursuant to Article 19 of the Basic Law of the Macau Special Administrative Region. For the last two decades or so, the criminal law system in Macau has maintained a similar legislative framework to Portugal—Macau's former colonizer—with distinctive characteristics of the continental legal system remaining.

In colonial times, only courts played a role in the judiciary. Despite the establishment of the Public Prosecution Office (the Prosecution Office) following the adoption of the Basic Law of Judicial Organization of Macau in 1991, the Prosecution Office in Macau was regarded as an extension of the Portuguese Public Prosecution Office. After the handover of Macau, the Basic Law of Judicial Organization (Law No. 9/1999) was amended to stipulate that 'the Prosecution Office is the only judicial organization to exercise the prosecutorial functions conferred by law',[4] which requires that the Prosecution Office 'fulfill judicial responsibilities and undertake judicial tasks for assisting judges with finding out the truth'.[5] This is consonant with the ex officio principle that shapes and underpins the criminal justice system in Macau, in which prosecutors are legally obligated to promote the legitimacy of criminal proceedings.[6] In particular, the Prosecution Office must lay charges against an accused person when there is clear and sufficient criminal evidence collected during the investigation period.[7] This means that Macau prosecutors have a very limited power of *nolle prosequi*—a prosecutorial decision to not proceed with a criminal charge. As stressed by Gao Jialing, a legal expert from the Macau Legal Translation Office, Macau employs a criminal law system based on the *mens rea* principle and the discretion of prosecutors

[2] Decree-Law n.° 58/95/M, Approves the Criminal Code. Retrieved from https://bo.io.gov.mo/bo/i/95/46/codpencn/declei58.asp.

[3] Decree-Law n.° 48/96/M, Approves the Code of Criminal Procedure. Retrieved from https://bo.io.gov.mo/bo/i/96/36/codpropencn/declei48.asp.

[4] Decree-Law n.° 9/1999, Approves the Basic Law of the Judiciary Organization. Retrieved from https://bo.io.gov.mo/bo/i/1999/01/lei09_cn.asp. Article 55, Basic Law of Judicial Organization (Law No. 9/1999).

[5] Article 42, Basic Law of Judicial Organization (Law No. 9/1999).

[6] Article 37, Criminal Procedure Code (Law No. 48/96/M).

[7] Article 265, Criminal Procedure Code (Law No. 48/96/M).

is strictly regulated to the point that only minor offences and violations can be dealt with lightly through a diversionary and non-judicial process (Gao, 1997).

In Macau's current criminal justice system, when there is evidence of criminality, the accused can be exempt from trial proceedings in only three ways. Namely: (1) acquittal archiving; (2) suspension of proceedings; and (3) withdrawal of the complaint/private charge brought by the claimant (victim). Acquittal archiving refers to non-prosecution of venial misdemeanours.[8] The Prosecution Office may suggest to the judge that the case file be archived should the prosecutor be satisfied with all legal prerequisites of an acquittal. The suspension of proceedings applies generally to crimes punishable by up to three years imprisonment, in which the Prosecution Office may impose mandatory orders and rules of conduct on the accused person in lieu of filing a formal criminal charge to have the case heard at court. Depending on the circumstances surrounding the accused's behaviours in the community, the criminal proceedings may be resumed or terminated after the suspension period ends. The exemption by complaint withdrawal, on the other hand, concerns the incidents involving semi-public crimes and crimes of private prosecution.[9] In these self-initiated legal actions, the accused person will not be indicted if the complainant or private prosecutor withdraws the complaint or private charge during the investigation period with the permission of the Prosecution Office.[10]

These three diversionary approaches are not implemented through *plea negotiation*, which is not mentioned in Macau's criminal law. Yet, they are ordinarily carried out with the consent of the prosecutor upon the consensus of the perpetrator and the victim. In this regard, these procedures display reconciliation as part of the case processing mechanism. In practice, however, acquittal archiving and the suspension of proceedings are hardly used. While there are approximately 4000 cases prosecuted annually in Macau, there are approximately no more than ten cases handled by means of the suspension of proceedings system, and

[8] Article 262, Criminal Procedure Code (Law No. 48/96/M).

[9] The criminal law of Macau contains a large number of accusations for semi-public cases. Among 185 accusations in the Penal Code, more than 30 are semi-public cases, such as theft and injury to bodily integrity.

[10] Article 40, Criminal Procedure Code. (Law No. 48/96/M).

there is often no record of acquittal archiving.[11] The most common way to exempt criminal responsibility appears to be through the complainant's withdrawal of their complaint. Every year, there are approximately 3000 such cases.[12] Against this backdrop, this chapter focuses mainly on the suspension of proceedings system and complaint withdrawal. Both systems involve a certain degree of private communication (or negotiation) between the perpetrator and the victim, with the effect that criminal proceedings are suspended or terminated. Yet, they do not necessarily involve bargaining or negotiation on charges and sentences as seen in some other continental jurisdictions, and this pattern of practice shows a stark contrast to the plea-based case dispositional schemes currently utilized in Mainland China, Taiwan, and Hong Kong.

This chapter first examines the status quo of the suspension of criminal proceedings and complaint withdrawal in terms of their legislative settings, discursive dimensions, and practical traits. Our analysis goes on to highlight the challenges facing the process of perpetrator-victim reconciliation in these programmes. It indicates that among the identifiable issues, the lack of communication channels is most detrimental to meaningful and effective negotiation between the parties affected by the offence. It then suggests that a formal mediation system presided over by prosecutors be constructed to widen the scope of criminal cases settled through reconciliation. Doing so would likely improve judicial efficiency and better assist the accused with their acceptance of fault and reparation of harm as well as reintegration into society.

[11] Macao Special Administrative Region Procuratorate, Retrieved November 3, 2023, from https://www.mp.gov.mo/zh_tw/standard/Statistical_data.html.

[12] For example, in 2020, 4449 cases were filed by the Public Prosecutor's Office, 6 cases were suspended, and 2929 cases of quasi-public and private crimes were filed due to the withdrawal of the claimant. In 2021, 4315 cases were filed by the Public Prosecutor's Office, and 5 cases were suspended. The number of semi-public and crimes of private prosecution cases filed because the litigants did not pursue criminal responsibility was 3306.

The Suspension of Proceedings

The suspension of proceedings system in Macau is akin to reprieve prosecution systems or conditional non-prosecution systems that have prevailed in continental legal systems.[13] Situated between formal prosecution and acquittal archiving, the suspension of proceedings takes place where the following conditions are met: (1) there is clear and sufficient evidence of criminality; (2) the act is serious enough to warrant a prosecution based on the perpetrator's circumstance, the severity of criminal behaviour, and the public interest; and (3) probation is appropriate with relevant mandatory orders and rules of conduct being imposed on the accused. If the accused successfully fulfils their obligations during the probation period, the Prosecution Office will no longer prepare the indictment. However, the breach of probationary conditions by the accused will result in the prosecution being resumed (Chen, 2012).

The suspension of proceedings system in Macau originates from Portugal, but in application it differs significantly. The Portuguese Criminal Procedure Code established the suspension of proceedings system in as early as 1987. Based on the statistics released by the Portuguese Prosecutor General's Office, there were 31,766 cases dealt with through the suspension of proceedings system in 2022 nationwide.[14] Among them, 14,948 cases were suspended at the investigation stage and 16,818 cases were suspended at the summary proceedings stage. In contrast, from the return of Macau to Mainland China (1999) to the end of 2022, only 39 cases were handled via the suspension of proceedings with an average of less than 2 cases per year, compared to approximately 4000 cases

[13] In reprieve prosecution systems or conditional non-prosecution systems, the Public Prosecution Office will not prosecute the criminal suspect whose behaviour has constituted a crime when the circumstances are relatively minor, with conditions and deadlines. Instead, they decide whether to terminate the proceedings according to the performance of the accused. If the criminal suspect fulfils the additional conditions within the time limit, the public prosecution organ will no longer bring a lawsuit against them. If a criminal suspect fails to fulfil their obligations within the prescribed time limit, a lawsuit shall be instituted.

[14] The prosecutor's comprehensive report (2022), 178, Retrieved November 3, 2023, from https://www.ministeriopublico.pt/sites/default/files/documentos/pdf/ramp_2022_final.pdf.

prosecuted to trial in Macau annually.[15] Perceptibly, the suspension of proceedings has yet to play a major role in Macau's diversionary justice. Three contributing factors seem to stand out.

First, the procedure design of the suspension of proceedings process is unsympathetic to the prosecutor. As stipulated in Article 263 of the Penal Procedure Code, the application of the suspension of proceedings requires the consent of all parties concerned, including the accused person, the complainant, and/or the victim. The complainant must declare their intention to become an assistant (and be qualified to become an assistant) during the prosecution stage.[16] More importantly, the accused and the complainant (assistant) and/or victim must personally, freely, and clearly give consent to the suspension of proceedings on the basis that they are aware of the legal consequences of criminal proceedings being suspended, the period and conditions of probation, and relevant mandatory orders and rules of conduct imposed on the perpetrator. In many respects, these stipulations speak to the importance of negotiated justice dispersed between individuals affected by criminal behaviours, and reflect a restorative function of criminal justice.

In reality, however, the victims (particularly those of public crimes) appear to be unwilling to become assistants (Yao & Gao, 2011). This could be due to the victim being uncomfortable with the idea of facing the perpetrator as it is likely to bring back memories of past traumas. A more plausible explanation perhaps is that victims lack confidence that negotiated and restorative justice will address their needs and interests. Therefore, the necessity of obtaining the consent of all parties has become a practical impediment to the application of the suspension of proceedings. Even if consent is successfully acquired, the prosecutor needs

[15] Public Prosecutions Office of the Macao Special Administrative Region, Retrieved September 11, 2023, from https://www.mp.gov.mo/zh_tw/standard/Statistical_data.html.

[16] In Article 58 of the Criminal Procedure Code, the assistant has the status of assisting the procuratorate, and their participation in the proceedings shall be subordinate to the activities of the procuratorate. In particular, the assistant has the following powers: (a) to participate in the investigation or preliminary examination, to provide evidence, and to request measures deemed necessary; (b) make a complaint independent of the prosecution (in cases where criminal proceedings are not possible without a private prosecution, the auxiliary may file a complaint independently even if the public prosecutor does not file a complaint); and (c) appeal against a decision affecting them, even if no appeal has been filed by the Public Prosecutor's Office.

to make a recommendation to the judge, who will then exercise the decision-making power as to whether the criminal proceedings should be suspended. As the whole process of seeking consent can be time-consuming and laborious, it is not uncommon that the Prosecution Office opts to go with the criminal prosecution, allowing the case to be decided by the court, which renders the practice of the suspension of proceedings nominal, if not entirely meaningless.[17]

Second, compared to its Portuguese counterparts, the scope of the suspension of proceedings is rather limited. In Article 263 of the Penal Procedure Code, it is provided that the crimes to be handled through the suspension of proceedings should be punishable by fine or a maximum imprisonment of no more than three years. In this light, the suspension of proceedings process can only be applied to misdemeanours. This is because crimes punishable by more than three years imprisonment in Macau's criminal law are generally seen as serious indictable offences which have a relatively high need for crime prevention.[18] Here, the term 'maximum imprisonment' refers to the maximum sentence that can possibly be imposed on a convicted individual, rather than the specific penalty that is handed down by the judge in a particular case.[19] Notably, the Penal Code of Portugal increased the required maximum sentence to five years under the suspension of proceedings in 1998.[20] The rationale behind this change is that by lowering the application threshold, the suspension of proceedings gets to reach a wider cohort of criminal cases deemed to have lesser degrees of culpability and severity. This way, Portuguese courts are arguably given more time and resources to handle more serious criminal cases. While Macau has yet to follow suit, whether

[17] Ibid., 8.

[18] Macau Penal Code, Article 48, paragraph 1. If having regard to the perpetrator's personality, living conditions, acts before and after the commission of the crime, and the circumstances of the crime, the court considers that mere condemnation of the facts and the threat of imprisonment are appropriate and sufficient to achieve the purpose of punishment, it may suspend the execution of a sentence of imprisonment not exceeding three years.

[19] In terms of institutional application of the suspension of proceedings, there are still some issues that have remained unaddressed by the legislature: (1) how to understand the maximum imprisonment in the event of crime coherency and (2) is it necessary to increase the required maximum abstract sentence to five years. These two issues have not been sufficiently examined theoretically and practically in Macau.

[20] Amendment of the Code of Criminal Procedure, Decree-Law n.° 59/98 of Portugal.

making the suspension of proceedings a more broadly applicable practice would increase cost-efficiency and the productivity of case disposition is certainly worth contemplating.

Third, although the suspension of proceedings is devised in view of rehabilitation and reparation of harms caused by crimes, it has long lacked an effective communication channel for the perpetrator and the victim to restore the broken relationship. There is a gap between what the programme can achieve in practice and what the programme is expected to achieve under the aegis of restorative justice.[21] In particular, the suspension of proceedings is not an effective way for the accused person to express their remorse or apologies. Neither is it one where the victim can speak about their traumatizing experience or express their needs so that effective and targeted solutions for harm reparation can be sought (Yao & Gao, 2011). The Portuguese scholar J. Figueiredo Dias claimed that the suspension of proceedings is not a truly consensual process, but simply the consent of one or more subjects of litigation expressed on the suggestions or statements made by other subjects of litigation (de Figueiredo Dias, 2011). Except for the Domestic Violence Prevention and Combating Act, Macau has not established a mechanism conducive to positive dialogue, communication, and negotiation between perpetrators and victims.[22] In many cases, opinions of the perpetrator parties are unilaterally solicited rather than being expressed in a free manner.[23] Without the genuine opportunity to admit mistakes, repent, and make up for the loss and damage incurred by the victim, the suspension of

[21] Public Prosecutions Office of the Macao Special Administrative Region, Retrieved September 11, 2023, from https://www.mp.gov.mo/zh_tw/standard/Statistical_data.html.

[22] Article 29, Domestic Violence Prevention and Combating Act. In the conciliation conference, during the suspension of proceedings, the examining judge may, at the request of the Prosecutor's Office, the suspect, the victim, or the auxiliary, convene a conciliation meeting between the suspect and the victim, with the aim of making the suspect aware of the inaccuracy of his conduct and giving him the opportunity to express remorse and obtain forgiveness from the victim.

[23] Article 263, Macau Criminal Procedure Law. If the offence is punishable by imprisonment for a maximum of not more than three years, even if it is punishable by a fine, or if the offence is punishable by a fine only, and if the following are true, the Public Prosecutor may recommend to the examining judge that by imposing mandatory orders and rules of conduct on the suspect.

proceedings is unable to properly attend to the victims' priorities and its philosophy premised on restorative justice is doomed to fail.

The Complaint Withdrawal Process

In Macau, criminality is classified as a public crime, a semi-public crime, or a crime of private prosecution, depending on the severity of the criminal behaviour and the specific complainant (victim) (Li, 2015). The prosecution of public crimes is a statutory obligation the Prosecution Office must discharge, whereas the prosecution of semi-public crimes is brought on the condition that the complainant enters a complaint.[24] Compared to public crimes, semi-public crimes warrant less serious levels of criminal responsibility, which, to some degree, resembles misdemeanours in most common law jurisdictions (e.g. the US and Australia). Defined in the Penal Code under a range of categories, semi-public crimes include *inter alia* simple offenses to physical integrity (Article 137), simple theft (Article 197), fraud (Article 211), property damage (Article 206), minor subtraction (Article 241), defamation (Article 174), and publicity and slander (Article 177). At the bottom of this criminality ladder are crimes of private prosecution. They refer to criminal acts that can only be dealt with upon legal action brought by the victim (private prosecutor). Ordinarily, it starts with police investigation before the case is handed over to the Prosecution Office. The Prosecution Office is in no position to initiate a criminal charge, and here their role is to notify the victim of the findings of investigation so that the private prosecutor can make an informed decision on entering a complaint on their own.

The victims of semi-public crimes and crimes of private prosecution can renounce their right to make a complaint.[25] But as soon as the victim makes a complaint, police will need to immediately inquire about the victim's intention to pursue the perpetrator's responsibility should the incident involve semi-public crimes or crimes of private prosecution. However, providing a statement of complaint does not necessarily mean that the victim has exercised their right to provoke private prosecution, which must be explicit and clear. If the victim expresses a desire to hold

[24] Semi-public crimes refer to Simple Offenses to Physical Integrity (Article 137), Simple Theft (Article 197), Fraud (Article 211), Damage (Article 206), Minor Subtraction (Article 241), Defamation (Article 174), Publicity and Slander (Article 177).

[25] Article 180 (1), the Macau Criminal Code.

the perpetrator criminally liable, police need to send the victim's statement to the Prosecution Office to officially open a case.[26] Notably, the law sets out an implied form of waiver of complaint and private prosecution. Article 61 (2) of the Penal Code stipulates that if the victim starts a civil action to seek damage or compensation, the right to complain regarding a criminal matter is deemed to have been waived. If that is the case, then the victim can no longer make a complaint or initiate a private charge.

Still, parties involved in the cases of semi-public crimes and crimes of private prosecution are granted relatively greater procedural autonomy. That is, the victim is allowed to withdraw the complaint at any point with the consent of judicial authorities.[27] A withdrawal made during the investigation period requires leave from the Prosecution Office, whereas a withdrawal made during the instruction or trial period should be approved by the investigating judge or the presiding judge respectively.[28] In the latter scenario, the judge ought to notify the accused about the victim's withdrawal so that the accused can declare whether they object to the withdrawal of prosecution within the prescribed time frame. In practice, it is common for the victim to submit a written statement of their intention to withdraw to judicial authorities, who will then immediately file the statement and notify the accused to comment on the withdrawal statement. In addition, the victim may also make a retraction statement in the form of a private document, which will then be filed into the case dossier for the accused to express their views on.[29] If the suspect does not object to the withdrawal of the complaint, the judicial authorities will give approval to the withdrawal in accordance with Article 108 (2) of the Macau Criminal Code and Article 40 of the Macau Criminal Procedure

[26] Article 39, Macau Criminal Procedure Code. The Public Prosecutor's Office shall, ex officio, take any measures which it considers necessary for the discovery of the truth and which are within its competence, participate in all proceedings in which a private prosecutor is involved, lodge complaints together with the private prosecutor, and appeal independently against the decision.

[27] Article 40, the Macau Criminal Procedure Code.

[28] Article 268, the Macau Criminal Penal Procedure Code. The purpose of the instruction is to provide judicial verification of the decision to file a complaint or investigation in order to decide whether to bring the case to trial.

[29] Article 40, Macau Criminal Procedure Code.

Code, thus declaring that the proceeding is no longer legitimate and filing it.

If the withdrawal is known during the investigation, it is approved by the Prosecutor's Office. If it is known during the instruction trial or trial, it shall be approved by the investigating judge or the presiding judge respectively. If the withdrawal is made during an instruction trial or a trial, the judge who has the authority to give approval shall notify the suspect that they may declare within the statutory period whether or not they object to the withdrawal. The participation of the prosecutor's office in criminal proceedings is terminated when the withdrawal of a complaint or private prosecution is recognized.

In many cases, the complainant puts forward certain conditions in the withdrawal statement, claiming that the complaint or private prosecution is revocable should the perpetrator meet the conditions (Leal-Henriques & Santos, 1995). This is, however, at odds with the legal principles. The Penal Code outlines that the withdrawal of a complaint or private prosecution is deterministic and cannot be accompanied by conditions, nor can it be given up or withdrawn without reservation (Leal-Henriques, 2014). The same is true for the 'no objection' decision made by the accused. Leal-Henriques, a Portuguese scholar in Macau, aptly pointed out that unlike renunciation being a purely unilateral act, retraction is inherently a legal act of both parties, and its legal effect hinges on the agreement of the aggrieved person and the accused (Leal-Henriques, 2014). That said, if the accused does not object to the withdrawal of complaint or private prosecution, the judge will have to approve the withdrawal in accordance with Article 108 (2) of the Penal Code and Article 40 of the Penal Procedure Code. After the withdrawal, no further complaint or private prosecution is allowed.

The Macau Prosecution Office filed a total of 8047 cases as of 2022. Among these, there were approximately 3000 cases involving semi-public crimes or crimes of private prosecution where the complaint or private prosecution was withdrawn by the victims.[30] This high rate of withdrawal is attributable, in part, to the relatively simple procedure and easier operation of complaints and private prosecution. Perhaps a more significant reason is that Macau is a small and highly organic society. Covering an

[30] Procuratorate statistics for the year 2022. Retrieved November 3, 2023, from https://www.mp.gov.mo/zh_tw/standard/Statistical_data_detail/article/lgn4hvoo.html.

area of 32.9 square kilometres and having only a population of approximately 660,000, Macau is geographically narrow, densely populated and has the characteristics of an 'acquaintance society'. Due to historical reasons, numerous ethnic groups, classes as well as multiple languages, cultures, and values have taken root in this small city. Diverse, complex, and heterogeneous societies are prone to social unrest and disorder, but Macau is harmonious and stable, which is divergent from other similar societies which tend to be laden with frequent political disputes and social contradictions.[31] In particular, there is an assortment of associations in Macao, covering all aspects of society, including politics, corporations, workers, women, returned expat Chinese, social welfare, education, students, culture and art, medical and health care, sports, religion, clan, and so on (Lu, 2008). At present, there are over 3000 communities officially registered in Macau, with an average of 200 members for each community. This structure is known as 'small government, big society' (Huang, 2016). Clearly, civil society functions as the cornerstone of social harmony and stability in Macau, promoting group unity and social trust, integrating different social classes, values, and concepts, and alleviating social confrontation and tension. It plays a pivotal role in maintaining social harmony and promoting political stability in Macao (Sun et al., 2006).

A considerable number of the withdrawal cases in Macau were intervened by social actors (e.g. lawyers or concerned third parties) who energetically function as facilitators of communication and mediation between perpetrators and victims. This is demonstrated by the parties' preference for the use of out-of-court settlement as the prime approach to resolving the dispute (Jiang, 2010). Out-of-court settlement is not new in civil law, but its popularity in Macau's criminal process is representative of the city's long-existing culture as a highly interconnected 'acquaintance society'. In many cases involving semi-public crimes and crimes of private prosecution, the perpetrator and the victim appear to be neighbours or colleagues, or even family relatives (Sun, 2018). As semi-public crimes and crimes of private prosecution display a low degree of culpability, harms caused by these crimes are generally trivial. Hence it is not uncommon

[31] The Social Security Situation in Macao Has Remained Stable and Sound. Government portal of the Macao Special Administrative Region of the People's Republic of China. Retrieved November 3, 2023, from https://www.gov.mo/zh-hant/news/893944/?utm_source=link%26utm_medium=share.

that the victim often does not prefer the involvement of judicial authorities, as judicial intervention may lead to greater costs, expenses, and time. In the eyes of victims, the judicial intervention in an 'acquaintance society' may not necessarily play out as the best protection for victims. Rather, it is adverse to the reconciliation, reparation, and restoration of social relations conducive to an effective means of dispute resolution accepted by both the victim and the perpetrator (Li, 2009).

Like many plea-based dispositional measures in common law and continental countries, the withdrawal of complaint or private prosecution entails the perpetrator's admission of wrongdoing, the victim's forgiveness and the abandonment of the trial process. More specifically, a victim's consideration of withdrawing the complaint and private prosecution revolve around two factors. First, it must be shown that the accused is willing to accept full responsibility and apologize to the victim for what they did. Second, the perpetrator agrees to make compensation for loss and injury caused by the crime (Tang, 2020). While it is imperative for the perpetrator and the victim to engage in productive conversations to discuss the impact and consequences of the crime, the Penal Procedure Code provides no guidance on the scope, form, and means of such negotiation. Foremost, it is not mandated that the prosecutor be present. This is compounded by the fact that the negotiation process and the content of settlement are not judicially supervised. Neither prosecutors nor judges are legally obligated to ensure that the outcomes of negotiation comply with the legal rules, public order, and social norms. This hand-off setting leaves concerned parties with no option but to take initiative to reach out to each other. In a better case scenario, parties retain the criminal lawyer to mediate and serve as a bridge for the perpetrator and the victim to exchange their opinions. However, the dearth of a regulatory or supervisory body makes the process of complaint withdrawal an informal practice of criminal justice, which is likely to beget a greater risk of undermining the integrity of the criminal process due to judicial authorities conceding the power of law enforcement to private parties on the ground.

Should a Formal Criminal Mediation System Be Established?

As discussed above, the suspension of proceedings and complaint withdrawal are two common trial-avoiding measures in Macau's criminal justice system. Both initiatives are devised to avoid the formal processing of an offender by the criminal justice system and advance a consensual form of justice. Yet, both initiatives also lack a working mechanism in favour of communication and negotiation between the perpetrator and the victim to talk about what happened, how they were impacted, and how the harm can be repaired. This makes the notion of plea-based case disposition in Macau almost void. The only exception perhaps is the use of mediation as prescribed in the Domestic Violence Prevention and Combating Act. Passed in 2016, the Domestic Violence Prevention and Combating Act provides that during the suspension of proceedings the judge may convene the mediation meeting between the accused and the victim at the request of the Prosecution Office.[32] The objective of mediation is to make the accused aware of the harm caused by their wrongdoing and to provide an opportunity for the accused to express remorse so that the victim can offer forgiveness. Nevertheless, this negotiation process applies exclusively to the cases involving intimate violence offences, which makes Macau one of the few civil law jurisdictions that has yet to establish a general criminal mediation system for fostering victim-perpetrator reconciliation. However, both from a cultural perspective and considering its actual judicial practices, a formal criminal mediation system should be established in Macau's criminal justice system.

First, this omission is unfortunate as Macau has a profound cultural foundation fit for plea-based restorative justice to thrive. For long, people in Macau have regarded familial and social harmony as the ideal social substructure (Yao, 2019). Particularly the philosophy of Confucius that promotes ritual, virtue, and benevolence has a significant bearing on everyone's social life and way of thinking. In a highly interpersonal society, people are more cautious about resorting to litigation and judicial processes when dealing with contradictions and conflicts (Ma, 2018). Instead, 'face-saving' turns out to be a priority concern (Ma, 2018). This is also illustrated by a heavy use of mediation as an approach to dispute resolution in civil matters in Macau. Therefore, when it comes to criminal matters, the introduction of mediation, as some scholars maintain, 'will demonstrate the respect for well-endorsed Chinese culture and Confucian philosophy, which can reflect the harmonious coexistence of culture, philosophy and law in the Macau legal system' (Robalo, 2016). In this context, there are always victims who are reluctant to face perpetrators

[32] Article 29, the Domestic Violence Prevention and Combating Act.

as adversaries. Hoping to settle the dispute in a peaceful fashion through negotiation, some victims prioritize apology and compensation over retaliation and punishment, while some defendants strive to temper sentences and restore relationships by actively making up to victims affected by their acts (Chen & Ge, 2006). On a larger scale, mediation has long been widely adopted by countries with a civil law system, such as France, Germany, Portugal, and the like. In these systems the will of perpetrators and victims to privately resolve criminal matters through non-judicial processes is respected, which has morphed into an essential component of case disposition in their criminal justice systems.[33]

Second, the judicial practices of Macau's criminal justice system are not merely punitive-oriented. The Penal Code stipulates that 'punishment and security measures are aimed at protecting legal interests and reintegrating the perpetrator into society'.[34] This suggests that penalty in Macau is assigned a dual purpose. On the one hand, it focuses on retribution, deterrence, and community protection to punish the deserving. On the other hand, it champions correction, rehabilitation, and social integration to promote public harmony. Therefore, although the ex officio principle requires prosecutors to engage in the pursuit of criminal cases, and, if necessary, submit the case for trial through the exercise of their prosecutorial power (Carvalho & de Processo Penal, 2015), not every criminal case is heard at court. This, therefore, explains the application of the suspension of proceedings and complaint withdrawal at the prosecutor's discretion as ways of performing restorative functions of criminal justice in Macau. While more work is certainly needed to improve the rehabilitative and corrective elements of these diversionary initiatives, they have laid a solid institutional foundation for the criminal mediation system to take shape. In a more practical sense, heavy-handed legal actions, including prosecution, sentencing, and imprisonment, are antithetical to the idea of reintegration, reform, and rehabilitation. Under normal circumstances, tensions between the perpetrator and the victim (and the society more generally) will not be mitigated by simply having the perpetrator go through nerve-racking criminal proceedings. As people are increasingly exposed to alternative justice schemes that are less tense, decorous, and procedurally rigid, the conventional style of prosecution,

[33] Ibid., 16.

[34] Article 40 Macau Criminal Law.

trial, and sentencing is likely to lose its momentum and gradually give way to more consensual approaches to criminality.

The Mediation System with the 'Macau Characteristics'

If a mediation system is discursively and institutionally warranted, then what should it entail? Indeed, Macau has instituted a number of trial-avoiding schemes, demonstrating a lenient perspective on criminal justice. Despite this, they are largely insufficient to nurture a meaningful interaction between the accused and the victim to materialize the conditions of restorative and negotiated justice. The lack of communication platforms has unsurprisingly resulted in relatively low application rates of the suspension of proceedings and complaint withdrawal, which leads us to consider a structural overhaul of these diversionary programmes in hopes of pursuing more efficacious reconciliation between the parties involved in the dispute.

In Portugal, for example, criminal mediation (or reconciliation) is an informal procedure wherein the perpetrator and the victim may reach a consensus on criminal responsibility and compensation by means of negotiation under the auspices of a neutral third party (Yu, 2015). Contextually, mediation in Portugal applies to crimes associated with minor injuries, victims' complaints, and private prosecution.[35] Covering predominately petty crimes, Portuguese criminal mediation is not applicable to crimes punishable by more than 5 years of imprisonment, sexual assault crimes, corruption, and bribery, crimes in which the victim is under 16 years old, and crimes where the summary procedure is applicable. A characteristic feature of criminal mediation in Portugal is that the mediation process is carried out by a third party. For example, the Minors Protection Act states that mediation in cases involving juvenile offences ought to be conducted by the General Council for Reintegration (DGRS)—an auxiliary institution under the leadership of the Ministry of Justice. Guided by the 'minimum intervention principle', DGRS is tasked with the overall supervision of juvenile crime cases, the application of mediation, and most importantly the facilitation of juvenile offenders' integration into society (Long, 2011). Operationally, mediation is

[35] Article 2, Portuguese Law No. 21/2007, Criminal Mediation System.

conducted by a professional arbiter, who, according to the Portuguese Law No. 21/2007, must have received proper training in mediation skills with relevant legal, managerial, and psychological knowledge. The mediator should also meet the strict requirements of age, degree, professional experience, and language competence among others.[36] The final decision-making power, however, lies with the prosecuting and judicial authorities who get to decide how the case should be disposed of on the grounds of a particular mediation outcome.

From a utilitarian perspective, Portugal's criminal mediation system has paid heed to the offender's need for rehabilitation; but it has yet to achieve the goal of efficiency. Apart from reducing the workload of judges, mediation by a third party increases the burden placed on already limited judicial resources. In this process, a mediation specialist is essential. It takes years of training to become a capable intermediary with the requisite experience, techniques, and skills. The fact that mediation is a mandatory approach to dealing with petty offences has oftentimes resulted in extra costs. Relatedly, it was found that mediation has also given rise to (undue) delays in case management by holding multiple perpetrator-victim meetings compared to a one-off trial that determines the case outcome.

In view of these drawbacks, it may not be unreasonable to license an existing law enforcement agency to fulfil the role of mediator for two reasons. First, the law enforcement agency (often as the handling officer of the case) is well equipped with first-hand information about the facts, circumstances, and evidence of the case. Second, the law enforcement agency has the required authority to regulate the mediation process and the power to execute the settlement agreement reached by the perpetrator and the victim. Having said that, in the context of Macau's criminal justice system a suitable candidate is the prosecutor. As stipulated in the Penal Procedure Law, the prosecutor in Macau not only presides over and supervises the investigation but also assumes the responsibility for discovering and collecting evidence in relation to the case. In cases where there is strong evidence of a crime and the specific perpetrator is identifiable, the Prosecution Office is authorized to initiate a formal charge against the suspect, and, more crucially, to oversee the entire criminal process with a full grasp of the circumstances of the case. This prosecutor-led model has

[36] Portuguese Law No. 21/2007, Criminal mediation system.

made prosecutors a dominant and decisive player in almost every aspect of the criminal justice system. As such, a new mediation system in Macau, like many plea-based case dispositional measures in continental jurisdictions, can be better operated by prosecuting agencies which have the legitimacy and authority to effectuate mediation in the interest of the parties' needs as well as efficiency. Able to suggest solutions in light of the circumstances of the case, the prosecutor is often accepted by parties as the impartial arbitrator not least because the judicial official is believed to be 'a person who upholds fairness without favouring and showing bias towards anyone in the exercise of his/her power' (Lu & Liang, 2011).

This way, prosecutors are in a better position to encourage voluntary negotiation between the perpetrator and the victim. Procedurally speaking, the proposed mediation process should start with the reconciliation meeting attended by all relevant parties, including legal representatives, as organized and supervised by the case-handling prosecutor. During this process, the prosecutor should have acquired the particulars of the case, understood the victim's demands, and recorded the offender's repentance and acceptance of criminal responsibility. Once a settlement agreement is formed, the prosecutor needs to review its content to evaluate the legality and enforceability of the settlement agreement and ensure that mediation has not been fruitless (He, 2016).

As prosecutors are state agencies with authorized power to implement criminal law, they are generally afforded with latitude to make discretionary decisions as to how a criminal matter should be dealt with. This means the prosecutor may decide to (not) endorse mediation according to the specific circumstances of the case. In Portugal's criminal mediation procedure, for example, the mediator may assess the prospect of success in terms of settlement before setting up the meeting. In the event of parties unwilling to engage in negotiation (or where there are other thorny obstacles to mediation), the prosecutor may stay the proceedings and switch to a criminal trial (Yu, 2015). A successful mediation process should normally entail certain procedural norms and standards as follows:

The consent of parties. The legitimacy of mediation rests upon the consent of the parties involved. Put differently, the voluntariness of parties is a prerequisite for an enforceable settlement agreement, which only arises where both parties get to make choices in the exercise of their free will (Su, 2005). This resonates with plea bargaining where guilty pleas should be made voluntarily, knowingly, and intelligently because it is said to reflect the concept of contractual freedom by which parties enter the agreement understanding their rights and obligations, as well as the legal consequences (Wang, 2013a, 2013b). Along the same lines, settlement between the perpetrator and the victim in criminal mediation should be deemed a free-willed 'contract' as a way of dispute resolution. Here, the perpetrator should be willing to admit their criminal liability and compensate for the victims' losses in exchange for exemption from the execution of a penalty. The victim will then give up their right to request a trial of the perpetrator to obtain the restitution as soon as possible.

The endorsement of prosecutors. As the arbitrators in the mediation process, the prosecutors' endorsement of perpetrator-victim settlement is crucial to the finalization of criminal cases. Without judicial checks and balances, the prosecutor should discharge the responsibility of reviewing the content of the settlement agreement, making a proper analysis of its authenticity, legality, and feasibility. Regarding semi-public crimes, the settlement agreement should play a similar role as the out-of-court settlement widely used in the complaint withdrawal: the victim revokes the complaint, with the prosecutor verifying the content of mediation and archiving the case as a result. In cases involving the suspension of proceedings, the prosecutor then ought to confirm the settlement agreement, monitor the implementation of the agreement conditions, and follow up on the perpetrator's performance under compulsory orders and rules of conduct, if any. Should the perpetrator violate the settlement agreement or breach relevant mandatory orders and rules of conduct, the responsible prosecutor is sanctioned to rescind the suspension of proceedings decision, triggering the resumption of criminal prosecution.

In constructing a mediation system with Macau's characteristics, the procedural settings should go hand in hand with the substantive framework—namely, the scope and content of mediation. Across most jurisdictions around the globe, criminal mediation is almost always limited to petty crimes, such as misdemeanours and juvenile offences. While the element of reconciliation is not invisible in serious crimes, Macau's mediation system should remain reserved for semi-public crimes and crimes of private prosecution. If a further specification on the categories of petty crimes falling within the purview of mediation is called for, it is then sensible to define them by the length of possible sentence. One example for reference is the use of criminal mediation in France where the applicable crimes are set as those with the fixed-term imprisonment of no more than two years (Wang, 2013a, 2013b), including *inter alia* offences of minor property damage, family court cases, and public order offences.

This arrangement appears to be in line with the composition of criminality in Macau, where most semi-public crimes and crimes of private prosecution do not trigger the heavy punishment of imprisonment.

More pragmatically, in the current judicial ambience of Macau, criminal cases suitable for mediation could have the following conditions: (1) petty crimes with a fixed-term imprisonment of no more than three years—with the exception of crimes of domestic violence prescribed in Law No. 2/2016, for which the maximum penalty shall be fixed-term imprisonment of no more than five years, and crimes with a penalty of fine or may be subject to a fine; (2) crimes related to familial relations (e.g. between parents and children); (3) juvenile crimes; and (4) negligent crimes. This is because the aforementioned crimes are said to cause minor personal and social harms. This paves the way for criminal mediation to take place as in those cases perpetrators may have not been physically or mentally developed and are hence unable to judge right from wrong, or the perpetrators' subjective malice is minor to the point that the perpetrator can be readily forgiven by the victim. In this regard, criminal mediation serves essentially as an alternative to criminal prosecution and trial of individuals committing petty crimes. It enables those perpetrators to be exempt from criminal liability and receive proportionate punishment while preparing to assume active responsibility for harm reparation and compensation as set out in the settlement agreement (Wang, 2013a, 2013b).

Considering this, the content of mediation should also consist of the perpetrator's acknowledgement of wrongdoing, apology to the victim, and compensation for property loss or damage, to say the least (He & Liu, 2009). For instance, in crimes involving acquaintances or family members, apology and repentance from the perpetrator is instrumental to reconciliation as well as forgiveness from the victim. There is no doubt that obtaining the understanding of the victim is key to the success of mediation, which further determines whether the goals of rehabilitation and crime prevention can be materialized on the ground. The willingness of the perpetrator to admit guilt and take responsibilities has a positive effect on offenders' social integration (Mao, 2015). On a relevant note, perpetrator's apology and repentance can often be demonstrated by restitution for (substantiated) losses associated with the offence, such as damage to property, or medical expenses. In most instances, whether the perpetrator could be forgiven by the victim depends largely on whether the victim is satisfied with the perpetrator's reparative effort (Chen, 2018).

The prosecutor is thus expected to review the content of the settlement agreement. Tests that can be run to assess the legality and viability of the agreement may include: (1) whether the agreement is entered by the parties voluntarily and knowingly in the exercise of their free will; (2) whether the agreement is lawful and seeks to pursue the aims of rehabilitation and crime prevention; (3) whether mandatory orders and rules of conduct are appropriate to the circumstances of the case; (4) whether the restitution is reasonable and in the public interest; and (5) whether the agreement contains improper arrangements, such as penalties that deprive personal liberty, violations of human dignity, and malicious circumvention of legal rules. If upon the examination a specific agreement is deemed unreasonable and unjustifiable, the prosecutor should be able to exercise their discretion to make amendments or request that the parties make changes accordingly. For example, where the restitution is set excessively high, the prosecutor should have the power to modify the amount in question in accordance with the compensation standards and the principle of equity as stipulated in the Civil Code of Macau. It follows that the prosecutor may then invalidate the settlement agreement if the parties refuse to accept the modification or refuse to make the amendments as requested.

Conclusion

Criminal law is the last line of defence in society. Strict enforcement of criminal law, characterized by criminal prosecution, trial, and punishment, represents a State's stern approach to crime. However, criminalization should only be relied upon as a last resort given the negative impact on individuals that indictment, conviction, and imprisonment bring in their wake. In other words, criminal law ought to be applied cautiously to manifest its 'modesty'—e.g. where there are other laws sufficient to deal with a certain unlawful act, criminal law should not apply; where there are diversionary programmes sufficient to hold the perpetrator accountable for wrongdoing, prosecution and judicial proceedings should be refrained from; and where there are lenient sanctions sufficient to serve the sentencing aims, harsh sanctions should not be applied (Zhang, 1995). In this chapter, we examined a number of trial-avoiding mechanisms and the way they are operationalized to reflect the 'modesty' of Macau's criminal law. Introduced to divert petty offenders from the criminal justice system, these trial-avoiding mechanisms manifest themselves in the praxis in ways such as the suspension of criminal proceedings and withdrawal of complaint by victims whose rights and interests are affected by transgressions. However, the realization of this modest aspect of criminal law is shaped by various factors—namely, whether the perpetrator accepts their obligations, whether the victim is willing to forgive and forget, whether a settlement agreement is reached in the public interest and also reflects the needs and expectations of all parties involved, among others.

In particular, the analysis of Macau's trial-avoiding justice schemes indicates that there is hardly a plea-based case dispositional system as there is in Mainland China, Taiwan, and Hong Kong. Where the prosecutor decides to suspend the criminal proceedings and the victim decides to withdraw the complaint, the law remains ambiguous as to whether the perpetrator is required to submit guilty pleas to the criminal charges. The focus of the diversionary practices tends to be on the reconciliation between the perpetrator and the victim to justify the stay of prosecution and judicial proceedings. Yet, our analysis also speaks to the reality that the suspension of criminal proceedings and complaint withdrawal have both saddled with the lack of a meaningful platform for the perpetrator and the victim to engage and discuss the effects of the offence.

This leads us to suggest that Macau introduce a mediation system to rationalize and catalyse its diversionary initiatives in the criminal process. Not only will it promote the 'modesty' of criminal law by creating a formal pathway for petty perpetrators to be discharged from criminal liability, but it is likely to enhance the quality of criminal reconciliation by generating case outcomes in alignment with the principles of legality, transparency, and accountability. Besides, establishing a mediation system in Macau is in line with a recent global trend of developing restorative justice as an alternative to conventional justice premised on deterrence and denunciation. From the perspective of a 'harmonious society', mediation in criminal cases is reasonably expected to yield a better effect on rehabilitation and crime prevention since the mediation process is, more or less, a process of education (Zhou, 2017). While a guilty plea is not required, it can help perpetrators better understand the harm caused by their offending behaviour, and prompt the perpetrator to make amends for the restoration of the relationship with the victim. It can, in turn, facilitate the perpetrator's integration into society to start a new life as a law-abiding citizen. On a more practical note, mediation used for semi-public crimes and crimes of private prosecution is likely to reduce the workload of judicial organs and further improve the efficiency of criminal proceedings. This is possibly more sustainable if prosecutors function as the mediator as opposed to a third party who lacks the necessary power and authority to oversee and enforce the settlement agreement.

References

Carvalho, P. M. & de Processo Penal, M. P. (2015), *Updated in Accordance with Amendments to the Criminal Code and the Criminal Procedure Code*. Almedina Press.

Chen, J. (2012). On the System of Temporary Suspension of Litigation in Macao and the Significance of Reference for Discretionary Non-prosecution. *Journal of Hebei Youth Management Cadre College, 4*, 70.

Chen, N. (2018). *Research on Penitence in Criminal Law* [Doctoral Thesis from Zhongnan University of Economics and Law].

Chen, G., & Ge, L. (2006). Preliminary Study on Criminal Reconciliation. *China Legal Science, 5*, 3–14.

de Figueiredo Dias, J. (2011). *Agreements on the Sentence in Criminal Proceedings*. Coimbra Editora Press.

de Fgueiredo Dias, J. (2021). *Criminal Law—General Part*. Social Sciences Academic Press.

Gao, J. (1997). *New Code of Criminal Procedure*. Printing Office of Macau Government Jurisdiction (2) Press.

He, T. (2016). Dual Solutions to Criminal Disputes: An Analysis Based on Model Construction. *Study in Law and Business, 1*, 43–54.

He, H., & Liu, L. (2009). Comparative Study of Criminal Mediation in the Context of Eastern and Western Legal Cultures. *People's Procuratorate, 11*, 56–59.

Huang, Z. (2016). *Small Government and Big Community, Post-Post-Modernity and Post-Traditional Life in Macau*. https://en.library.ipm.edu.mo/

Jiang, H. (2010). *A Preliminary Study on the System of Out-of-Court Settlement in Minor Criminal Cases*. Business China Press.

Leal-Henriques. *Commentaries and Comments on the Macau Penal Code* (Vol. 2). King of the Books Press.

Leal-Henriques, M. (2014). *Macau Criminal Law Notes and Reviews* (Vol. 2). King of the Books Press.

Leal-Henriques, M., & Santos, S. (1995). *Annotated Penal Code* (Vol. 1). Lisbon Press.

Li, Y. (2009). Introduction to Macau's Semi-Public Crime System. *People's Procuratorial Semimonthly, 20*, 57–58.

Li, Z. (2015). *General Introduction to Macau Criminal Procedure Law*. Social Sciences Academic Press.

Long, F. (2011, July 29). *Overview of the Criminal Mediation System in Portugal*. People's Court News, p. 6.

Lu, Y. (2008). A Preliminary Study on the Phenomenon of Associations in Macau. *Social Organizations in China, 20*(10), 55.

Lu, Y., & Liang, F., translation (2011). *Macau Criminal Procedure Law Tutorial* (Part 1). The Centre for Legal and Judicial Training Press.

Mao, Y. (2015). *The Value and Realization of Restorative Criminal Responsibility* [Doctoral Thesis from East China University of Political Science and Law].

Ma, S. (2018). Strategy Selection and Certification of Rural Dispute Resolution Under the Background of "Modern Acquaintance Society." *Hubei Social Sciences, 2*, 5.

Robalo, T. L. A. S. (2016). Criminal Mediation in Criminal Proceedings in Macau, Chinese and Portuguese versions, Study on the 20th Anniversary of Macau Criminal Law and Code of Criminal Procedure, 893–915.

Su, T. (2005). The Theoretical Basis of Criminal Mediation System. *Forward Position, 11*, 121–122.

Sun, G. (2018). Conviction and Sentencing of the Acts Committed by Relatives Under the Economic Principle. *Economic Research Guide Press, 2018*(32), 198.

Sun, Y., Shaolin, N., & Dongchuan, S. (2006). Reflections on the Status of Macao Community in the Harmony and Stability of Macao. *Theoretical Exploration, 1*, 130.

Tang, Y. (2020). Independence Shaping and Substantive Construction of the Defendant's Right of Consent to Withdraw Suit. *Law Review, 5*, 91.

Wang, H. (2013a). Re-Perfection of the Reconciliation Procedure of Public Prosecution Cases in China under the Comparative View of China and France. *China Legal Science, 6*, 131–140.

Wang, C. (2013b). The Judicial Value of Mediation in Criminal Procedure. *People's Tribune, 33*, 94.

Yao, J. (2019). Since the Reunification in 1999, Macao Has Ensured People's Livelihood and Improved Social. *Governance and Administrative Reform, 10*, 6.

Yao, H., & Gao, G. (2011). On Victims' Participation in Litigation Under Restorative Justice Model. *Hebei Journal, 3*, 136–142.

Yu, F. (2015). Analysis of Mediation System in Portugal. *Southeast Judicial Review*, 523–534.

Zhang, M. (1995). The Modesty of Criminal Law. *Studies in Law and Business, 4*, 55–62.

Zhou, W. (2017). Analysis on the Criminal Mediation System of Procuratorial Organizations. *Legal System and Society, 21*, 34–35.

The Many Cultural Manifestations of Convictions Through Pleas in Greater China: An International Perspective

Enshen Li

Introduction

Over the past few decades, plea-based case dispositions have grown by heaps and bounds. The plea bargaining system in the US is the most prominent illustration (Alschuler, 1979; Langer, 2004), but many similar initiatives—though termed differently (e.g., charge negotiation, resolution discussion or plea resolution)—have developed exponentially in the European, Latin American and Asian criminal law regimes (Brook et al., 2016). While there is variation across different legal jurisdictions, one perceptible commonality of many types of plea-based dispositional measures appears to be what Máximo Langer (2021: 378) terms the 'administratization of criminal convictions'. That is, convictions are being buck produced through a highly bureaucratic and administrative manner in the criminal process. According to the American criminal lawyer, this trend is global and features in two perspectives. First, the administratization of criminal convictions speaks to a broad utility of trial-avoiding mechanisms whereby one's conviction is determined by *non-judicial,*

E. Li (✉)
School of Law, City University of Hong Kong, Hong Kong, China
e-mail: enshenli@cityu.edu.hk

E. Li et al. (eds.), *Criminal Case Dispositions through Pleas in Greater China*, https://doi.org/10.1007/978-981-97-1856-6_11

administrative officials. Second, this lack-of-trial criminal process is, more often than not, associated with the neglect of defendants' procedural rights. Building his thesis on a comparative analysis of cross-national data from 26 jurisdictions, Langer (2021: 386) contends that the administratization of criminal convictions has taken place 'in many corners of the world'.

Langer's theory has many merits. One in particular is that it meticulously points to a discursive and operational shift in today's criminal justice systems that have fundamentally warped the criminal process by prioritising the efficient disposition of cases above constitutional rights and the rule of law. Increasingly, the criminal process is becoming more streamlined and simplified, which is primarily measured by speed, quantity and work ratio as opposed to 'factual, legal and moral accuracy' (Bibas, 2004). As a result, criminal convictions are no longer a product of a fair (contested) trial but an object in the plea-centred assembly line with little to no quality control and assurance (Schulhofer, 1992). In addition, the administratization of criminal convictions highlights a power shift among law enforcement authorities in the criminal process—it vests power in police (or other investigative agencies) and prosecutors to determine the criminal proceedings of one's case and their guilt. The role of judges is, instead, reduced to little more than a rubber stamp for case outcomes.

The concept of 'the administratization of criminal convictions' is certainly credible and well-founded. Nonetheless, there is also reason to believe that, in practice, there is divergence in the way different plea-based case dispositions operate, considering the nuances in the way plea-based case dispositions play out across different legal systems and social conditions. Even Langer (2021: 403–404) acknowledges that some regimes may appear to be an exception to rather than an example of his theory. Though not specified in his empirical work, this divergence tends to stem from regime-specific cultural foundations and geneses that have shaped each individual criminal justice system. Over the last few decades, this cultural significance has been aptly studied in the context of Anglo-Saxon and Continental jurisdictions. But the scholarly dearth of the interaction between indigenous cultural dynamics of socio-legal arrangements and plea-based dispositions across Asian jurisdictions is unfortunate. This book is prepared to fill this void. Looking at the 'Greater China' region as a case study, we intend to tease out the cultural distinctiveness of Mainland China, Hong Kong, Taiwan and Macau to identify the normative and operational peculiarities of plea-based case dispositions in each jurisdiction and how they are in line with or antithetical to this plea-informed administrative process of criminal convictions.

The Many Cultural Faces of Plea-Based Case Dispositions in Greater China

As illustrated throughout this volume, efficiency, productivity, and greater need for fast case processing have become matters of common concern across Greater China. By and large, it is influenced by a desire to ensure predictability, calculability of case results and, ultimately, cost savings via a more economic criminal process. Yet, the extent to which this procedural rationality is sought and manifested varies from region to region. In many respects, the local context of law and culture plays a vital role in shaping the disparities.

Mainland China

In Mainland China, plea leniency reveals significant parallels with the country's pervasive criminal policy of 'leniency to those who confess, severity to those who resist'. It reinforces China's confession-based practice by enabling procuratorates to become the de facto adjudicator of case outcomes. Reflecting a process of bureaucratising criminal convictions (Li, 2023), Chinese procurators are afforded discretionary power to decide who gets criminalised, through their new powers over underlying facts, charging and sentencing. This is exemplified in two particular ways. First, procurators border on entering the territory of the police through 'early intervention' to steer the direction of investigations. Second, procurators making sentencing recommendations to judges upon the accused's guilty pleas is a prerequisite to the closure of criminal cases (Lin et al., Chapter "Plea Leniency in Mainland China: Legislation, Characteristics and Effects").

By creating a marked disconnection between trial and conviction, Chinese procuratorates reach criminal convictions more 'efficiently' by assuming much of the investigatory and judicial duties, meaning the procedural requirements associated with the trial are not only absent but legitimately circumvented. This has prompted commentators to depict procurators in plea leniency as 'cooks' (He, Chapter "Plea Leniency and Prosecution Centredness in China's Criminal Process"). That is to say, procurators 'prepare the food' (collecting the evidence in relation to the case), 'cook the food' (seek and secure guilty pleas) and 'present the food' (the plea affidavit) to their 'customers' (judges) for review. Because courts are legally mandated to 'respect' the procurators' decision, the judicial role in plea leniency has been marginalised with minimal responsibilities of oversight, quality control and correction of errors. In practice, the judge's deference to prosecutorial discretion is evident. This is accompanied by defence lawyers encountering more obstacles when representing the accused individuals in plea leniency cases, not least because their role of the advocate gets increasingly diminished to give way to a speedy approach to case disposition. Challenges facing defence lawyers are multifaceted, including, *inter alia*, tight time frames to prepare a proper defence case, uncertainties of case results should defence lawyers adopt aggressive defence strategy, as well as general difficulties of competing against prosecutors on an equal footing in the state-controlled criminal process (Mou and Chen, Chapter "Guilty Pleas and New Challenges to Criminal Defence Practices in China").

However, while plea leniency in Mainland China strives for procedural rationality of conviction, it is generally done in a way to better seek 'substantive rationality'—namely, final objectives achieved by more economic actions associated with less procedural hurdles (Weber, 1968). In the parlance of Chinese authorities, efficiency and crime control are wedded to each other. This is poignantly illustrated by the infamous 'Strike Hard' campaigns that were once the centre of criminal justice during 1980s and early 2000s. In this signature anti-crime movement, severity and swiftness were upheld as the dominant tenors of law enforcement and punishment. Swiftness was reflected in the speedy process of investigatory, prosecutorial and adjudicative activities as well as the disregard of procedural rights afforded to suspects in the law (Liang, 2005). Across a substantial number of cases, offenders were imprisoned or executed within a few days or weeks of commencing the investigation, making the judicial system a rubber-stamp for decisions made in secret by police and procuratorates (Trevaskes, 2007). While police were required to complete their investigations within a short period, the criminal cases were tried even faster through the judicial process to produce sentencing decisions for immediate imprisonment and execution. At the same time, 'Strike Hard' campaigns severely targeted designated criminals with disproportionately tougher penalties, ranging from hooligans to underworld mafias. Together with the appearance of public trials and sentencing hearings during crackdowns, summary and harsh punishment invigorated societal justice in reform China. Overall, 'Strike Hard' campaigns in many ways repeated the features of political campaigns in Mao's China: mass parades, rallies, massive imprisonment and executions (Li, 2018).

Thanks to legal civilisation and modernisation, the campaign-style penal tactics have become less visible over the past decades. But trading procedural fairness for 'substantive justice' has never lost its momentum in the Party-state's lexicon of crime control. This, to a large extent, explains the continued heavy application of plea leniency in today's China. While the government has been gradually retreating from its indiscriminate 'iron fist' approach to crime and disorder (Li, 2018), plea leniency represents a more nuanced and delicate approach to dealing with public instability. It retains the efficiency of crime control yet makes sure that conviction is an inevitable outcome of the process. This new arrangement makes perfect sense as plea leniency, since its conception, has been fundamentally devised to serve the goals of 'timely and effectively punishing crime, optimising judicial resources and increasing efficiency of criminal justice' (*The 2019 Guiding Opinions on the Application of the Plea Leniency System*, Section 1). Here, the bureaucratisation of criminal convictions through plea leniency manifests itself in the scheme's tunnel vision and excessive reliance on procuratorates as the exclusive authority in resolving criminal cases. Defendants, on the other hand, are not afforded more rigorous protections. Nor are they given greater legal rights to challenge their pre-determined charges, verdicts and sentences.

In any event, expediting procedure is to optimise substantive outcomes. The procuratorate-driven mode of plea leniency appears to revolve around how to produce goal attainment (optimise the chance of conviction) more efficiently in line with the Party-state's crime control agenda. This is not at all surprising because conviction, in the eyes of Chinese authorities, is not only a demonstration of justice being served but a conduit to address public sentiment towards social disorder, especially in most high-profile criminal cases (Huang, 2012; Li, 2015). Against this backdrop, plea leniency and conviction go hand in hand to produce their intended effects on maximising 'social effects through substantive justice'. This way, both efficiency and crime control are materialised. In a foreseeable future, this composition is likely to be continuously weighed heavily with China's law enforcement agencies to serve as an agent of social control with a higher purpose of political stability for maintaining the Party's monopoly over power.

Taiwan

In Taiwan, plea-based dispositional measures have received little attention in the criminal justice system. Seemingly, this challenges Langer's observation of a global trend towards the bureaucratisation of criminal convictions. Due to a lack of sufficient data, Langer (2021: 403) remarked that 'it is not possible to assess whether Taiwan might be an exception'. This volume, however, suggests two reasons for why plea bargaining in Taiwan works against the global trend. First, unlike most plea-based initiatives around the world, judicial power has remained robustly influential over plea bargaining in Taiwan. If the prosecutorial supremacy has become the norm of plea leniency operations in Mainland China, then plea bargaining in Taiwan's criminal justice system is, by contrast, somewhat under the heel of judges. It operates in a 'paternalistic' framework in which judges play a role as a 'guardian of the accused' as well as 'an enforcer of moral discipline' (Lin, Chapter "Judicial Paternalism and the Stagnant Bargaining Process in Taiwan"). Here, the judicial superiority results in and amplifies the prosecutors' reluctance to engage in plea bargaining. This is simply because the effort to obtain guilty pleas by prosecutors is susceptible to judges' interference; judges can actually lay their hands on the outcome of the case regardless of the prior agreement reached between the accused and the prosecutor. The judge can call off a plea deal if they are of the opinion that the plea agreement in question is unfair, unsatisfactory, or unsafe, either substantively or procedurally. Second, plea bargaining in Taiwan does not offer an economic alternative to existing expedited proceedings. Plea bargaining is legally coupled with more onerous procedural conditions for its enforcement, and thus it has yet to demonstrate an advanced level of efficiency compared to other simplified trial procedures, such as summary judgements. At any rate, plea bargaining is submerged by current expedited proceedings, as crimes falling with the purview of plea bargaining overlap extensively with those dealt with through simplified trial procedures. Collectively, they have made plea bargaining a rather unpopular choice of case disposition in terms of cost-effectiveness and time-efficiency.

Discursively, Taiwan's court-centred mode of plea bargaining is an embodiment of the jurisdiction's long-existing inquisitorial legacy of criminal justice. An inquisitorial legal system was first imported to Taiwan under Japanese rule, and inherited by the *Kuomintang* (KMT) after it lost the civil war and retreated to Taiwan. During the entirety of the pre-2002 period, the court in Taiwan's inquisitorial system played a genuine investigatory role in establishing the facts of the case (Hou, 2012). Just like its Continental law counterparts, the court in Taiwan was perceived as the truth-finder and justice achiever (Su, 2017). This licensed judges to direct and intervene in the activities of investigation and prosecution, with broad powers, for the sake of discovering objective facts and maintaining the integrity of criminal justice. Markedly, the court combined the roles of both the judiciary and the prosecution, and gathered the evidence in ways they deemed appropriate. The year of 2002 marked a watershed moment where efforts were made to move Taiwan's criminal justice system towards an adversarial system. The admirability of Anglo-Saxon legal systems played a major part in this development. Equally importantly, a waning sense of public trust—provoked over time by considerable high-profile wrongful conviction cases and the publicity of judicial corruption—has urged Taiwanese authorities to reconsider the judicial role and its deficiency in the alignment of courts' decisions with the morality of grassroots citizens. Along the way, it is hoped that the mighty power of judges will be reduced to reshape the court as an impartial adjudicator during the trial. This attempt seemingly reached its pinnacle when the Citizen Judge Act was enacted in 2020 by the Legislative Yuan to officially let 'lay jurors' (citizens) participate in the court's decision-making process of conviction and sentence (Chin, 2019).

Still, it is argued that the legislative effort to distance Taiwan's criminal justice system from an inquisitorial framework has borne little fruit (Su, 2017). Dubbed as a 'hybrid system', the reformed criminal justice framework has continued to see courts function as an energetic player, as judges remained obligated to diligently and thoroughly investigate evidence, specifically regarding 'maintaining justice or discovering facts that are critical to the interest of the accused' (Su, 2017: 206). There is much evidence that Taiwanese authorities are unwilling to bend over backwards to turn judges into a complete passive observer in a holistic way (Lewis, 2009). This is particularly the case when the 'hybrid system' goes on to give judges greater power over criminal proceedings. Mainly, it empowers the judges to select appropriate criminal procedures for case disposition, in that the judge is virtually in an unchallenged position to decide whether a particular procedure should be initiated or dismissed. For example, the judge may choose to cancel the plea bargaining procedure and instead call for a regular trial process or vice versa. More likely than not, this is driven by the judge's concern over the default procedure in terms of finding the 'truth' about the case. It suggests that, unlike a typical adversarial system where the judge serves as a referee, Taiwan's 'hybrid system' does not refrain the judge from taking centre stage and conducting the investigation-trial. As Brian Kennedy (2003: 24–25) aptly pointed out, Taiwanese courts are caught in a dilemma. On the one hand, the reformed adversarial system requires judges to perform an impartial duty, deciding one's guilt based on the prosecution and the defence proving their case. On the other hand, judges are under constant pressure from Taiwanese society, their supervisors and the stakeholders in the criminal process to handle the case in a way that is 'satisfactory and justifiable' in every respect. This, unfortunately, cannot be done by taking on a hands-off approach by courts to merely reviewing evidence or hearing witness testimonies at trial. On this view, the citizen judges system is introduced to somehow relieve courts from this direct collision course on the ground. Though the extent to which this new initiative can achieve its intended goal remains unknown, it speaks to the lawmakers' original intention of 'drawing a clear distinction between the duties of prosecutors and those of judges, in order to establish the impartial status of the court' (Su, 2017: 207). The corollary, however, is the declining status of plea bargaining in Taiwan's criminal justice system.

Hong Kong and Macau

Hong Kong represents a different case. Embedded in British common law system for more than a century, the legal system in Hong Kong has been equipped with the liberal idea of the rule of law, constitutionalism and an independent judiciary upholding fair and equal justice (Han, 1993). As such, the criminal justice system in Hong Kong is predicated predominately on an *Anglo-Saxon method* of administering justice, underpinned by due process and adversarialism associated with common law principles including, *inter alia*, the presumption of innocence, proving guilt beyond reasonable doubt ('golden thread'), the right to remain silent, the privilege against self-incrimination and double jeopardy. Post-colonial Hong Kong continued to adopt criminal laws from those passed by the British Parliament in London, making only having minor alterations to align this legislation with local conditions (Li, 2001). Having been promised that it can retain its common law system, post-1997 Hong Kong is regulated by the Basic Law as its overarching constitution. Adopted by the National

People's Congress of China to enshrine the principle of 'One Country, Two Systems', the Basic Law allows Hong Kong to administer its own sets of law with a high degree of autonomy (Chen, 2017). It entrenches a wide range of essential rights and freedoms set out in the Hong Kong Bill of Rights Ordinance. In addition, the Basic Law provides for the separation of powers, granting Hong Kong courts authority to conduct constitutional review on local legislation and executive actions within the limits of Hong Kong's autonomy.

Considering this, Hong Kong's preference for an English model of plea bargaining is nothing but comprehensible. Particularly, although adversarial competition is the defining feature of Hong Kong's criminal justice system, plea bargaining has morphed into a highly relevant method of case resolution (Cheng, Chapter "The Courts, the Prosecution, and the Defence in Plea-Based Case Dispositions in Hong Kong"). It epitomises a strong mark of negotiated justice where the prosecution and the defence (legal counsel) strive to work out an appropriate and mutually satisfactory *agreement* about the criminal charges. Unlike plea practices in Mainland China and Taiwan, plea bargaining in Hong Kong entails negotiation between the prosecution and the defence. It generally occurs by an accused putting forth a guilty plea in exchange for some concession provided by the prosecution (Cheng, 2023). The most common form of plea bargaining in Hong Kong is the negotiation of a guilty plea in exchange for a reduction in charges, though this process may also take the form of negotiations for less serious charges or factual bargains. Importantly, plea bargaining in Hong Kong generally does not include direct sentence negotiations or recommendations, as sentencing remains in the exclusive jurisdiction of the court (Cheng, 2023).

Like many common law countries, the frequent use of plea bargaining in Hong Kong is typically attributed to the professed benefits that it offers in increasing the effectiveness and efficiency of the criminal justice process. By foregoing the trial process and reducing the number of parties involved in proceedings, there is a wide assumption that plea bargaining can '[save] resources and financial expenditure, reduce court backlogs and prosecutorial workloads, and spare accused persons and victims prolonged proceedings' (Flynn, 2011: 371). This is further exemplified by the Hong Kong Court of Appeal pushing forward a sliding scale of sentence discounts to encourage early guilty pleas. Borrowed from England and Wales, such a sentencing strategy for plea bargaining abides by the notion that the earlier the accused pleads guilty, the greater the reduction they can receive on their sentences. Notably, courts in some jurisdictions are discouraged from making lenient sentencing decisions for every plea bargaining case (e.g., Australia). But the judiciary in Hong Kong has clearly voiced unconditional support for plea bargaining through the adoption of the percentage-based sentencing policy. With the judicial endorsement, it appears that the major players in Hong Kong's criminal justice system have formed a shared vision of relying upon plea bargaining as a solution to their heavy workloads and high cracked trial rates.

Similarly to Hong Kong, Macau was only handed over to China from the Portuguese administration two decades ago. However, it represents an exception to the universal espousal of plea-driven case resolution. Instead of constructing a specific plea-centric mechanism, Macau clings to its deep-seated simplified procedures as a primary measure of finalising criminal cases that involve limited culpability and harmful consequences. Characterised by programmes like the suspension of criminal proceedings and the withdrawal of complaint, Macau's simplified procedures help to avoid trials but do not utilise guilty pleas as a requisite element of doing so. Despite being under heavy influence of the Continental legal system, Macau has never fully embraced the notion of negotiated justice (e.g., admitting guilt in exchange for lenient punishment). This is illustrated by the fact that this Special Autonomous Region has yet to develop a criminal reconciliation procedure conducive to negotiation, communication and conflict resolution between the offender and the victim (Li et al., Chapter "Prosecution or Mediation: Perpetrator-Victim Negotiation in Macau and the Way Forward"). On the contrary, it licenses prosecutors to exercise the latitude of choosing a specific criminal procedure befitting for the type and level of crime, regardless of whether the accused has pled guilty. Diverging from plea-based initiatives in Mainland China, Taiwan and Hong Kong, Macau's plea-free simplified procedures alleviate pressures from prosecutors engaging in the demanding task of acquiring guilty pleas to facilitate case disposition. It follows that, in Macau, seeking convictions is not the main concern of prosecutors, who appear to distribute a great deal of effort on diversion as well. As Macau is fundamentally an 'acquaintance' and a less crime-laden society, it is not uncommon that criminal cases are settled through an informal process of restitution, compensation and restoration between the offender and the victim with very little, if any, interference from law enforcement agencies.

The Uncommon Commonalities of Plea-Based Case Dispositions in Greater China: An International Perspective

Plea-based case dispositions in Mainland China, Taiwan, Hong Kong, and Macau each exhibit notable and distinct features. This is hardly surprising given that criminal justice as a social artefact is intertwined and meshed with the social changes, economic arrangements and especially political considerations that have driven the dynamics of change and the strategic principles underpinning contemporary arrangements of criminal law and punishment. In this regard, plea-based initiatives in the four entities of Greater China are mostly subject to various local legal, social and political conditions that have interacted with and impacted the way in which crime and public disorder are understood, perceived and tackled.

In short, our analysis of plea-based case dispositions in Greater China makes a valuable addition to Langer (2021)'s remark of 'the adminstratization of criminal convictions'. It reveals practical variations and exceptional circumstances, but, overall, plea-based initiatives in the selected Eastern societies are replete with many of the same problems facing their Western counterparts in the US, the UK, Australia and the like. From a comparative perspective, those shared issues are not uncommon—no matter which system of criminal justice is adopted (e.g., due process, crime control, adversarial or inquisitorial), there lacks a working mechanism that can sufficiently address questions regarding the fairness, legality and proceduralism of plea-based justice. In particular, the concern lies primarily in the risk that plea-based case dispositions can easily undermine the integrity of the criminal process. And this can be done in a myriad of ways regardless of the values and principles each different type of criminal justice system upholds.

One prominent example is the tendency for plea-based case dispositions to exert significant pressure on the accused that can compel them to plead guilty (Redlich & Shteynberg, 2016). Predominantly, the high financial burden associated with going to trial, tied with the likelihood of a harsher sentence being imposed if found guilty, can act as incentives that pressure the accused into admitting guilt. For those that are already vulnerable, such as indigenous, mentally impaired or lower-class persons, these pressures have a more arduous effect (Flynn & Freiberg, 2018). Vulnerable defendants tend to lack not only the knowledge and ability to participate in informed negotiations (if any) in relation to the charges against them, but also the resources to access legal representation (Schulhofer, 1992). This creates a significant power imbalance between the prosecution and defendant, which only exacerbates the pressure upon them to plead guilty. Under plea bargaining, charge resolution and other similar schemes, defendants are often left with little choice but to plead guilty and relinquish their right to a fair trial, thus being stripped of the ability to maintain their innocence. This consequently has the potential to compel innocent persons to plead guilty, the likelihood of which is only heightened as the sentencing differential—that is, the difference between the likely sentence that would be imposed at trial and the sentence offered during the plea process—increases (Wilford et al., 2021).

The forgoing speaks to a significant normative question of plea-based justice—namely, whether or not a *guilty plea* entered by an accused is *truly* voluntary. Both Western and Eastern practices base convictions on voluntary guilty pleas, yet coercion *with specific* coerced *acts/omissions* is *widespread*, and in many jurisdictions it has become an unspoken rule of law enforcement. While physical torture remains off limits, it is not unusual that guilty pleas can be induced by threats or promises, or drawn out from basal voluntariness—e.g., duress, intimidation, persistent importunity or sustained or undue insistence or pressure.

Indeed, voluntariness as a core tenet of negotiated justice has been the subject of intense debate on its conception, connotation and content (Redlich et al., 2016). In the common law procedure of plea bargaining, for example, not only is voluntariness a key determinant of legally binding guilty pleas, but it is a critical precursor to the legitimate circumvention of court proceedings and the waiver of a set of procedural rights conferred on the accused. An earlier debate on whether plea bargaining represents a voluntary process suggests that there is no generally accepted theory of plea voluntariness and how it is consistent legal standards. On the one hand, it is argued that the situation imposed by plea bargaining on the accused is 'intrinsically coercive' (Brunk, 1979: 528), and thus the defendant can only act involuntarily to accept negotiated pleas (Kipnis, 1976; Luna, 2022; McCoy, 2005; Smith, 1986). Kipnis (1976), for instance, compares plea bargaining to the gunman scenario to demonstrate the inherent presence of involuntariness in the former. In his view, the process of plea bargaining can be likened to a victim handing over his or her wallet in response to the demand of an armed robber.[1] This is because 'both the gunman and the prosecutor require persons to make hard choices between a very certain smaller imposition and an uncertain greater imposition' (Kipnis, 1976: 98). The comparison is particularly acute when there exists the probability of harsh punishment (e.g., the death penalty) if the defendant chooses to go to trial. Therefore, the more attractive the offer, the more likely it is that the defendant's acceptance is involuntary (Caldwell, 2011).

On the other hand, some legal theorists challenge this 'systematic coercion' narrative by claiming that it is not the nature of plea bargaining which overbears the defendant's will to plead guilty. Rather, the centrality of involuntariness rests upon 'psychological/moral unfreedom' (Wertheimer, 1983: 639) or 'social unfreedom' (Brunk, 1979: 532) as a result of undue influences from the inner workings of the bargaining process. According to this line of analysis, plea bargaining resembles, structurally, a contractual negotiation process (Scott & Stuntz, 1992). It gives rise to agreements that have legal standing despite being made under external pressure—just like labour agreements formed in response to threats of strike, which are somehow legally enforceable (Philips, 1981: 210). However, a plea agreement is naturally 'non-binding' if the defendant's exercise of free judgement during negotiations is precluded. In Wertheimer's (1983) account of the two-pronged voluntariness test, a guilty plea is rendered involuntary if the defendant is compelled to enter into a plea agreement without his or her volition, and through someone's 'wrongful act', e.g., a threat made by the prosecution. In a similar vein, Brunk (1979) propounds a nuanced theory of (in)voluntariness. He posits that the voluntariness of guilty pleas is likely to be undercut if the accused's conduct is not free from constraints imposed by other persons or social institutions (e.g., law enforcement personnel or other extra-legal actors). Such impositions require the defendant 'to perform an action as a means to the achievement of a desired end [that is] less desirable than some other that will normally achieve the same end' (Brunk, 1979: 545). Here, the normal course to achieve the same end (finding a defendant

[1] Many have expressed the dissenting voices regarding this analogy. Philips (1981), for example, opines that the gunman scenario is not appropriate in the plea bargaining context because while the law illegalises what a gunman does, it permits the prosecution to impose the choice situation to reach plea agreements.

guilty) refers to an adversarial trial that necessitates procedural protections, which, if ideally practised, is more desirable than the course of plea bargaining.

Apparently, the controversy on voluntariness has not impeded the proliferation of plea-based case dispositions throughout the world. In most Anglo-Saxon countries, the overwhelming majority of criminal cases (approximately 94–97%) are disposed of through plea bargains compared to those convicted by jury or a judge (Brook et al., 2016). To justify the practice of plea bargaining, the US Supreme Court, for example, addressed the constitutionality of plea bargaining and established that a defendant's guilty plea must be 'knowingly, voluntarily, and intelligently' entered (Primus, 2015). The court's evaluation of a knowing, voluntary and intelligent plea, as enunciated in a number of high-profile judgements, involves several different yet correlated questions, mainly concerning the volitional component of the test. They include, for example, whether the defendant's decision is independent of threats, false promises or misrepresentations (*Culombe v. Connecticut*).[2] In addition, cases have also considered whether the defendant's will is overborne (*Boykin v. Alabama*),[3] and whether the confession is likely to be dishonest or untrustworthy (*Blackburn v. Alabama*).[4] Acknowledging that the US criminal justice system is 'a system of pleas, not a system of trials' (Henderson & Levett, 2019: 81), the Supreme Court has concurred that the structural coercion of plea bargaining is inevitable and tolerable. In discussing coercion in *United States v. Speed Joyeros, S.A.* vis-à-vis the prosecution's offer of lesser imprisonment, the Court maintained that 'requiring plea negotiations to be free from "any coercion" would contradict the basic notions of bargaining' (Redlich & Summers, 2011: 3). This position is articulated in *Brady v. United States*, in which it was held that the defendant's decision to plead guilty in the hope of avoiding a substantially higher penalty, including the death penalty, is deemed voluntary unless it is attained by any duress or inducement, either direct or indirect, express or implied, and however slight.

Still, how to ensure that the defendant's willingness to admit guilt is not influenced by criminal justice agencies engaging in deceptive or

[2] *Culombe v. Connecticut*, 367 U.S. 568 (1961).

[3] *Boykin v. Alabama*, 395 U.S. 238 (1969).

[4] *Blackburn v. Alabama*, 361 U.S. 199 (1960).

coercive behaviours is fraught with uncertainty. For instance, the strategies of prosecutors to extract confessions are diverse. Carried out with a singular aim of obtaining the defendant's confession (as early as possible), they consist of, *inter alia*, overcharging, threats to recommend mandatory minimum sentences, threats to investigate and indict friends or family members, pre-trial detention with unaffordable bail, and the so-called trial penalty. It is true that the past few decades have seen investment in the US judiciary and legislature to safeguard voluntariness in the face of irregularities of state authorities. Evidence, however, indicates that none of the protective measures have been particularly effective, including the constitutional right to adequate counsel assistance 'serv(ing) as a first safeguard to secure the voluntariness and accuracy of the plea' (Davis, 1972: 133).

In a pioneering study conducted across ten major urban jurisdictions in the US, Alschuler (1975: 1313) discloses that defence attorneys are 'subject to bureaucratic pressures and conflicts of interest grounded on the guilty plea'. According to his findings, a paradox exists where the voluntariness of a guilty plea seems to be reliant on the assistance of counsel who has a huge interest in urging the defendant to plead guilty. This is different from the common view that defence lawyers act as an advocate in the adversarial system, and instead defence counsel tend to form a cooperative relationship with prosecutors during the bargaining process. Rather than offsetting any irrationality on the prosecution's part, counsel are keen to engage in a trade-off where they accede to the prosecution's demands for one client in exchange for some benefits in sentence or charge for another, characterised as 'bureaucratic symbiosis' (Alschuler, 1975: 1579). Notably, this practice is commonly associated with pressure exerted by prosecutors on defence attorneys to accept plea offers (Hessick III, 2002).

If reciprocity has catalysed a non-confrontational relationship between counsel and prosecution, then defence lawyers, including public defenders and private attorneys, are also financially incentivised to encourage defendants to plead guilty as opposed to assisting them with the right to trial (Alschuler, 1975). The preoccupation with pleas accrues from enormous caseloads facing most public defenders who are paid on the quantity of cases finalised. In the same vein, the rapid disposition of cases through pleas can keep practices of private attorneys moving and profitable (Leclerc & Euvrard, 2019). To maximise economic gains, rarely do defence lawyers devote time to conducting case investigations, filing motions, interviewing witnesses or preparing possible defences (Joy &

Uphoff, 2014). Such an observation lends itself to a strong assertion: 'the defence attorney is himself (herself) a frequent source of abuse' (Alschuler, 1975: 1313).

This leads to two consequences. First, plea bargaining facilitates the covering up of a large amount of prosecutorial misconduct. Not only prosecutors are relieved from proving one's guilt beyond a reasonable doubt before a competent, independent and impartial court, their 'effort' to reach the plea agreement is barely challenged by counsel and gets 'archived' once the plea-led conviction is recorded by the court. Second, plea bargaining is more prone to false convictions than trials. It has been consistently found that innocent people are routinely coerced into pleading guilty to crimes they did not commit (Wilford et al., 2019). While there are many contributing forces, it is axiomatic that custodial interrogation can create a compulsive ambience where threats of violence, psychological manipulation, emotional pressure and many other oppressive tactics can render guilty pleas involuntary (Primus, 2015). Significantly, this is also attributable to the fact that the inadequate, if not entirely ineffective, assistance of counsel has been pervasive throughout the plea barganing system.

In Greater China, similarly, plea-based case dispositions are not immune from the problem of voluntariness. At a legislative level, like the US, voluntariness is ostensibly prescribed as a basis of valid guilty pleas. In Mainland China, for example, the 2019 *Guiding Opinions on the Application of the Plea Leniency System* stipulates that the admission of guilt and acceptance of punishment are required to be voluntary and fact-based. The *Guiding Opinions* states in detail that, during police interviews, criminal suspects must not be compelled to admit guilt in exchange for leniency. Procuratorates and courts are supposed to assess (1) whether the guilty plea was entered as a result of violence, threats or inducements that led the defendant to go against their will in admitting guilt and accepting punishment; (2) whether the guilty plea was entered by a defendant with a normal mental state and cognition; and (3) whether the defendant understood the nature of admitting guilt and accepting punishment and the legal consequences it might lead to. In the meantime, the law places much of its faith in defence lawyers playing a salient role in assuring the defendant's volitional choice of confessing. Under the *Criminal Procedure Law*, lawyers are expected to help defendants fully apprehend the nature and legal consequences of entering into a plea. To reinforce this, criminal justice agencies are mandated to inform defendants about their right to discuss plea options with lawyers. For those who are unable to access their own legal representation, criminal justice officials are obligated to notify a duty lawyer from legal aid services to provide legal assistance.

There is little research to explore whether voluntariness can in fact be conceived in the way intended by the legislation. Yet, the available literature has alluded to the uncertainty of defendants accepting plea deals in the exercise of free will. This uncertainty mainly stems from the fact that plea leniency operates largely as a procedurally unfair system. Simply put, there are a series of fundamental structural impediments that make plea leniency distinct from a rights-oriented system (Li, 2022a). Borrowing Tom Tyler (2003)'s notion of procedural justice, studies show that plea leniency basically lacks opportunities for defendants to tell their side of story. In addition, this confession-centred programme works in a way that is inconsistent with the production of neutral results. While applying disproportionately to relatively minor crimes, it gets neglected as an approach to handling serious and heinous crimes. Worse is the fact that plea leniency has yet to foster a mechanism that earnestly addresses the interests and concerns of the defendants (Li, 2022a). Contrary to the legislative purpose, there is a non-linear correlation between guilty pleas and reduced sentences. On the whole, plea leniency undercuts, rather than promotes, the fundamental rights of defendants.

It comes as little wonder, then, that the voluntariness of guilty plea is a far-fetched concept in plea leniency. Inherently a process of power imbalance, plea leniency exacerbates an adversarial feature that is already weak: defendants are in a less favourable position to have their voices heard. Indeed, the high detention and conviction rates in Mainland China raise serious doubts over the degree to which defendants can reject the procurator's plea offer. This is particularly true when the role of Chinese defence counsel has been reduced to symbolic significance in plea leniency (Zhang et al., 2024). In addition to the findings of Mou and Chen (Chapter "Guilty Pleas and New Challenges to Criminal Defence Practices in China"), research provides that when representing their clients, defence lawyers in Mainland China are largely confined to three peripheral roles—'explainer', 'persuader' and 'observer'. Instead of negotiating the charge and sentence on the defendant's behalf, it is found that lawyers have found themselves in a position of only being able to help defendants gain a simple understanding of plea leniency while encouraging their acceptance of the proposed sentence (Li, 2022b). In many ways akin to the US, pragmatic considerations also impact the defence counsel's conduct: a desire to maintain a beneficial relationship with procurators and an unwillingness to challenge the generally accusatory, draconian, and conviction-centred nature of Chinese criminal proceedings. Overall, plea leniency catalyses an emasculated role for lawyers, who function primarily as a mechanical constituent of the country's increasingly monotonous assembly-line version of criminal justice. With procuratorates turning into the genuine decision-maker in the plea leniency process, the majority of defence lawyers have become accustomed to a sluggish pattern of criminal defence, resulting in the neglect of due process and anything associated with an adversarial process. What is then left to judges seems to be an administrative task of certification to verify the 'voluntary nature, authenticity and legality of the guilty plea' (He, 2023: 454). Even then, this verification is carried out mostly verbally, which, for the sake of saving time, does not involve an evidence-based and thorough inquiry about the undisciplined and unethical practices of procurators.

In Taiwan, the attempt to guarantee the voluntariness of guilty pleas takes a different path, albeit the effectiveness of this path remains at least equally questionable. Under Taiwan's plea bargaining system, courts take on a paternalistic role in approving or rejecting the plea agreement. Judges are licensed to make a decision on the validity of the plea agreement to their liking in spite of the defendant's true intention. This means that the defendant's choice of confessing can be readily set aside should the judge deem the plea agreement inappropriate in a substantive or procedural sense. Furthermore, if plea leniency in Mainland China necessitates a mandatory presence of defence lawyers, the assistance of counsel is not at all required in Taiwan's plea bargaining process. There are six types of criminal cases in which defendants must be legally represented according to the *Code of Criminal Procedure*. Plea bargaining cases are mostly excluded from this list. Typically, the moment in which defence attorneys get to meet their clients is after the client has already pled guilty. It follows that lawyers are not supposed to provide legal opinions in conflict with the defendants' earlier pleas (Article 455–5, the *Code of Criminal Procedure*). More telling is that defence lawyers in Taiwan are expected 'not only to work for the interest of defendants, but also for justice and public interest' (Su, 2017: 213). Together with prosecutors, judges and all other public officials, defence lawyers form a 'coalition' seeking to ensure justice is served and perform their legal duties in the public interest. This duality of the role of lawyers clearly gives rise to a collision of values in their practice of legal defence. The quality and depth of legal assistance provided by defence counsel as an adversary of prosecutors is thus limited, with accused individuals involved in plea bargaining cases bearing the brunt of the consequences.

Hong Kong and Macau, though both were once Western colonies, followed divergent rules of plea voluntariness in their criminal justice systems. Macau has been almost vague and silent on what constitutes voluntariness given there is no formal plea-based system, while Hong Kong continues to cling to the principles of English common law, at the core of which is that ***judges should not*** ordinarily ***participate*** in ***plea negotiations***. Like in Mainland China and Taiwan, courts in Hong Kong ought to confirm the defendants' willingness to plead guilty. They are, however, restricted from giving sentence indications should defendants elect to accept a plea agreement. For one, this is to prevent courts from imposing unwarranted pressure on defendants in their plea decisions. A more compelling reason is that Hong Kong courts are not legally empowered to engage in bargains with defendants and the authority of plea bargaining is assigned solely to the prosecution.

In reality, however, this could not be further from the truth. Particularly, the introduction of the sliding scale sentence discounts in 2016 manifests the Hong Kong judiciary's strong desire to promote the speedy admission of guilt. While it seems reasonable to award greater sentence reductions for guilty pleas made earlier, an inevitable outcome of this sentencing rule is that defendants are likely to confess merely to dodge a heavier sentence, putting the voluntariness of their guilty pleas on the line. In *The Timing of Guilty Pleas: Lessons from Common Law Jurisdictions (2023), Kevin Cheng* offers a timely scrutiny of this salient issue. Drawing upon a critical and comparative analysis, he argues that the legislative effort to prompt early guilty pleas through a percentage-based sentencing practice is both futile and unjust. Comparing Hong Kong to England and Wales, Cheng challenges a well-held presumption that early guilty pleas can help fix a cracked trial—one that does not proceed as scheduled but is eventually dismissed because the case has already reached an outcome. This is because, unlike extant literature generally assumes, cracked trials are not caused by tactical defendants 'playing the system' in the form of delaying their guilty pleas. The criminal process in Hong Kong does not operate in a way conducive to the manipulation of defendants. Rather, it is adept at pushing defendants into pleading guilty. Young and underprivileged defendants are more likely to hastily enter the plea agreement due to their absence of legal knowledge and counsel assistance. So are those who have already been pressured to make confessions during police interviews and/or remanded in custody pending trial. On top of it, 'trial penalty' applies readily to defendants opting for late guilty pleas or jury trials. In this context, the sliding scale of sentencing discounts is devised to incentivise guilty pleas, with little regard to questions of conscious volition and procedural fairness arising from this sentencing practice.

Relatedly, defence lawyers in Hong Kong are generally competent, independent, and adversarial-spirited. Nonetheless, when it comes to plea bargaining cases, they have the capability and tendency to shift roles seamlessly from a fierce advocate to a cooperative player. In many ways resembling their counterparts in Mainland China and Taiwan, Hong Kong lawyers are found to be more preoccupied with advising their clients on the benefits of early guilty pleas over all else. Rather than challenging the prosecution's case, defence counsel—particularly legal aid lawyers—are seen as sitting at the same table with the prosecution in pursuit of guilty pleas as a common objective (Cheng, Chapter "Behind the Scenes: Exploring the Legal and Cultural Factors of Taiwan's Plea Bargain System"). This explains the high rate of guilty pleas in Hong Kong, as evidence consistently shows that a defendant's decision to plead guilty is heavily influenced by their legal representatives (Cheng, 2013, 2014). Apart from defence counsel's aspiration to urge their clients to accept the plea agreement, guilty pleas are usually entered by defendants in the wake of defence counsel's advice on 'the legal consequence of not pleading guilty'—namely conviction and harsher punishment. With the ability to assess the accuracy and reliability of legal advice, counsel assistance in Hong Kong, unfortunately, does not help defendants make free choices but further undermines the voluntariness of guilty pleas.

Conclusion

In this concluding chapter, I provided a summary note of the discursive and operational characteristics of plea-based case dispositions in Greater China. Langer's proposition of the 'administratization of criminal justice' lays a conceptual framework for us to appreciate a global trend of trial-avoiding mechanisms in optimising the chance of conviction through guilty pleas. The current volume is organised with the aim of contributing to this line of scholarship. It is hoped to shed light on the cultural diversity of plea-based programmes in Chinese-speaking societies which have hitherto been understudied by jurists, criminologists and social scientists. While efficiency, predictability and bureaucratisation have become the underlying principles of 'administratized' criminal proceedings, our volume offers a nuanced, delicate and regime-specific scrutiny of the cultural foundations and geneses that have informed and underpinned the local administration of plea-based justice, in order to understand their idiosyncrasies in operation on the ground. In the climate of different needs, interests and priorities, measures of plea-based case dispositions are carried out in culturally distinct fashions in Mainland China, Taiwan, Hong Kong and Macau. But the unexpected commonality across the otherwise varied practices happens to be the neglect of individual rights and procedural fairness in seeking guilty pleas. What is at issue is the concern over the legitimacy of plea-based case dispositions due to the lack of effective mechanisms guaranteeing the true voluntariness of guilty pleas.

It would be highly undesirable to abolish this process in its entirety—doing so would only further burden the criminal justice system by increasing depleting resources. That being said, the key focus for fortifying the legitimacy of plea-based case dispositions should be on the promotion of transparency and uniformity across proceedings. Although plea voluntariness may still remain questionable, taking these steps would be likely to improve, at a minimum, procedurally fair outcomes for defendants and increase the accountability of plea bargaining to the public. One way of facilitating this is to introduce formal guidelines to oversee the process of plea-based case dispositions, such as the UK's 'Attorney-General's Guidelines on the Acceptance of Pleas and the Prosecutor's Role in the Sentencing Exercise'. These guidelines cover the responsibilities and conduct of prosecutors by outlining factors to be considered in deciding whether to instigate plea negotiations, setting requirements in the determination of facts between the accused and prosecution, and requiring a formal record to be kept of these agreed facts. The adoption of a similar framework in Greater China jurisdictions (and also expanded to other criminal justice agencies such as judges) could increase both the visibility and accountability of plea-based case dispositions by alleviating perceptions that efficiency is the main motivation for the process, providing more scrutiny on decisions and reducing pressures on defendants to plead guilty. This is certainly not a panacea for all normative issues associated with plea-based case dispositions; but doing so would increase the transparency of plea-based programmes and promote uniformity across prosecutors' decisions, ultimately improving the integrity of the criminal justice system.

References

Alschuler, A. (1975). The Supreme Court, the Defense Attorney, and the Guilty Plea. *University of Colorado Law Review, 47*, 1–72.

Alschuler, A. (1979). Plea Bargaining and Its History. *Columbia Law Review, 79*, 1–43.

Bibas, S. (2004). Plea Bargaining Outside the Shadow of Trial. *Harvard Law Review, 117*(8), 2463–2547.

Brook, C., Finannaca B., Harvey, D., Marcus, P., McEwan, J., & Pomerance, R. (2016). A Comparative Look at Plea Bargaining in Australia, Canada, England, New Zealand, and the United States. *William & Mary Law Review, 57*, 1147–1224.

Brunk, C. (1979). The Problem of Voluntariness and Coercion in the Negotiated Plea. *Law & Society Review, 13*(2), 527–553.

Caldwell, M. (2011). Coercive Plea Bargaining: The Unorganized Scourge of the Justice System. *Catholic University Law Review, 61*, 63–96.

Chen, H.-Y.A. (2017). The Hong Kong Basic Law and the Limits of Democratization Under "One Country, Two Systems." *International Lawyer, 50*(1), 69–86.

Cheng, K. (2013). Pressures to Plead Guilty: Factors Affecting Plea Decisions in Hong Kong's Magistrates Courts. *The British Journal of Criminology, 53*(2), 257–275.

Cheng, K. (2014). The Practice and Justifications of Plea Bargaining by Hong Kong Criminal Defence Lawyers. *Asian Journal of Law and Society, 1*(2), 395–412.

Cheng, K. (2023). *The Timing of Guilty Pleas: Lessons from Common Law Jurisdictions*. Cambridge University Press.

Chin, M.-H. (2019). Lay Participation in Taiwan: Observations from Mock Trials. *Asian Journal of Law and Society, 6*(1), 181–207.

Davis, S. (1972). The Guilty Plea Process: Exploring the Issues of Voluntariness and Accuracy. *Valparaiso University Law Review, 6*(2), 111–134.

Flynn, A. (2011). Fortunately We in Victoria Are Not in That UK Situation: Australian and United Kingdom Legal Perspectives on Plea Bargaining Reform. *Deakin Law Review, 16*(1), 361–404.

Flynn, A., & Freiberg, A. (2018). *Plea Negotiations: Pragmatic Justice in an Imperfect World*. Palgrave Macmillan.

Han, A. (1993). Hong Kong's Basic Law: The Path to 1997, Paved with Pitfalls. *Hastings International & Comparative Law, 16*, 321–342.

He, X. (2023). Plea Leniency and Prosecution Centredness in China's Criminal Process. *The China Quarterly, 254*, 448–465.

Henderson, K., & Levett, L. (2019). Plea Bargaining: The Influence of Counsel. In B. Bornstein & M. Miller (Eds.), *Advances in Psychology and Law* (pp. 73–100). Routledge.

Hessick III, A. (2002). Plea Bargaining and Convicting the Innocent: The Role of the Prosecutor, the Defense Cousel, and the Judge. *Brigham Young University Journal of Public Law, 16*(2), 189–242.

Hou, C. (2012). An Overview of the Criminal Justice System in Taiwan. In J. Liu, B. Hebenton, & S. Jou (Eds.), *Handbook of Asian Criminology* (pp. 297–308). Springer.

Huang, X. (2012). Re-legalization or De-legalization? Netizens' Participation in Criminal Justice Practices in China. *British Journal of Criminology, 52*(4), 724–743.

Joy, P., & Uphoff, R. (2014). Systemic Barriers to Effective Assistance of Counsel in Plea Bargaining. *Iowa Law Review, 99*, 2103–2130.

Kennedy, B. (2003). Taiwan's Criminal Justice System: Clash of Cultures. *American Journal of Chinese Studies, 10*(1), 21–27.

Kipnis, K. (1976). Criminal Justice and the Negotiated Plea. *Ethics, 86*(2), 93–106.

Langer, M. (2004). From Legal Transplants to Legal Translations: The Globalization of Plea Bargaining and the Americanization Thesis of Criminal Justice. *Harvard International Law Journal, 45*(1), 1–64.

Langer, M. (2021). Plea Bargaining, Conviction Without Trial, and the Global Administratization of Criminal Convictions. *Annual Review of Criminology, 4*(1), 377–411.

Leclerc, C., & Euvrard, E. (2019). Pleading Guilty: A Voluntary or Coerced Decision? *Canadian Journal of Law and Society / La Revue Canadienne Droit Et Société, 34*(3), 457–478.

Lewis, M. (2009). Taiwan's New Adversarial System and the Overlooked Challenge of Efficiency-Driven Reforms. *Virginia Journal of International Law, 49*(3), 651–726.

Li, E. (2015). The Cultural Idiosyncrasy of Penal Populism: The Case of Contemporary China. *British Journal of Criminology, 55*(1), 146–163.

Li, E. (2018). *Punishment in Contemporary China Its Evolution, Development and Change*. Routledge.

Li, E. (2022a). Haste Makes Waste: Why China's New Plea Leniency System Is Doomed to Fail. *Asian Journal of Comparative Law, 17*(1), 1–30.

Li, E. (2022b). Chinese Courts' New Plea Leniency System: Scrutinizing the Efficacy of Mandatory Defense Counsel. *The China Journal, 88*(1), 78–99.

Li, E. (2023). Bureaucratising Criminal Convictions in China. In E. Johnston & A. Pivaty (Eds.), *Efficiency and Bureaucratisation of Criminal Justice: Global Trends* (pp. 69–87). Routledge.

Li, P. K. (2001). The Executive-Legislature Relationship in Hong Kong: Evolution and Development. In J. Y. Cheng (Ed.), *Political Development in the HKSAR* (pp. 85–100). WSCP.

Liang, B. (2005). Severe Strike Campaign in Transitional China. *Journal of Criminal Justice, 33*(4), 387–399.

Luna, S. (2022). Defining Coercion: An Application in Interrogation and Plea Negotiation Contexts. *Psychology, Public Policy, and Law, 28*(2), 240–254.

McCoy, C. (2005). Plea Bargaining as Coercion: The Trial Penalty and Plea Bargaining Reform. *Criminal Law Quarterly, 50*(1–2), 67–107.

Philips, M. (1981). Question of Voluntariness in the Plea Bargaining Controversy—A Philosophical Clarification. *Law & Society Review, 16*(2), 207–224.

Primus, E. (2015). The Future of Confession Law: Toward Rules for the Voluntariness Test. *Michigan Law Review, 114*(1), 1–56.

Redlich, A., & Summers, A. (2011). Voluntary, Knowing, and Intelligent Pleas: Understanding the Plea Inquiry. *Psychology, Public Policy, and Law, 18*(4), 626–643.

Redlich, A., & Shteynberg, R. (2016). To Plead or Not to Plead: A Comparison of Juvenile and Adult True and False Plea Decisions. *Law and Human Behavior, 40*(6), 611–625.

Redlich, A., Bushway, S., & Norris, R. (2016). Plea Decision-Making by Attorneys and Judges. *Journal of Experimental Criminology, 12*(4), 537–561.

Schulhofer, S. (1992). Plea Bargaining as a Disaster. *Yale Law Journal, 101*, 1979–2009.

Scott, R., & Stuntz, W. (1992). Plea Bargaining as Contract. *Yale Law Journal, 101*, 1909–1968.

Smith, D. (1986). Plea Bargaining Controversy, The. *Journal of Criminal Law & Criminology, 77*(3), 949–968.

Su, K.-P. (2017). Criminal Court Reform in Taiwan: A Case of Fragmented Reform in a Not-Fragmented Court System. *Washington International Law Journal, 27*, 203–240.

Trevaskes, S. (2007). Severe and Swift Justice in China. *British Journal of Criminology, 47*(1), 23–41.

Tyler, T. (2003). Procedural Justice, Legitimacy, and the Effective Rule of Law. *Crime and Justice, 30*, 283–357.

Weber, M. (1968). *Economy and Society: An Outline of Interpretative Sociology* (Vol. 1). Bedminster Press.

Wertheimer, A. (1983). Legal and Extra-Legal Voluntariness: A Response to Philips. *Law & Society Review, 17*(4), 637–646.

Wilford, M., Shestak, A., & Wells, G. (2019). Plea Bargaining. In N. Brewer & A. Bradfield-Douglass (Eds.), *Psychological Science and the Law* (pp. 266–292). Guilford Press.

Wilford, M., Wells, G., & Frazier, A. (2021). Plea-Bargaining Law: The Impact of Innocence, Trial Penalty, and Conviction Probability on Plea Outcomes. *American Journal of Criminal Justice, 46*, 554–575.

Zhang, L., Lu, H., & Hu, M. (2024). An Empirical Study of Publicly Appointed and Privately Retained Defense Lawyers in Plea Bargaining: The Chinese Experience. *Crimal Law Forum.* https://doi.org/10.1007/s10609-024-09482-2

Index

E. Li et al. (eds.), *Criminal Case Dispositions through Pleas in Greater China*, https://doi.org/10.1007/978-981-97-1856-6

SPRINGER NATURE

GPSR Compliance

The European Union's (EU) General Product Safety Regulation (GPSR) is a set of rules that requires consumer products to be safe and our obligations to ensure this.

If you have any concerns about our products, you can contact us on ProductSafety@springernature.com

In case Publisher is established outside the EU, the EU authorized representative is:

Springer Nature Customer Service Center GmbH
Europaplatz 3
69115 Heidelberg, Germany

The manufacturer's authorised representative in the EU is Springer Nature Customer Service Centre GmbH, Europaplatz 3, 69115 Heidelberg, Germany. If you have any concerns regarding our products, please contact ProductSafety@springernature.com

Printed and bound by CPI Group (UK) Ltd, Croydon, CR0 4YY
01/10/2026
02225854-0010